FRIENDS WITH JESUS

Experiencing the Depths of Spiritual Intimacy

John 13-16

David A. Christensen

THE
REPHIDIM
Project

ISBN-13: 978-0692749470
ISBN-10: 0692749470

THE
REPHIDIM
Project

To Janie, my best friend on earth and my soul mate for life.

ACKNOWLEDGEMENTS

Many thanks:

To Dr. S. Lewis Johnson, who first stimulated my love for Jesus' words through his lectures entitled *Greek Exegesis of the Upper Room Discourse* in the summer of 1983 at *Grace Theological Seminary*.

To Mark Halfacre, Corey Decker and Lynn Sarver, for their careful editing and insightful suggestions which improved this book immensely.

To my friends at Galilee Baptist Church, where I preached a series of messages on John 13-17 in the early 1990s.

TABLE OF CONTENTS

PROLOGUE

"Friends, just friends," we say as if mere friendship were a lesser love. We celebrate romantic love over friendship love – Eros over Philia – in our modern world, virtually ignoring friendship as if it is of little value. Oh, we know we need friends. Everyone should have a few who share life from a healthy emotional distance, but we don't think of friendship as true love. We don't connect intimacy with friendship. Intimacy is reserved for romance, not friendship. Intimacy is reserved for the sexual union, not mere affection. We forget that the best romance is grounded in friendship. The aged couple, long past sexual intimacy, live for the love of friendship. Friendship may well be the deepest, least natural and most intimate of all loves, for it is love chosen purely for the sake of the one chosen.

The ancients considered friendship to be the greatest of all loves. Cicero promoted the virtue of friendship in *Laelius de Amicitia*. Aristotle devoted a whole book in his *Nicomachean Ethics* to friendship. He wrote, "Friendship is a single soul living in two bodies." C.S. Lewis in his book, *The Four Loves: An Exploration of the Nature of Love*, wrote extensively about the value of friendship, exploring the ancient philosophers and the importance they placed on friendship.

> Inevitably that sort of love was most prized which seemed most independent, or even defiant, of mere nature. Affection and Eros were too obviously connected with our nerves, too obviously shared with brutes. You could feel these tugging at your guts and fluttering in your diaphragm. But in Friendship – in that luminous, tranquil, rational world of relationships freely

chosen – you got away from all that. This alone, of all the loves, seemed to raise you to the level of gods or angels.[1]

Jesus said:

> You are My friends, if you do what I command you. No longer do I call you slaves, for the slave does not know what his master is doing; but I have called you friends, for all things that I have heard from My Father I have made known to you. You did not choose Me, but I chose you, and appointed you, that you should go and bear fruit, and that your fruit should remain, that whatever you ask of the Father in My name, He may give it to you. This I command you, that you love one another. (John 15:14-17)

The characteristics of friendship love are clearly seen in Jesus' words to us in that upper room the night before he died for us. Friends immerse themselves in a common cause. They unite in purpose for life. Friendship revolves around a central cause unifying friends in the experiences of life. Friendship love is expansive. There is a fermenting quality to friendship that allows the love to grow and deepen over time. Friendship love is selective and discriminatory. Not just anyone is a friend, and friends of friends must choose to share the love. Friends are loyal to each other. Friends share a loyal love with the friends of their friends as they mutually devote themselves to a common mission in life. Friendship is born out of and grounded in companionship. Friends form a joint company of people around a common interest. Camaraderie and fellowship characterize friendship. Friendship is built on trust because friendship is revealing and we won't reveal ourselves to someone we don't trust. There is mutual transparency among trusted companions. Friendship, Lewis says, "is an affair of disentangled, or stripped minds. Eros will have naked bodies; Friendship naked personalities."[2]

Jesus strips himself before us and shares his most intimate teachings in what we call "The Upper Room Discourse." Chapters 13-16 of the Gospel of John are Jesus' most intimate words for us, His friends. He calls us to the intimacy of friendship with Him. He draws us into His friendship by inviting us to be transparent and open with Him. He invites us to enter His love by opening our hearts to Him as He opens His heart to us. We will see all the ingredients of friendship love in His words. Jesus doesn't want us just to serve him out of duty and obligation. Jesus wants us to enjoy the depths of spiritual intimacy with Him as our forever friend. His friendship is both personal and communal as all true friendship is. The beauty of friendship love is that it adds rather than subtracts. It is not exclusive but expansive. We join with Him and many other friends in the cause for which Jesus died, and, as we join with His friends, our own friendship with Him is expanded.

I invite you to take your Bible in one hand and this book in the other to explore the wonder of our friendship with Jesus. Jesus will teach in true Semitic style, circling again and again, to touch on the themes of friendship love so we will follow His ever expanding message through these chapters. Jesus invites us to go deeper and stay longer with Him as we walk through life. He wants us to be His friends forever.

LOYALTY:

THE PRELUDE TO INTIMACY

1
WASHING UP FOR SUPPER

John 13:1-11

Matthew Kelly, the *New York Times* bestselling author, wrote: "Human beings yearn above all else for intimacy. ... Our desire for happiness is ultimately a desire for intimacy. If we have intimacy, we can go without an awful lot and still be happy. Without intimacy, all the riches of the world cannot satisfy our hungry hearts. Until we experience intimacy, our hearts remain restless, irritable, and discontented."[1] Kelly wrote about the intimacy of marriage, but the truth is hardly confined to romantic love. True friends experience the happiness that comes from intimacy. More importantly, we were made for intimacy with God. Our human hearts yearn for the intimacy that can only come in communion with God. In the often quoted words of Saint Augustine, "You have made us for yourself, O Lord, and our heart is restless until it rests in you."

A relationship without intimacy is dreadful and boring. A friendship without sharing is dreary and dead. There is no happiness. The human heart yearns for intimacy, and the deepest intimacy is spiritual intimacy, so the deepest happiness is spiritual happiness. Jesus invites us to enjoy the spiritual intimacy of friendship with him. Religion, sadly, turns friendship into formality and relationship into responsibility. It is all obligation and duty without enjoying the relationship. Responsibility is a part of any relationship, but responsibility by itself produces no joy. Intimacy produces the joy in our relationship.

John 13 is Jesus' invitation to intimacy, not the intimacy of romance but the intimacy of friendship. The intimacy of friendship begins when I pull back the curtain covering my soul and allow another to see inside. In the same way, the intimacy that Jesus invites us to enjoy with Him begins as He pulls back the curtain and shares His heart with us inviting us to share our hearts with Him. John chapters 13-16, "The Upper Room Discourse," show us Jesus. He reveals the inner workings of His heart that we might enter into the intimacy of friendship with Him. Theologian James Boice called these chapters "Christ's love letters" because they stress the intimacy of spiritual friendship.[2] Jesus is pulling back the curtain and revealing Himself to us – inviting us to enter into friendship with Him. As He peels back the layers, we see deeper into His love.

LAYERS OF LOVE

Intimacy is a many-layered love. According to Matthew Kelly, there are seven levels of human intimacy:

> (1) the level of clichés
> (2) the level of facts
> (3) the level of opinions
> (4) the level of hopes and dreams
> (5) the level of feelings
> (6) the level of faults, fears, and failures
> (7) the level of legitimate needs[3]

Jesus, of course, does not have needs we can meet, for He is complete in the love of the Godhead – three persons in the unity of perfect love. However, He invites us to move deeper into his love by leaving the level of facts about him and moving through the level of our faults, fears and failures leading us to share our true needs that only He can meet.

It is Thursday night of Passion Week. It is the night before he is crucified. Jesus has gathered in the upper room to share a special night with those who are closest to him. John 13 is the drama that precedes the teaching. The first movement in this holy drama shows us that Jesus loves with a forever love (13:1). I don't think we should be surprised that the verse which begins this whole intimate teaching by Jesus should open with an emphasis on Christ's special love for those who are His own. This verse makes as sharp a distinction as any verse in the New Testament between God's love for the world and God's love for His own. There is a world of difference between the two.[4] James Montgomery Boice wrote, "God has done some things for all men, that is, everyone in the world. ... On the other hand, God has done all things for some men. These are His own. They do not lack and never will lack any good thing."[5]

Yes, God loves the entire world in a general way, but God loves we who worship Him with a special love. The Greek literature of the day used this expression as a term of endearment for very close relatives.[6] This is family language. If you have trusted in Christ, then you are part of His family, and the love that He talks about in these chapters is a family love. You are special to Him because you are His own. Jesus loves you as you are – warts and all! Victor Hugo, explaining the death of M. Myriel, the blind Bishop in Les Miserables, described the love of his sister with these famous words: "The supreme happiness of life consists in the conviction that one is loved; loved for one's own sake – let us say rather, loved in spite of one's self." Jesus loves us in spite of ourselves, and we find our deepest happiness in His love.

Jesus knew that the time of His departure from this world had arrived, so he gathered His disciples for supper - *having loved His own who were in the world, He loved them to the end*. To the end of what? To the end of His life? To the end of ours? The expression would be better translated "to the utmost." He loved fully. He loved completely. All the love that an infinite God can possess is the love with which He loves His own. His love for us has no limits. That kind of love will always do what is best for us. In essence, the rest of the upper room discourse is our Lord's attempt to demonstrate that love. For Him to expound that love for His disciples (and by extension for us) completely will take the next three chapters.

Jesus dramatizes His love by washing their feet. Foot washing is the "perfect love token" as one writer put it, leading us to the second movement in the drama (13:2-5). Jesus is becoming vulnerable, opening Himself to rejection, revealing His heart. True friendship requires self-disclosure. Jesus takes the initiative and discloses His heart to the disciples. Intimacy calls for sharing the inner person with friends. It is the opening

15

of self to another. Jesus will share His deepest passions and values with us in the next few chapters. He wants us to know what He most deeply cares about in life and why He will die for us, but before He talks about His heart, He shows His heart. Jesus stoops to serve us because serving us is at the heart of who He is. In the process, He becomes vulnerable to misunderstanding and rejection.

A TEST OF HUMILITY

It is in the middle of supper. The hum of conversation fills the room. Arguments, jokes, serious discussions and silly teasing go on as they do among any group of men who have traveled together, lived together and eaten together for three years. Outside the dangers abound. Inside a sense of security resides. The disciples were arranged in what was called a "triclinium," an arrangement of couches set around a low central table with one end open for the servants to replenish the food. The couches were arranged in a "U" pattern, close to one another so that the disciples could reach the food in the center. A pillow was placed at the head of each couch, and the disciples would recline on their left arm and eat with their right hand. No utensils were used. Rather a piece of bread was used to dip into the common food containers and eat. This arrangement left their feet on the outside of the triclinium and servants could rinse the feet without interrupting the conversation.

Normally, a servant would take a basin and a pitcher of water. The feet were not placed in the basin, but rather the water was poured over the feet and caught in the basin so that the dirt from the dusty streets was rinsed into the basin. Then the servant would wipe the feet with his hands to get rid of the dirt and then dry the feet with a towel. There had been no servant to perform this important service – and no disciple volunteers – so Jesus rises in the middle of the banquet, leaves his couch and goes over to the wall where the toiletries are kept. He removes his clothes, except for his loincloth which is the probable force of this expression and ties the long towel around him. Then he begins to wash the feet of each disciple in turn.

John makes a deliberate point in this passage to emphasize that what Jesus did here, he did in the full consciousness of who he was. Here was no mere man who lived a wonderful example. He was fully conscious of His deity and, yet, still chose to wash their dirty feet. He knew that it was time to die (vs.1). Even more important, He knew that His destiny was in His hands (vs.3). Only God controls all things, including death. He knew that what happened was by His choice, His decision. It was within His power to change the course of human history. He was fully conscious of who He was yet chose to serve those who should serve Him.

J. I. Packer writes: "This is what God does for those He loves – the best He can; and the measure of the best that God can do is omnipotence! Thus, faith in Christ introduces us into a relation big with incalculable blessing, both now and for eternity."[7] Jesus teaches us here that love does not give us what we want. Love gives us what is best. Jesus, our Creator and Sustainer, pledges Himself in this drama to serve us with all He has and all He is. I think it is harder to accept the truth that Jesus delights to serve us than it is to preach the truth that we ought to serve Him. We are far readier to serve Him humbly than we are to accept His service to us. We are uncomfortable when He humbles Himself before us, so we make that humility merely an example of how we should function. What Jesus does here is far more than an example. It is incarnational truth.

The most humbling test is not to give forgiveness but to accept forgiveness. The test of humility is not to give service but to accept service. It is more humbling to allow another to serve me than for me to serve another. In our human relationships, we often substitute service for intimacy. I will humble myself to serve you, but I dare not confess that I need you to serve me. It is even more so with the Lord. Our pride keeps us from accepting His forgiveness and admitting that we need His service. Until we are willing to accept that we need the Lord to serve us, we will never enjoy the sweetness of our relationship with Him. Here is the starting point, the lesson of Peter. Jesus confronts his pride with a tender touch.

We do not know the order of the foot washing. Some suggest that Jesus began with Peter, but the most normal reading of the text would imply that Jesus had washed several feet before he came to Peter. John Chrysostom, a church father, believed that Jesus washed the feet of Judas Iscariot, the traitor, before he came to Peter.[8] Alfred Edersheim suggests that Jesus, as the host, would have been seated on the right side of the "U" in the middle of a set of three couches nearest the open end. John and Judas would have reclined on either side of Jesus, and Peter would have been on the far end of the "U."[9] Jesus began washing feet with John and proceeded around the table. The normal order for the rituals of the

Passover Supper proceeded to the left of the host. If this is true then, ironically, Judas accepted the foot washing but Peter did not. If Peter reclined on one end of the "U" and Jesus started at the other end, then Peter would have been the last to have his feet washed by Jesus. By the time he came to Peter, there must have been dead silence in the room. The hum of conversation had stopped. Embarrassment and confusion filled the room as Jesus silently went about his work. When He came to Peter, Peter refused. His revulsion grew with each disciple and exploded when Jesus arrived at his feet. Peter curled his feet up under him and incredulously said, "Lord, are you trying to wash my feet?!"

Open confrontation. Like so many things we do in service, Peter's action seems to demonstrate humility. Doesn't Jesus realize that this is degrading? He seems concerned for the position of Christ. In fact, he is offended. His pride is wounded. Jesus must confront that pride in Peter as He must confront that pride in us. It is possible to be very devoted to the Lord but very wrong at the same time. Jesus explains that he doesn't understand this all now but he will one day. That is so true of love. We do not understand why, if God loves us so, He lets bad things happen to us. So we respond with a mixture of pride and fear. "No way will you wash my feet." Now Jesus makes the choice clear for He cannot ignore such a confrontation. "If I do not wash you, you have no part with me." The pronoun used here is very important. Jesus does not say you have no part *in me*. He says you have no part *with me*. He is talking about fellowship and intimacy, not conversion. As theologians like to say, "He is talking about communion, not union."

A Scottish preacher wrote: "Peter is humble enough to see the incongruity of Christ's action, yet proud enough to dictate to his master."[10] We cover ourselves in the robe of humility which hides the pride of our self-sufficiency. A fundamental requirement for enjoying our friendship with the Lord is that we let Jesus wash our feet. Feet smell. Feet are dirty and letting someone wash our feet is humbling, but we need to be humbled by our need before we can experience the intimacy of His love. As long as we are holding back, as long as we are retaining our self-sufficiency, there will never be intimacy. Intimacy only comes when we throw ourselves completely into the loving arms of our Lord and say, "Do what you will." The choice is ours! We can enter into intimacy by letting Jesus wash our dirty feet, or we can curl up our feet and refuse His love.

VULNERABILITY AND SELF-DISCLOSURE

The depth of love between two people is always limited by the less mature of the two. The truth is readily apparent when we look at a parent and a teenager. The intimacy of the friendship between a parent and a teen is limited by the teen. The level of intimacy between two lovers is defined by the emotional limitations of the immature lover. The weaker person sets the boundary for how deep the love can go by putting up walls that hinder intimacy. In our relationship with God, we are the weaker lover. Our emotional limitations hinder the depth of our intimacy with Jesus. Perfect love exists among the three persons of the Godhead, and Jesus offers perfect love to us. How deep we grow in our friendship with Jesus will be determined by how open we will be with Him. Our willingness – or unwillingness – to be vulnerable with Jesus determines the depth of our intimacy.[11]

Intimacy begins with self-disclosure. The DNA of friendship is mutual self-revelation.[12] Friends share their hopes and dreams, their hurts and struggles, their passions and problems. The level of our transparency limits the level of our intimacy. Jesus will open His heart to the disciples that night in ways they could not anticipate. He will share His passion with them, and they will see His agony in the Garden. That night will be filled with deeply intimate moments, although they cannot know all this as He washes their feet. Jesus invites them to open their hearts to His penetrating gaze by allowing Him to wash their dirty feet. He invites them to trust Him enough to be transparent with Him. He desires that they become His friends. He gives the same invitation to us today.

As a pastor, I am invited into the hearts of many people. They open up to me and share their hurts, and I listen in love. The result is a powerful bond between us, but that bond goes to a deeper level when I open my heart to another and let that person serve me in love. I saw this very clearly with a good friend. He had shared some of his private hurts with me, and I had responded in love. Our friendship was good but not deep. Later I was going through a private struggle caused by some deep emotional wounds. I took the risk. I opened my heart to him. I shared a moment of deep vulnerability through many tears. I allowed him to wash my feet, and our friendship deepened instantly.

Real love frees us to confess our needs, and, when we confess our needs, friendship flourishes. Christ knows how ugly we are. He still chooses to love us to the utmost, fully, completely, the very end of ends, eternally, without limit. When we are confident of his love, we can accept his washing and then enjoy the love he offers to us. Vulnerability frees us for intimacy with the one who loves us infinitely, leading us to the final movement of the drama. Jesus restores with a gentle grace (13:9-11).

Verse 9 is typical Peter. "Fine, if that is the choice then please give me a bath!" He means it as an expression of his love, but it is another expression of his pride. It is possible to be very devoted to the Lord, yet very wrong. It is possible to be very humble and committed for all appearances and yet still be refusing to let Christ do as He pleases inside. I am always leery of public commitments for that reason. I have seen too many people, including myself, confess loudly over the years while fighting God inwardly. It is the Peter syndrome. He has no idea what the next twenty-four hours will bring. He cannot even imagine it. Often the louder the confession, the deeper the failure.

Once again, Jesus must correct. What follows is a classic statement of friendship with the Lord. A guest would normally bathe before attending the banquet. But as he walks through the dusty streets in his sandals, his feet would get dirty. So he needed only to have his feet washed not his whole body. Jesus is saying here that everyone in that room except Judas the traitor has already spiritually bathed. They were all saved people. The early church fathers liked to use this analogy for the Christian life. You are bathed in Christ when you trust him as your savior, but as you walk through life, your feet get dirty. You don't need to get another bath. You don't need to be saved again and again and again. You only need to have your feet washed.

Ray Stedman writes: "The bath gives us part in him, the foot washing gives us part with him."[13] He goes on to point out that the Holy Spirit doesn't "stutter." He doesn't say, "You must be born again and again and again and again." You are born again once. But the only way to maintain fellowship is through regular confession and cleansing. Sin breaks our communion with the Lord. Confession restores that intimacy, a major theme throughout the upper room discourse. Jesus is talking about communion, not union, fellowship not salvation in these passages. John, in 1 John 1:9, is talking about fellowship as well when he writes: "If we confess our sins He is faithful and just to forgive us our sins and to cleanse us from all unrighteousness."

Jesus is teaching a distinction in this verse between fellowship and conversion; between communion and union. The word for bathe is different than the word for wash. The word "to bathe" is a Greek construction which indicates that the bath occurred in the past, but the cleansing continues today. The verb emphasizes the continuing status of the person. The word "to wash" is a Greek construction which means "to get his feet washed" or "to let his feet be washed." There is a responsibility on us to come regularly to get our feet washed by Christ. Our character has been bathed in the grace of Jesus, and we do not need another bath. What we need is to allow Jesus to wash the daily dirt regularly off of our feet.

Oh, how many Christians never learn to enjoy their relationship with Christ because they refuse to come regularly and get washed up by Jesus! The Lord loves you. He loves you with an unconditional, everlasting love. He loves you to the end of time and beyond. He loves you to the infinite utmost. He wants to express that love regularly by washing your feet. But if there is something that stands between you and Him there can be no intimacy. If the dirt is not rinsed off, you will not enjoy the love as He desires.

PEELING THE ONION

Imagine yourself like an onion. You are a person with many tightly wrapped layers of "skin." The outer layer is what people see when they first get to know you. We carefully construct our outer layer. We want to control what people see. It is the layer we show when we gather on Sunday morning in church. There are many other layers to each of us, but we only allow people in when we trust them with our inner layers. As the layers are peeled back one by one a person can see deeper into us – comes to know us better. Now imagine Jesus' invitation in this chapter as a knife cutting through our layers. The deeper the blade penetrates, the tougher the resistance but the closer the intimacy. If this sounds painful, it is! It is called the Social Penetration Model for understanding friendship. I know it sounds clinical, and we like to think of friendship as simply a warm, fuzzy feeling, but the truth is that the "knife through the onion" analogy is accurate. No wonder Peter recoiled. So do we! We recoil out of the fear

21

that Jesus might see something we don't want Him to see in us. We fear rejection so we must learn trust. Emory Griffin writes: "Trust is the climate for transparency, but no closeness takes place until the knife moves inward. Social Penetration theory labels the inward thrust of the blade into a willing onion self-disclosure. It's the process through which people get close – the stuff of friendship."[14]

Suppertime was an important family time in our home when the girls were young. I tried to avoid missing suppertime even when I had evening meetings. Suppertime and the next hour or so until bedtime were family time. But there was a requirement for supper. We all must "wash up." If you will pardon this "homely" analogy, the one requirement for enjoying fellowship with the Lord is that we have to wash up for supper. Jesus wants to dine with us. He wants to commune with us. He wants to love us and share life with us. He wants to serve us. The upper room discourse is Jesus for the last time before His death sharing intimate times with those who are special to Him. He teaches us how much He wants to do the same with us.

Christianity is not meant to be endured. Christianity is supposed to be enjoyed. But the one requirement for such friendship is that we wash up regularly. Get the dirt and the grime of our day rinsed away. Take care of the sinful attitudes and actions which inhibit our relationship. Confess the anger and the frustrations that come between us and get right with the Lord every day. Then you will enjoy His love to the fullest extent. Don't hold back your secrets. Begin today. He is waiting with arms open wide. He will not reject you. He loves you to the utmost! You can trust His love. Jesus wants to be your friend.

> An Arabian proverb defines a friend as one to whom one may pour out all the contents of one's heart, chaff and grain together, knowing that the gentlest of hands will take and sift it, keep what is worth keeping and with the breath of kindness blow the rest away.[15]

2
WASH WHOSE FEET?

John 13:12-20

A s I sit at my desk typing these words, I look across my study at a quote stitched carefully by hand on a pale, white fabric background set inside a silver frame. The quote is by Ugo Bassi, a 19th-century Italian priest who was executed by a firing squad for his work as a chaplain with the Italian nationalist movement. Bassi wrote:

> Measure thy life by loss
> Instead of gain,
> Not by the wine drunk, but
> The wine poured forth.
> For love's strength standeth
> In love's sacrifice;
> And whoso suffers most
> Hath most to give.

Bernice "Bunny" Foss stitched that quote and gave it to me as a gift. Bunny grew up in a small town in Maine, educated in a one-room schoolhouse. From those humble beginnings, she went on to serve as a missionary for 36 years in the Belgian Congo, now called the Democratic Republic of the Congo. She came home after being diagnosed with cancer, but God led her to what she called her "bonus years" teaching missions and spiritual life at New England Bible College.[1] Bunny influenced my life, the lives of other faculty, and many students during those years with her gentle, servant's heart.

St. Bede's Episcopal Church in Santa Fe, New Mexico, has only one entrance into the sanctuary. A hand-lettered sign hangs over the door which reads: "Servant's Entrance." There is no other way into or out of this church except through the service door.[2] We live in a consumer society even when it comes to church. For many people, churches are like stores in a mall. They pay their money in return for merchandise which we call worship, programs or ministries. People select a church because it meets their needs, and if it ceases to meet their needs, then they seek a new store. Christians shop for a certain worship "experience" and migrate to a church that provides that experience. The church, certainly, is supposed to meet our needs. The church is not supposed to leach the life from the souls of men. On the other hand, if everyone waits to be served then who does the serving? We often act like we entered church through the entrance reserved for honored guests instead of the servant's entrance. If we enter through the servant's entrance, then we understand that we are there to serve not be served, and it is as we serve that we are served.

THE ORDER OF THE TOWEL

The church is made up of needy people joined corporately to meet each other's needs. God designed the church to be reciprocal in nature. It is people having their needs met by meeting the needs of others. If you want your needs met in church, then you must be willing to meet the needs of others. We serve to be served. We are served to serve. Mutual service is the nature of the church. Jesus is teaching us the wonderful principle of service in John 13. True friendship involves mutual service. The overflow of our love for Jesus is our love for each other. The overflow of our love for each other is humble service. Mother Teresa tells the story of two friends who came to see her. They brought a large sum of money to use for feeding the poor through her work. She asked them, "Where did you get all this money?" The couple told her they were married two days earlier but had decided not to have a large wedding banquet. They chose to bring the money that they would have spent on their wedding banquet to Mother Teresa. She asked them, "Why?" They replied, "We love each other so much, and we wanted to share our love with other people, especially with those you are serving."[3]

They were following the example of Jesus, who taught us the principle of humble service. Jesus has just finished demonstrating His love by washing their feet. This drama was designed to be an example to us of how we ought to function as well, but foot-washing is more than an example. It is a principle. Jesus delights to serve us. We start to understand friendship when we begin to understand that Jesus loves to serve us. That concept is foundational to friendship. To be friends with Jesus is to accept his service to us. We begin to enjoy the Lord when we let Him wash our feet with His love, and we build friendships with other Christians as we follow his example of humble service by washing the feet of others.

There are Christians that believe foot washing is an ordinance which we are to practice like communion and baptism. I graduated from a Brethren Seminary. The Brethren Church teaches that we are to wash each other's feet regularly whenever we participate in communion. The service is a beautiful and tender expression of this principle of humble service. I wonder, "Does anyone come to a foot washing service with dirty feet?" Jesus washed dirty feet, and He calls us to wash dirty feet. Jesus is teaching a principle not a practice here. The principle is that we ought to serve one another, and our greatest service is to wash the dirty feet of others. As Jesus daily washes our dirty feet we ought to daily wash the dirty feet of others.

We are told in the Gospel of Luke (22:24) that an argument broke out among the disciples at dinner that night. They were bickering about which one of them was the greatest! They were bickering about self-interest while Jesus was teaching them about self-sacrifice. Jesus shows us that He honors humble service, but it is not just any service. The greatest friends of Jesus are those who wash the feet of others. Those closest to the heart of Jesus are those who serve others with His heart.

For many years, I taught at New England Bible College. My father, as President and Chancellor, had initiated a ceremony that we performed at graduation each year, and I continued that tradition. It was called "The Order of the Towel." Each graduate was given two items; a hand towel draped over an arm and a small square of the towel to be placed in a pocketbook or wallet. I would challenge the graduates who had just received their baccalaureate degrees that the towel was their personal business card, unlike any other business card. They should keep it in their wallet or purse as a reminder of who they were – a servant of Jesus Christ. The towel should be kept in their office or study as a reminder that no servant is greater than his/her master, and no one who is sent is greater than the one who sent him/her. I would close the brief ceremony by saying, "Graduates, tonight you are entering, as Dr. Vernon Grounds once said: "into the highest and noblest of all fraternities – the order of the towel."

We are not taught here to wash Christ's feet. In many ways, that would be easier. If Jesus Christ were here in this room, we would gladly wash his feet. We would kiss his feet for He is the Lord. But Christ's feet need no spiritual washing. He does not sin. People sin and they sin against us. We are to wash their sins with our loving confrontation and forgiveness just as Jesus washes our sins with His loving confrontation and forgiveness. This service is not just any service. It is the service of forgiveness. I do not mean that we atone for anyone's sin. Only Christ can atone for sin. But we wash the feet of other believers when they get dirty by lovingly correcting them in their sin and then forgiving and restoring them when they confess and repent. Dr. H.A. Ironside pointed out that when we wash each other's feet, we must take care of the temperature of the water. We are tempted when others have wronged us to fill the pitcher angrily with boiling water and say, "Stick your feet in here! How does that feel." Other times we are tempted to fill the pitcher with ice water which is just as bad for the relationship. Ray Stedman says that some Christians come with no water at all. They "dry clean" the feet. Scrape off the dirt and make sure it hurts.[4] Make her pay for the rest of her life for what she has done to me. "I may have to wash his feet, but he will feel it!"

This kind of spirit only brings misery to everyone. Jesus goes on to teach us that humble service is the recipe for happiness (13:16-17). Do you want to be happy? Jesus gives us an important clue to deep and abiding happiness in verse 17. The word "blessed" is our sanctified version of "happy." We are uncomfortable talking about happiness as a value. It sounds so selfish to want happiness. We would rather talk about being blessed than being happy because it sounds more spiritual. Yet the Greek word here means to be happy – to exist in a "state of true wellbeing."[5] It is the same Greek word used over in the Beatitudes where Jesus repeatedly says, "Happy are the humble for they shall inherit the earth." (Mt. 5:5)

26

OUR HAPPY DANCE

Real happiness – God's kind of happiness – comes from serving others not out of duty but out of joy. John Piper illustrates this principle with an analogy drawn from marriage. Suppose that I take my wife out to celebrate our anniversary. I tell her that I am taking her out for our anniversary because it is "my duty." Will she feel honored? Will she be happy? Will I find happiness in serving her out of duty? No! Serving her out of duty does not honor her at all. It belittles her. Serving her with joy honors my wife. If I tell her that nothing makes me happier than to be with her on our anniversary, this brings happiness to us both.[6] All true servants of Jesus understand this principle of happiness.

I grew up in Pakistan and heard the stories of "Praising Paterson" and "Praying Hyde" from an early age. R. McCheyne Paterson and John Hyde were Presbyterian missionaries to the Punjab region of India, now Pakistan, whose nicknames describe their personalities. John Hyde practiced a life of intense prayer which led some to consider him rather morose. A young lady tried to have some fun with John Hyde, so she asked him, "Don't you think, Mr. Hyde, that a lady who dances can go to heaven?" He quietly responded, "I do not see how a lady can go to heaven unless she dances."[7] He understood the spirit of true servanthood.

Are Christians supposed to be happy? Yes! God wants us to be happy. He wants us to enjoy life in Him, but we have such a shallow, superficial view of happiness that we reject such notions. Real happiness means to enjoy the pleasure of God in what we do. Everything else is substitute happiness. Everything else is saccharin compared to the pure sugar of His pleasure. Jesus teaches us how to be happy here. There are two ingredients to this recipe. We are happy when we first know and then do what Jesus teaches us here. We find a double condition governing our happiness in John 13:17. The first condition is a factual expectation. It is expected that we know these things about the servant not being greater than his master. The happiness doesn't come from the knowing it comes from the doing. The second conditional sentence - "if you do them" – is a construction that emphasizes probability but not actual fact. Our happiness is based on the probability that we will do what a servant does. If we do what a servant does then we will find happiness.

The first conditional clause, "If you know these things," is a Greek construction that assumes they already know these things. We know that we are not greater than Jesus and that if He modeled servanthood, then we should as well. I know that, but I do not practice it very well. In fact, we practice it in reverse. I know what my wife should do to make me happy. Wives know exactly what is wrong with their husbands. Children figure that their parents could improve in certain ways, and they know just how they can improve. We all know how others could change so that we could be happy. The truth is that we will never find happiness that way, not real happiness. The person simply never does what we want them to do and even if they did the result would be self-centered and shallow.

We will not enjoy God's happiness until we learn to serve those we love. The second conditional clause implies that we may not always put the doing into action. It is up to us to serve and so enjoy happiness in our service. Contrary to everything that our culture teaches us, we are happiest when we are serving others! We enjoy God's pleasure when we seek to serve rather that seek to be served. I observed this lesson in my life as a freshman at Philadelphia College of Bible. It was a Friday night, and all of my friends were out on dates or other enjoyable activities. I was stuck in my dorm room, dateless and alone. We didn't have access to electronic entertainment like students today, so I was feeling bored and depressed. I decided to wander over to the student lounge in the main building just for something to do. The only other person in the lounge was a freshman girl I knew casually from some classes. She was sitting at a table with tears in her eyes as I walked up to greet her. I sat down and asked what was wrong. She poured out her heart to me. Her parents were missionaries in one of the South American countries, and she had received word that her father was gravely ill. She did not have any way to contact her parents (this was before the days of cell phones and the internet). She was worried about her father. She also struggled with the reality that life was so different in America, and she did not fit in with other students. We talked for an hour or two that night since I, too, had grown up on the mission field and understood the struggles of life in America for MK's (missionary kids). I walked back to my dorm room that Friday night suddenly realizing that I no longer felt down or depressed … and it wasn't because I had a date! I never even had another lengthy conversation with her again. My happiness was the direct result of serving another student who needed help at that moment. In a very small way, Christ's love brought me great joy in serving another.

WHERE IS THE HAPPINESS IN HURT?

Mother Teresa wrote: "Joy must be one of the pivots of our life. It is the token of a generous personality. Sometimes it is also the mantle that clothes a life of sacrifice and self-giving. ... True love is love that causes us pain, that hurts, and yet brings us joy."[8]

Robertson McQuilken was president of Columbia Bible College and Seminary which became Columbia International University. He was a renowned Bible conference speaker, teacher, and administrator. In 1991, he resigned to take care of his wife, Muriel, who had Alzheimer's. It hurt to watch her fade away. Serving her needs was exhausting. He rarely became irritated with her. What would be the point? Yet once he lost it all. It was back in the days before they had resorted to a diaper and she had an accident. He was trying to clean up the accident, and she kept getting in the way. He got more and more frustrated with her until he slapped her on the calf to get her to move. It was not a hard slap, but he was overcome with guilt. In 44 years of marriage, he had never so much as touched her in anger. Never was he even tempted. He sobbed for her forgiveness even though she could not understand his words. So he turned to the Lord for solace.

A few weeks later he was in the same condition. He was mopping frantically while trying to keep her hands from "helping." Then he heard over the radio the booming voice of Chuck Swindoll saying, "Men! Are you at home? Really at home?" McQuilken writes: "In the midst of my stinking immersion I smiled, "Yeah, Chuck, I really am." Do I ever wish I weren't?" We think, "How sad. Where is the happiness in that?" McQuilken writes:

> I think that my life must be happier than the lives of 95% of the people on planet earth. It's just as well I have ... memories of past conversations, for she hasn't spoken a coherent word in months - years, if you mean a sentence, a conversation - though occasionally she tries, mumbling non-words. Would I never hear that voice again? Then came February 14, 1995. Valentine's Day was always

special at our house because that was the day, in 1948 Muriel accepted my marriage proposal. On the eve of Valentine's Day in 1995, I read a statement by some specialist that Alzheimer's is the most cruel disease of all, but that the victim is actually the caregiver. I wondered why I never felt like a victim. That night I entered in my journal: "The reason I don't feel like a victim is - I'm not!" When others urged me to call it quits, I responded, "Do you realize how lonely I would be without her?" After I bathed Muriel on her bed that Valentine's Eve and kissed her goodnight (she still enjoys two things: good food and kissing!), I whispered a prayer over her: "Dear Jesus, you love sweet Muriel more than I, so please keep my beloved through the night; may she hear the angel choirs."

The next morning, I was peddling on my Exercycle at the foot of her bed and reminiscing about some of our happy lover's days long gone while Muriel slowly emerged from sleep. Finally, she popped awake and, as she often does, smiled at me. Then, for the first time in months, she spoke, calling out to me in a voice clear as a crystal chime, "Love ... love ... love." I jumped from my cycle and ran to embrace her. "Honey, you really do love me, don't you?" Holding me with her eyes and patting my back, she responded with the only words she could find to say yes: "I'm nice," she said. Those may prove to be the last words she ever spoke.[9]

It hurts to love sometimes. We must risk love anyway. It costs to serve sometimes. We must risk serving anyway. Sometimes people betray our love. We must love anyway. Jesus will soon know the awful sting of betrayal. In fact, he predicts the betrayal here. He is teaching us that humble service prepares us for betrayal in verses 18-19. Jesus quotes from Psalm 41:9. The psalm is David's lament over his betrayal by a close friend, and Jesus looks at his friend and disciple, Judas Iscariot as he predicts the coming betrayal. Jesus is still reaching out to Judas. He has already washed the feet of the traitor as His act of love, and now he appeals to him again in the form of a warning. Jesus loved so deeply that he even served his betrayer! If you have ever been betrayed by someone you love, then understand the model he leaves for us. Humble service prepares the heart to love even in betrayal!

Jesus teaches about service here to prepare the disciples for the betrayal. There are few things more devastating to our faith than to be betrayed by someone we love. If we are unprepared, then we can easily fall away from the Lord in the aftermath. So Jesus prepares for that betrayal by predicting it. If you know ahead of time that even those you love and trust the most can betray you, and you still choose to serve them humbly, then you will be ready for the betrayal, and it will not shipwreck your faith.

Jesus continues in verse 20 to teach us that welcoming His servants is welcoming Him and welcoming Him is welcoming God into our lives. When we receive Jesus Christ's forgiving, cleansing, washing service then we really receive God. That is easy enough to accept. We understand the truth that Jesus represents God to us, but the first part of the principle is harder to accept. God uses human ambassadors to do His work. When we receive the washing work of other believers, we really receive Christ, who sent them into our lives. The reverse is just as true. When we reject the help of other believers who are trying to show us where we've blown it, we are really rejecting Jesus Christ. That principle paints this whole servant concept in a different perspective. Friendship with Jesus is a communal friendship.

If we have made a mess of things and are in danger of making matters worse and someone comes to us to try and get it straightened out, we are to remember that the person is sent by Jesus Christ, Himself. Jesus is standing in front of us. We are not to resent it. We are not to react with the attitude, "you have no right to do this. You have no right to treat me this way. You have no right correct in this way." That kind of resentful spirit will only end up destroying us and those we love. We must accept the warnings through other Christians with a humble spirit because, if we don't, we will end up like Judas Iscariot!

THE BANYA OF JESUS

Do you long to have a deeper friendship with the Lord? You have repented and confessed your sins to Him, and you have accepted His cleansing for those sins, but you still struggle with guilt. You have a sense of friendship with the Lord, but you have no friendship with other

31

Christians because you are unwilling to risk rejection and unwilling to accept correction. I have a theory. The theory is that no one is completely whole until they experience both vertical and horizontal forgiveness. Wholeness comes only when our feet are washed by the Lord and when our feet are washed by the people we have wronged by our sin. Sin has both vertical and horizontal ramifications. We wrong the Lord and we wrong other people. We will only find wholeness when we confess to the Lord and experience his washing, and we go to those we have wronged and experience their washing.

If you have wronged someone, you will never experience friendship until you accept their service to you. The other side is just as important. You may not have forgiven the person who has wronged you. You hold it against them for what they did. In a thousand little ways, you make them pay for it. You are either frigid or scalding but either way, there is no real friendship. There never will be friendship until there is mutual service to each other. Go to that person who has wronged you and offer the washing of forgiving, restoring grace. This is Christian friendship at its best, and the pleasure is deep and abiding.

Mutual service is necessary for spiritual friendship. Jesus serves us, and we serve Jesus. We serve others, and others serve us. The welcoming of service and the giving of service are both necessary for true friendship with each other and with Jesus because we represent Jesus to each other. We bond in mutual service.

When I was in Russia teaching some seminars, I was invited to participate in a banya after church on my last Sunday night. They insisted that I experience banya with them so I could appreciate their culture! Banya is more than a sauna. It is a bonding experience between Russian men around the shared experience of a steam room. We met around 11 p.m. in a building behind the house. The building had several rooms. There was the kitchen/dining room where we ate together. There was the changing room and the steam room. They explained to me that a banya involved several parts. We undressed and entered the steam room. There were five of us that night. They were all naked, but they allowed the two of us who were American to wear shorts. The steam room was heated almost to a boiling temperature, and we sat on wooden racks in a room perhaps eight feet square. Periodically, leafy branches of a birch tree were put in water and spattered around the room and on the rocks to create steam. A sand glass timer was used to ensure that no one stayed too long in the room. We left the room and spent some time eating pizza together in the dining area before returning to the steam room. After the second steam room experience, we went outside into the February night and rolled in the snow before returning to the steam room. This time, I was instructed to lie down on the rack and birch branches were used to hit me on the back, front, and feet to stimulate blood circulation. The host "served" me in this kind of Russian massage. After several cycles I had to take my leave since it was 2 a.m. and I had to leave the house where I was staying by 6 a.m. to catch my flight home to America. Sometimes men will stay all night in a banya together. The local missionary/pastor who hosted the banya told me that he often accomplishes more ministry with men in the banya than anywhere else.

There was one peculiar feature of the banya that they explained to me. When we approached the steam room, there were racks to hang towels and a collection of odd hats to wear. These hats were the only pieces of attire they would wear into the steam room. The hats seemed childish. One hat was an admiral's hat. Another was a general's hat. There were other similar hats to wear. I was given a hat with the explanation that there were no generals or privates in the banya. Stripped of all our trappings of success except for the parody of the hats, we were equals in the banya! Nobody was higher than anyone else in the banya. No one had a higher standing than another in the banya. The banya was a place of friendship where we could share ourselves with each other.

Jesus invites us into His banya. We share in His friendship as we share in the friendship of each other. We welcome His service to us as we welcome the service of those who represent Jesus to us. We offer our service of cleansing to one another in the banya of Jesus, our host. Jesus welcomes us to His banya every day.

3
THE DARKNESS WITHIN

John 13:21-30

Jesus has a problem. He wants to spend his last evening on this earth in close friendship with those who are His own. Therefore, He must get rid of the traitor. True friendship excludes traitors! There can be no friendship with those who betray us. They say that Benedict Arnold found little comfort with the British soldiers after his betrayal. At one point he supposedly asked a British officer what the Colonial army would do if they ever caught him. The British officer replied that they would probably cut off his leg which had been wounded in battle and give the leg a military burial. Then they would hang him without it.

Before Jesus continues this special supper in John 13; before he begins his fellowship teaching; and especially before He introduces the ordinance we call Communion; He deals with the traitor. He excludes Him from the communal friendship. To be friends with Jesus is to be friends with Jesus' friends. Friendship requires loyalty.

FROM WITHIN NOT WITHOUT

Jesus makes an important announcement in the middle of that last supper. "Truly, truly, I say to you, that one of you will betray Me." It is not one of the Pharisees or one of the enemies but one of his closest friends who would betray Him. In fact, Luke's account (22:21) indicates that Jesus also added: "one who eats with Me." Jesus has just predicted the betrayal in verse 18 where He quoted from Psalm 41:9. Psalm 41 is a psalm of David written after he was betrayed by one of his closest friends, someone who ate with him; yet turned against him.[1]

It is nearly dark now. King David is walking barefoot near the top of the Mount of Olives weeping as he goes. His group of faithful soldiers and advisors along with their women and children walk with him through the gathering twilight. The Levites carrying the Ark of the Covenant join him along with Zadok and Abiathar the priests. His son Absalom has betrayed him and taken over the kingdom, and David is fleeing for his life once again. It is one of the darkest moments of David's life. It is precisely at that moment that someone tells him that Ahithophel is one of the leaders of the conspiracy with Absalom. "How can this be? I am King of Israel. God, I was faithful to you. For years, I was on the run in the wilderness while King Saul hunted me like a wild animal. Now as an old man, I am hunted by my own son. And Ahithophel? My trusted advisor; the one who lived with me in the wilderness; the one who ate with me and served with me; the one who advised me and fought with me; the one who stood by me in countless battles and saved my life; Ahithophel is with Absalom." The news is too much for David. He turns once again to the Lord and says, "O Lord, I pray, make the counsel of Ahithophel foolishness."

Psalm 41 was most likely composed by David after the event was over, so it is fitting for Jesus to quote it here. The story of Ahithophel does not end there. Ahithophel advises Absalom to pursue David immediately with his army before David has time to regroup for he knows that David is an old warrior and given time he will strike back. Absalom does not follow Ahithophel's advice but instead waits for a day to gather his forces before going after David. It is all the time that David needs because, when the battle is joined, his experienced warriors defeat the army and kill Absalom. What about Ahithophel? He is nowhere to be found because, when Absalom did not follow his advice, Ahithophel left the palace, went to his home, put his things in order and hanged himself – a remarkable picture of Judas![2]

Jesus considers the story of David and Ahithophel as he makes his announcement. He is troubled. Betrayal hurts. Here was a man who had lived and eaten and worked with the Master for three years. Now he was betraying him. Friendship runs the risk of betrayal. Those we love always have the greatest power to hurt us, and Jesus is hurt deeply. The darkness of betrayal always comes from within not without.

PRETENDERS!

The announcement has startled the disciples. Jesus has been predicting his betrayal for nearly a year now. It shouldn't have startled them, but it did. They were looking all around at each other wondering who it was. They had no idea it was Judas. They could not imagine it. They could not even understand how someone from within their group could possibly do such a thing. We think that we can look around in a church and pick out the traitors. We can't! We look around and say that David or Susan live up to certain standards of morality so they must be spiritual people. Judas lived up to every possible standard and never was a believer at all. Even after living and working close together for three years they had no idea who it was. Traitors are pretenders, and they are experts at pretending. They are good at convincing everyone that they are spiritual people when in fact they are hypocrites.

This fact should drive us to examine ourselves constantly to see if we fit the category of a pretender. The disciples do not point the finger at Judas. Matthew and Mark tell us that they were asking, "Is it I, Lord? Is it I?"[3] We must start with that same attitude if we are ever to understand the lessons of Judas.

Picture the supper. The disciples were arranged in a U-shaped fashion around a low table. The open end of the table allowed for food to be served. They reclined on a series of couches or pillows arranged in groups of three facing the center table where the food was located. Now there are all sorts of conjectures about the seating arrangement that night. I conclude, with Edersheim,[4] that the host was reclining on the center couch of a group of three couches on the right-hand side of the "U." This was the location where the host would recline so as to be nearest the food being served and where he could easily start the Passover rituals which proceeded around the table to his left. We know that John, the beloved disciple, was reclining to Jesus' right. Since they reclined on their left arms and ate with their right, this would mean that John would only have to lean backward to speak quietly with Jesus. As he did so, he would be reclining on Jesus' chest and looking up into his face. Peter reclined across the table down one of the arms of the U. Peter was far enough away so that he could not talk privately with Jesus, so he motioned to John to ask the Master. John leans back and asks very simply, "Lord, who is it?"

THE SOP OF CHOICE

I believe that Judas was reclining immediately to Jesus' left at the juncture of the U formation. Jesus speaks quietly to John in answer to his question while everyone else is busy talking about the announcement. He can whisper to John that he will identify the traitor by giving him the sop without the others hearing the full information because John is only inches away. So I believe that only John and perhaps Judas to his left hear this exchange. The rest of the disciples were unaware of the exchange of words. They see Jesus take the sop and hand it to Judas, but they do not understand the significance of his action.

The "sop" was a piece of unleavened bread which the host would dip in the common bowl and scoop out a piece of lamb along with a sauce made of mashed fruit and bitter herbs. Jesus hands the "sop" to Judas. According to custom, the host would give the honored guest the choicest piece. We know from the other accounts that Judas also had asked, "Is it I?" along with the other disciples.[5] He played the game to the very end. The disciples could not have known all that went into that simple exchange but they would have seen what Jesus did and quieted down to watch the master and Judas.

If Hollywood was portraying this scene, the music would crescendo, and the eyes of each would look deep into each other. The moment would be frozen in time as Judas hesitated, trying to read the eyes of the master. He knew he was found out. He knew his cover was blown. He knew the moment of truth. This was Christ's last attempt to reach Him, knowing well that Judas had already passed the point of no return. The lesson here is that Jesus was in full control of the situation. Jesus took the initiative. Jesus didn't just react to Judas, but He forced Judas to make a choice. "This is your last chance Judas. We will play this game no longer." Jesus knew all along it was a charade. Now he exposes the pretender, at least to himself.

Jesus knows the pretenders from the beginning. God is not surprised by hypocrites. In fact, Jesus has been slowly backing Judas into a corner for a year now. Eventually, in His perfect time, He forces the traitor to make a final decision, teaching us two lessons. God is in full control even of traitors. Yet, Judas is fully responsible for his decision. Judas was part of God's design. Yet, Judas is guilty of betrayal. The same is true today. God eventually forces pretenders to make their choice. He takes the initiative. He is in control.

THE POINT OF NO RETURN

The treachery of Judas' heart formed slowly over time. Traitors do not suddenly materialize. They develop through a lengthy process. They do not suddenly decide to reject the Lord. A hard heart slowly develops until it reaches the point of no return. This process of hardening has been going on for some time, and it culminates on this fateful night. Spiritual warfare is going on in the heart of Judas.

> But Judas Iscariot, one of His disciples, who was intending to betray Him, said, "Why was this perfume not sold for three hundred denarii and given to poor people?" Now he said this, not because he was concerned about the poor, but because he was a thief, and as he had the money box, he used to pilfer what was put into it. (John 12:4-6)

> During supper, the devil having already put into the heart of Judas Iscariot, the son of Simon, to betray Him, Jesus, knowing that the Father had given all things into His hands, and that He had come forth from God and was going back to God, got up from supper, and laid aside His garments; and taking a towel, He girded Himself. (John 13:2)

> After the morsel, Satan then entered into him. Therefore, Jesus said to him, "What you do, do quickly." (John 13:27)

39

Satan was playing with the mind of Judas. He was tempting him with ideas, circumstances, thoughts, and plans. We can see here the anatomy of sin. Sin begins in the mind. Satan's door into the mind of Judas seems to be his lust for money and success. Satan cannot read our thoughts, but he can influence us through the people and circumstances around us. He uses those circumstances to trigger ideas. As we dwell on those ideas, plans begin to take shape, and emotions drive us to plan more. Up until now, no one has been hurt. Judas has just been playing the game. But now Jesus makes him decide. Jesus knows his mind and he forces him to take action. It is only after Judas takes this seemingly innocent action of receiving the bread that Satan controls him. In other words, Judas opened the door and invited Satan to control him by taking that bread from the hand of Jesus. It is the point of no return.

When Jesus gives up on a person, there is no hope. *What you do, do quickly.* The timetable has been taken out of the hands of Judas. Jesus is in control of the timetable for the crucifixion. Friday, the fifteenth of Nisan was Jesus' appointed day. It was not Judas' plan. It was not the plan of the Sanhedrin. They wanted to wait until after the Passover. But Jesus forced the hand of Judas. If it was going to happen, it had to happen tonight. The heart is hard. The decision is fixed. Jesus can see it in his eyes and orders him into action. Judas may be possessed by Satan, but he obeys Jesus!

HONORED TO THE END

Still no one understands. Even John apparently was too shocked to understand the enormity of what was happening until he looked back on it later. Two thousand years later, I find it hard to comprehend how a man who walked with Christ, tasted of His salvation, and was enlightened by his teaching, could betray Him to His death. The only comfort is to realize that Judas, too, was part of God's plan from the first; yet fully responsible for his decision.

Judases are never people we expect. Judas was the treasurer of the group. He was a leader. Even now they thought that Jesus was instructing him on some financial responsibility. It is interesting that the most important position at the Passover was not the person to the right of Jesus but the person to his left. The host would place the honored guest at his left to begin the service of the meal. The host would give the most honored guest at the meal the first "sop." Taking the sop was a pledge of loyalty. Jesus has been honoring Judas all night long.

I am amazed at the patience and love of Jesus. The disciples did not recognize the traitor because Jesus had done nothing but honor the very one he knew was against him. The disciples had come that evening arguing about who would sit in the place of honor. I can hear Jesus saying, "Come over here Judas. I want you to sit by my side. I want to talk with you." I do not know what was said that evening, but I can hardly believe that Jesus did not talk graciously and lovingly with Judas during the evening, reaching out to him the closer he drew to the betrayal.

So today, traitors are great pretenders. They are almost always people in leadership roles. They are people who fool us with their gifts, their skills, their success, and their zeal. The traitor is the kind of person who sweeps us off our feet with his or her abilities. He comes into a fellowship and quickly becomes a successful leader. We thrill to the testimonies and the gifts of the person. Only later do we ever find out that he was never a believer at all. He was a Judas. He betrays His master by turning away. Traitors are never who you expect them to be.

LEAVING THE LIGHT FOR THE NIGHT

Judas leaves. John, who has been watching this whole thing and hearing but not quite understanding what is happening, records his editorial comment. As he looks back later, he remembers the blackness of the night through the open door and finds it appropriate for Judas. The most expensive upper rooms were rooms which had their own external entrances via a set of outside stairs. Most people joined groups of Passover guests at common meals in rooms surrounding the courtyard. But it is most likely that Jesus ate His final Passover in an expensive upper room, and not the more common rooms below, allowing people to come and go privately. It also meant that John could look through the open door and see the dark night outside.

Judas took the sop and "went out immediately, and it was night." Nobody coerced Judas. He acted on his own. It was his choice to excommunicate himself from the friendship of Jesus and His followers. As Judas paused for just a moment, he was framed in the doorway. The contrast, between the warmly lit room and the blackness outside, framed John's growing realization that Judas had now left the spiritual light to join the forces of darkness. It is hard to believe, but traitors leave the warm light of Christ's love for the blackness of their own sin. The result is that they are excluded from any real friendship with the master no matter how religious they might seem at the time.

Joe (not his real name) was one of my best friends. We started Bible College together as freshmen. We studied together, prayed together, and worked together through three years of college. We spent hours discussing and exploring theological issues in countless dorm room "bull sessions." Many a late night was spent cramming for exams together. Joe had come from a small town and grew up in relative poverty. His father was disabled, and his mother supported the family as best she could, but with several children it was a hard life on the "wrong side of the tracks." Joe put his faith in Christ through the ministry of a local Baptist Church youth group and excitedly went off to Bible College to become a pastor until that summer following our junior year in college.

Joe worked long hours as a security guard along with a full load of classes that year. One of his research papers was on the life and writings of the German philosopher Friedrich Nietzsche and he poured himself into his research. We took an Old Testament Bible class together that spring and the professor offered us an option for the final exam. We could choose to do a portfolio on all the prophetic books instead of taking a final exam. Joe and I both chose to do the portfolio. I had my reasons. I was getting married a week after school ended and wanted to get as much done before final exams week as possible. Joe was in love too and wanted to leave quickly to see a young lady back home for the summer. We worked hard on our portfolios, and we both put together some excellent binders full of information, charts and resources on each of the prophetic books. We turned in our binders on the day of the final exam only to have the professor tell us that he had changed his mind. We had to take the final exam. We were angry, of course, but the professor would not budge. I chose to take the exam without studying and barely passed. Joe refused and flunked. He never came back to school.

I lost touch with Joe during my senior year but caught up with him after I graduated. He was a philosophy student at the local university. We met and talked for many hours. Joe had left school that spring very angry with God and with Christians. His anger grew when he returned home to find out that the family of the young lady he loved (and thought she loved him) had turned against him because of his poverty-stricken family background. His pastor did not support him, and he felt like the church turned against him. So Joe turned against God. He became an ardent atheist. He followed the teachings of Nietzsche whom he originally critiqued in Bible College. Joe was angry and bitter. Christians were hypocrites, and God didn't exist. He walked away from all he once believed, never to return so far as I know. I was heart-broken. My friend was gone. He had rejected Jesus, and he wanted nothing more to do with me as a friend of Jesus.

Joe had been on fire for Jesus. If you had asked me during our early years at Bible College if Joe would deny Jesus, I would have thought you crazy. He was passionate about his faith and a good friend to me. Yet Joe made a choice. He chose to walk out of the light into the night. No longer friends with Jesus, he was no longer a friend with me – by his choice, not mine. We were walking different paths now. Joe wanted nothing to do with Christians because he wanted nothing to do with Christ. To be friends with Jesus means to be friends with Jesus' friends.

4

LOYAL LOVE AND THE CROWING COCK

John 13:31-38

If you have ever been in a place where friends or family have gathered to discuss important information but have felt uncomfortable because one of those present in the group was not united with the others in spirit, then you understand what is happening in John 13:31. Tension fills the room until the person leaves, and suddenly everyone begins to talk freely and openly, and the fellowship is sweet. Friendship is based on loyalty, and when a person is working at cross purposes with the group the loyalty is divided and the friendship hindered. True friendship is inhibited by disloyal people.

Three figures dominate John 13: Judas, Jesus and Peter. Judas betrayed Jesus, and Peter denied Jesus; so the chapter begins and ends with disloyalty. True friendship requires loyalty. Judas has just left the upper room and even though the disciples never recognized him as a traitor, there is an almost palpable sense of relief at this point. There must have been some sense, call it a sixth sense if you will, that had made them increasingly uncomfortable around him, because John makes a point of emphasizing his departure. His departure was critical to the developing friendship of the group. Judas had to go before Jesus could teach them the critical lessons of the next few chapters. He begins with loyalty.

We are loyal to Jesus when we accept his glory (13:31-32). That sounds easy enough. We'd be glad to accept the glory. It's the suffering and pain we don't want. Yet, the glory Jesus talks about in these verses includes the pain and suffering. We cannot accept the glory without the pain any more than we can accept the crown without the cross. There are three ways in which the concept of glory is used in these two verses, and we cannot pick and choose which aspects of Christ's glory we want to accept. We take it all, or we don't take it at all!

THREE GLORIES

First, we see the glory of His choice (v.31a). Jesus said, "Now is the Son of Man glorified" – right now, in this decision, in this choice. Christ displayed His greatness in His decision regarding Judas. Jesus had seen the coming storm clouds and, rather than avoid the storm; he had chosen to walk right into it. Jesus knew the coming pain, and he chose to accept the coming suffering. His choice was glorious.

> 13:1 - Jesus KNOWING His hour had come
> 13:3 - Jesus KNOWING that He was going back to God
> 13:11 - He KNEW the one who was betraying Him
> 13:18 - I KNOW the ones I have chosen

The events surrounding Judas' betrayal were initiated not by Judas but by Jesus. He offered the sop and dared Judas to make his choice. He told Judas, "What you do, do quickly." Jesus saw the storm brewing and walked right into it. He chose to take the pain and suffering of betrayal and disloyalty, and his choice demonstrates His glory.

Next, we see the glory of His cross. "And God is glorified in Him." This is a reference to God the Father. So when was the Father glorified in the Son? The glory was in the cross. It was in the cross that the greatness of God's character was displayed. He could have wiped out the world for its sins, but He chose to die on a cross for the sins of that world. His desire to glorify the Father drove the Son to the cross. The opening words of His prayer in the Garden of Gethsemane express His motivation. "Father, the hour has come; glorify your Son, that your Son may glorify you" (John 17:1).

Finally, we see the glory of His crown. Now the tense switches to the future. "God will also glorify Him in Himself, and will glorify Him immediately." This is a reference to the resurrection, ascension and glorification of the Son with the Father in Heaven after His work on earth is done. And all of this glory will happen immediately - quickly! His glory consumed Jesus on His last night on earth. He pleaded with the Father in His prayer: "I glorified you on the earth, having accomplished the work which you have given me to do. Now, Father, glorify me together with yourself, with the glory which I had with you before the world was" (John17:4-5).

We can only be loyal to God when we are willing to accept all aspects of His glory. There is glory in suffering for Christ – a glory we should willingly embrace. There is glory in triumphing in Christ – a glory that follows the pain. We must take the pain now if we want the glory later. We are loyal to Jesus when we accept His glory – all of it as a package deal. Such acceptance requires a life commitment of loyal love.

A CONFESSION OF LOYAL LOVE

Amy Carmichael (1867-1951), the Irish missionary to South India sent out by the Keswick Convention of England, labored for fifty six years in her adopted homeland without ever returning to Ireland. She founded "The Dohnavur Fellowship" in 1901, a community originally devoted to rescuing young girls who had been dedicated to the temples and expanded to provide service to many others in India. Her ministry was born in sorrow and grew through pain. Death seemed to follow her everywhere in those early years of struggle. Her spiritual "mother," Mrs. Hopwood, died. Amy often had visited her in the hill country of Ooty for times of refreshment. Soon after, Lulla, a favorite child, died suddenly and within months her spiritual mentor, Thomas Walker, died of ptomaine poisoning. Ponnammal, her support and confidant, contracted cancer and soon passed into heaven. Then Arulai, her close friend in the ministry, almost died. As Arulai, her "star," lay dying, Amy walked the small compound praying. She pleaded with God. "Did He have to take them all?" God didn't. Arulai recovered and the "Sisters of Common Life" were formed. It was a fellowship devoted to the common life and determined to avoid a distinction between the sacred and the secular. There were seven young Indian women, including Arulai, who joined Amy in her group. They all

47

bound themselves together by a "confession of love." Every young lady gladly accepted this confession to become part of the sisters.

> *My vow: Whatsoever Thou sayest unto me, by Thy grace I will do it.*
> *My constraint: Thy love, O Christ, my Lord.*
> *My confidence: Thou art able to keep that which I have committed unto Thee.*
> *My joy: To do Thy will, O God.*
> *My discipline: That which I would not choose, but which Thy love appoints.*
> *My Prayer: Conform my will to Thine.*
> *My Motto: Love to live, live to love.*
> *My Portion: The Lord is the portion of my inheritance.*[1]

We are loyal to Jesus when we love each other (13:33-35). Everybody wants to be loved! One man, whose wife had left him for another man, told me between sobs, "I just wanted to be loved unconditionally – for who I am not what I do." Children gravitate toward love. They will respond to love far more effectively than authority. When our two girls were little, I used to give them single red roses for Valentine's Day each year. They were thrilled. The first time I did it, Kari walked around and around with her rose shouting "Thank you, Daddy." She didn't even want to let go of it to put the rose in a vase. A few Sundays later, Katie was riding home in the car with me, and she said, "Do you know what Dad? Uncle Dan loves me!" Then with eyes wide open she looked up at me and said, "Dad, he leaned over at the end of church and whispered, 'I love you.'" Wow! Everybody wants to be loved!

So it should not be a surprise that Jesus begins this little section with a very tender expression, "little children." This is the only place in the gospels where this expression is used, and it is a term of endearment. "Little children" was a term that the Rabbis used for their personal pupils, so it is noteworthy that Jesus used this term only after Judas had left. Now He can talk affectionately to those He loves and who love Him with a loyal love.

All loves are not the same. Not everybody experiences the loyal love Jesus is talking about here. The love that binds the disciples together with Jesus is different than the love God has for others in this world. Jesus had told the Jewish leaders that they would seek Him and would not find

Him because they were unable to go where He was going (John 7:34). Jesus says that they are unable to come with Him. Here in this passage He uses the same language but leaves off the part about seeking and not finding. The disciples will seek Him, and they will find Him. Furthermore, Jesus specifically says that they cannot follow Him now but will follow later (v.36). So there is a major difference between the disciples and the Jewish leaders. The disciples are part of a community of love that the Jewish leaders will never experience.

Jesus is saying that only by faith in Him can anyone experience His love. Many people in this world never experience His love because they refuse to repent of their sins and trust Christ with their lives. They continue to live for themselves just like the Jewish leaders. Jesus' point here is not so much to distinguish between the disciples and the Jews as it is to lead into the new commandment that will bind them together with Him. Jesus is saying, "Look, I know that when the perfect example of love is gone, you will wish that He was here with you. I am leaving this world, and after I am gone, you will seek my example of love and wish that I could be present in your midst or that you could be with me, and you cannot come for now." The perfect example of perfect love will leave this world so how will people ever learn how to love as Christ loved? Through His people. Where will people look to find divine love demonstrated? They will see it only in us! We continue that legacy. We are a new community of love, so we need a new commandment to love.

A NEW COMMANDMENT

How is this command new? (John 13:34) God had commanded the Israelites to love both fellow Israelites and strangers in the Mosaic Law (Lev. 19:18, 34). "You shall love your neighbor as yourself." Jesus had repeated this command (Mark 12:31). Jesus, ratifying the Mosaic Law, commanded us to love God and love our neighbors as the two greatest commandments of all time. How, then, can Jesus say to His disciples "a new commandment I give to you, that you love one another" on the night before He died on the cross?

There are two Greek words commonly used for "new." In many contexts, the two words for "new" are used interchangeably, but sometimes – as here – there is an important distinction. The first word emphasizes new with respect to time, new in reference to something that has recently come into existence. The second word emphasizes new with respect to quality. Jesus used the same word in John 13:34. The emphasis is on new as opposed to something that has become worn out or damaged by age.[2] The same word is used in John 19:41. Joseph of Arimathea has a "new tomb" in which no body had been laid. The tomb was not a tomb that was new because it had been recently carved out of the rock. It was a new tomb in the sense that it was fresh and had never been used before. The new commandment to love one another is new in the sense of fresh, as opposed to the old commandment that had become worn out by usage. Jesus says, "A fresh commandment I give to you, that you love one another."

The freshness of the command to love one another rests on the foundation of a new standard for love and a new basis for love. The new basis for our love is the cross. We are to love with a "cross love." Jesus goes on to say that we are to love one another "as I have loved you." Here is the new standard for our love. The Mosaic Law commanded us to love our neighbors as ourselves. Loving another as I love myself is a high calling but a humanly doable calling. I can (sometimes) attain to loving someone as I love myself. It is a fleshly standard – a human standard – for love, but at least it is humanly attainable. The fresh commandment for the new covenant is founded on the standard of Christ's love for us. He is our standard. His love is an infinite measureless love which can only be extended to others on the basis of the cross and our relationship together under the banner of the cross. So as Christ loves us, we love others. The vertical dimension of love is played out in the horizontal dimension of the church.

THE MESSINESS OF A LOCAL CHURCH

Christ's love is not a sickly sweet, sentimental, worldly love which gives the other person whatever he wants. Real love involves rebuke and correction as well as support and encouragement. The same Jesus, who loved Peter enough to choose Him, also loved him enough to rebuke him. One of the marks of a Christian is how he relates to other Christians. Love is a characteristic of genuine Christian relationships and God gives the world the right to decide whether Christianity is real or not based on how we love one another (vs. 35). That is a scary thought. A final test of our discipleship is how we love one another in the church – the visible, tangible, local church. We can love one another in the body of Christ – the church universal – much easier than we can love one another in the local church. We can love people in the body of Christ at a distance. We have to love people in the local church up close and personal. We rub each other the wrong way. Personalities clash. We must work together, pay bills together, make decisions together, disagree with each other and compromise with each other to achieve common goals. Serving together in the local church can get messy. We don't have the luxury of distancing ourselves from people in the average sized local church. Love in the local church looks very different than love in the universal church. Love up close looks very different than love from a distance.

People leave a local church. I take it personally when they do! I try not to take it personally as a pastor. I hide it well. I am "professional" about it. I know they are not leaving the church universal. We are still part of the body of Christ. We are still unified by the Spirit and the cross. I know that there are many other good local churches around and that people have choices. I still take it personally as a pastor. That is the true confession of most pastors. One of our elders commented at a meeting that it feels like people rip themselves away from us when they leave the church. He misses them because they are no longer part of his life. I agree. It stings. It should sting because we are part of one another in a local church in a way we are not part of one another in the universal church. It often stings far more than it should because people say hurtful words when they leave. One man left our church to go to another church over what I considered a minor disagreement. He, obviously, did not consider it minor. Shortly after he left the church, there was a tragic death in the family. I called to offer my sympathy and prayer. He said, "You only called because you feel guilty that you didn't meet our needs." It was not true. I genuinely wanted to express my love, and it hurt to hear those words. Another man had disappeared from the church after serving with us in many ways over some years. I contacted him to see what had happened. I told him I thought we were friends, and I had hoped that he would have shared with me as a friend his concerns before leaving the church. He quickly said, "We were never friends at all." He felt no friendship toward me. It hurt. His words were like a knife slicing into my soul. True love is reciprocal, and loyal love is the mark of true friendship.

God designed the local church as a community. We cannot make it on our own. We cannot choose to do our own thing and go our own way

51

in life and expect to be healthy Christians. We need each other. The world will be far more impressed with how we care for one another than they will be with our programs and our buildings. I need you, and you need me to grow. We cannot make it on our own. Sadly, more and more Christians are opting out of the local church in favor of the universal church. George Barna in his 2005 study identified the growing trend of Christians who are leaving local churches to work out their faith through kingdom living with small groups of friends. He points out that 70% of Americans relied on the local church for their primary spiritual experience in 2000, and only 5% turned to alternative forms of Christian community. Barna predicts that by the year 2025 only 33% of Christians will see the local church as their primary focus for faith experience while another 33% will turn to alternative forms of community and another 33% will use the media for their primary spiritual experience. Christians increasingly are committed to *the* church, not *a* church. They want to *be* the church not *go* to church.[3] These Christians do not see the local church as an effective model for spiritual life and growth. They want more spiritual reality and less religious structure.

The truth is that most Christians I know who have opted out of local churches do so for less idealistic reasons. The local church is simply too messy and uncomfortable for them. The local church places demands on them. Being committed to the body of Christ, as opposed to the local church, makes it much easier to love because we can choose our friends. We can love those we like and who like us. We can serve in soup kitchens once in a while and go on a mission trip, but we don't have to love weekly those we don't like. We don't have to serve on a committee that makes decisions about what to do with limited resources. We do whatever we want because we don't have to answer to anyone else – at least anyone who disagrees with us! We can avoid those messy relationships that drain us in any local church. The local church forces us to love those we don't like. The local church is God's visible expression of Jesus to the world, and it is in the local church where his command to love one another is tested.

NO PLASTIC SAINTS ALLOWED

The early church in Acts was hardly utopian although many paint an idealistic picture by glossing over the uncomfortable details of the New Testament record. The early church argued and fought about decisions.

Factions developed between fractious Christians. Sin and failure filled the church in Acts from the very beginning. These Christians were not plastic saints. Many were not even people we would like, but they were the people who filled local churches. As hard as it is, we need to work together with people in a local church who seek to demonstrate the love of Christ to the world around us. It is hard, but we need each other. We are flawed people, and church gets messy, but failure is part of the package. We are all saved by grace, and we must extend grace to one another. We have to love one another in our failures.

I read a cute story somewhere about a little girl in a Sunday School class who became frustrated with her drawing of the animals in Noah's Ark. Her older brother tried to comfort her. "Don't worry," he said, "It took the great artist Michelangelo fifteen tries until he finally got the sixteenth chapel right." Well ... here is poor Peter trying for the umpteenth time to get it right and failing again (John 13:36-38). Peter bypasses the whole teaching about the new commandment to talk about his agenda. He wants to know where the Lord is going. Peter is like so many of us. We are more focused on our concerns than His mission. Local churches are filled with "Peters!" Our agenda is more important than the Lord's teaching. So we rush on ahead seeking to follow our goals and plans only to end up failing the Lord again.

We could talk about Peter's impatience or his pride here. We could study the process whereby he fell into sin, but I want to focus on the point this passage makes in its context. Chapter 13 starts with Judas, the traitor but ends with Peter the denier. Both men are disloyal to the Lord at this critical moment in human history. The disloyalty of each man leads to very different results. Judas will die as the "Son of Perdition." Peter will become one of the foremost apostles and founders of the Christian faith. What makes the difference? Let me ask it another way? Could Jesus have forgiven Peter's denial and refused to forgive Judas' betrayal? No. I think we would have to conclude that Jesus would have forgiven Judas just as well as Peter. So the difference is not in degree of failure but rather in each man's response to failure. Judas and Peter both fell. They both were disloyal to the Lord. Peter responded with repentance and Judas did not. There is all the difference between heaven and hell - between friends with Jesus or enemies of Jesus.

Anyone can fall. Anyone can fail. Every one of us fails. Every one of us sins. It is how we respond to that sin which makes the difference. Jesus is presenting a contrast between the response of Judas and the response of Peter. Peter will repent. Judas did not. One of the lessons of loyalty is that when confronted with our own disloyalty we surrender. We repent. We turn to God for forgiveness. Everyone sins but those who want friendship with Jesus repent. They turn around and come back to Jesus and accept His washing and enjoy His friendship once again.

John 13 is the prelude to Jesus' extended discourse to his friends preparing them for the future. The prelude to deeper friendship starts with a prediction of utter failure! The irony of intimacy is that intimacy often rises from the ashes of despair. Failure can become the foundation for a deeper spiritual friendship if we run to Jesus with our guilt and let Him embrace us in our shame. Peter will be more passionately in love with Jesus after his denial than before, and he will experience a deeper friendship with Jesus because of his failure and subsequent restoration. So can you. So can I.

Dr. John Duncan (1796-1870) was a professor of Hebrew and Oriental Languages at New College in Edinburgh and an ordained minister in the Free Church of Scotland. His passionate love for the Jewish people and his knowledge of Hebrew led many students to call him "Rabbi Duncan." He was helping to serve communion one Sunday when he noticed a woman in a front pew who was crying quietly. She refused to take the cup that was offered to her by an elder. This warm-hearted scholar left his place behind the table and walked over to the elder serving communion. He took the cup and handed it to the woman. He looked into her teary eyes and said, "Take it woman - it's for sinners!"[4]

A local church is not a gathering place for the self-righteous but a hospital for sinners. You are welcome. I am welcome. A local church is to be a place where healthy friendships take place, but such friendships require us to wash each other's feet with forgiving love. Our friendship with Jesus calls for us to allow Him to wash our dirty feet regularly. Our friendship with each other calls for mutual foot washing. Those who do not follow Jesus are not part of the friendship we share with Jesus. True friendship requires loyalty to the Lord and each other, and that loyalty is tested by the fires of Satan and the failures of saints. Loyal love is the foundation for true friendship.

THE TRANSPARENCY
OF TRUST

5
A FOREVER FAITH

John 14:1-6

> Blessings on thee, little man,
> barefoot boy with cheeks of tan,
> trudging down a dusty lane
> with no thought of future pain.
> You're our one and only bet
> to absorb the National Debt.
>
> Little man with cares so few,
> we've got lots of faith in you.
> Guard each merry whistled tune,
> you are apt to need it soon.
> Have your fun, boy, while you can,
> you may be a barefoot man! [1]

Are you afraid of the future? Facing the future is part of growing up. We cannot stay in our comfortable cocoons. Life is tough. Problems come. Childhood friends move away. I haven't seen my best friend in high school for years now. Facing the future without your best friend can be terrifying to contemplate. The disciples were afraid on this night before the crucifixion. Jesus' words were disturbing. He has just told them that He is leaving them, that there is a traitor in their group and that Peter, another friend, will deny Him three times that night! Their friendship with Jesus and each other will be deeply tested in the next few days. They must grow up fast. So Jesus says in John 14, "You must trust me no matter what happens in the next few hours." The future is secure in me.

Friendship – true friendship – is founded on faith. No human friend can guarantee the future for us, so we have to trust the friend for the future. When we pledge our friendship, we pledge our loyalty in the face of the unknown future. Jesus pledges His friendship to us. We can experience that friendship only by faith as we face the unknown future.

DON'T BE TROUBLED ... TRUST!

The word for "troubled" is important here. It was sometimes used of surging water or the storm waves of the sea. If you have ever been on a boat in the ocean when the waves were tossing it about, then you have some idea of what this word implies. These surging, raging emotions can destroy a person if they are not dealt with effectively. The same word is used three times to describe the emotional life of Jesus Himself most recently in 13:21. So we know that it is not sin to have troubled emotions. Emotions are not sinful. They are part of the normal human experience. Some people, obviously, are more emotional than others, but the emotions are not wrong. It is what we do with emotions and how we handle those emotions that can be sinful.

Jesus knows that the disciples are troubled here, so He says to them, "Stop letting your heart be troubled." It is a command, and the command implies that we can do something about a troubled heart. We do not have to be ruled by the emotions. We can challenge those emotions with God's truth. Jesus is saying here that we can do something about our emotions. The key to dealing with fear and worry is in our power. We can choose to let the fears overwhelm us, or we can choose not to let those fears overwhelm us.

The antidote to fear is faith. Faith drives out those fears. Faith controls the raging emotions which threaten to overwhelm our souls. Two commands follow this first command. "Believe in God ... Believe in Me." Jesus commands faith as the answer to fear. Don't be troubled ... trust! Trust God and trust me. Jesus uses the word "believe" twice, and the form is ambiguous. There are four ways these verbs could be translated. 1) Both verbs are imperatives (commands). 2) The first verb is an indicative (statement of fact) and the second is a command. 3) The first verb is a command and the second is a statement. 4) Both verbs are indicative making factual statements. It is a matter of interpretation since all four translations are grammatically correct. The question boils down to the precise point that Jesus is making in this verse.[2]

Many argue that Jesus was commanding both faith in God and faith in Him. The two verbs should be translated the same way according to many. However, I think that Jesus recognized they had faith in God already, but they needed to trust Him. I think that Jesus said, "You trust (statement of fact) in God, trust (command) in Me also."[3] He had just predicted that He is leaving the disciples and that Peter would deny Him three times before the cock crowed. These are troubling predictions that raise doubts about what Jesus is doing. Jesus was not commanding them to believe God. They were pious Israelites. He knew they believed God. Jesus was commanding them to trust Him. After all, He was the one troubling them with these predictions.

These verbs are talking about continuing faith, not initial faith. Jesus knows that they have believed in God. Every Jew believes in God. Jesus knows that they continue to believe in God, yet now they are afraid. They fear because they doubt Him. Jesus knows they have trusted Him in the past. They have followed Him for three years now. He is saying that they must continue in that belief. It is precisely in the moments when we struggle with our emotions – when we face the unknown – that we must be reminded to continue to place our trust in Jesus as our friend.

Jesus does not say here, "believe what I am telling you." He says, "Believe in me." There is one kind of faith which trusts the words which are spoken, but there is another kind of faith which trusts the one who does the speaking. The second kind of faith is the key to dealing with emotional turmoil, and it is the key to intimacy with Jesus. We must trust not only what God says in the Bible, but we must trust Jesus as a true friend. We must know that Jesus would never, ever do anything that is not in our best interest. We must trust Him implicitly no matter what we face in life. The testing of trust leads to the intimacy of friendship.

The Spanish mystic, John of the Cross (1542-1591), wrote his famous work entitled *The Dark Night of the Soul* after his arrest and confinement. He taught that God draws us into a deeper intimacy with

Him through "the dark night of the soul" because God wants to purify us for Himself.[4] God invites us to enter a new intimacy through experiencing loss. When Jesus seems most distant, He is inviting us to follow Him into deeper intimacy. The distance of Jesus is the door to friendship. Jesus is now inviting the disciples into closer friendship by withdrawing from them as they enter their dark night of the soul. He does the same with us. Klaus Issler writes: "By extending such an invitation, God considers us ready for a new and deeper level of intimacy with him. By means of such periods of dryness, God purifies our faith, and in the process, he dislodges what we hold dear, including our false fixed ideas about God. Paradoxically, God desires to draw us closer to Himself by being temporarily distant and hidden."[5]

The pain was etched into his face and seared into his eyes. A colleague in ministry, a gifted teacher, he was experiencing the depths of the pit. His wife of a few years had left him for another man. He had been wrestling through many long nights of tearful prayers. I didn't know what to say. A long silence filled the office broken only when he lifted his eyes to meet mine, and, with tears welling up, he said that God seemed so far away in his pain – at first. When he needed him the most, God seemed the most distant – initially. Now he was beginning to understand at last. Now God seemed closer than before. Now his prayer times had become sweeter than he had ever known in his life. He said, "I've never felt closer to the Lord. I wouldn't wish this experience on anyone, but I wouldn't trade it for anything either!"

"Trust me," Jesus says, "even when I'm distant. You must learn to trust me in the darkness if you want to experience the depths of spiritual intimacy."

NEVER MOVING AGAIN!

Many years ago, when our children were small, we moved into a new house. Moving is such a hassle and getting settled takes time. Shortly after moving into our new home, our four-year-old daughter Kari was asking my wife, Janie, some theological questions. She asked, "Mommy, why did Jesus die?" Janie said, "Well Jesus died for us so that when we die we can go to heaven with Him." "What's heaven?" Kari asked. "Well, heaven is a place where Jesus is making a new home for us," Janie said. To which Kari quickly replied, "But Mommy, you said you never wanted to move again!"

A move to heaven is one move we will be glad to make. Jesus says, "In my father's house are many dwelling places." *My father's house* is a reference to heaven. Jesus promises His friends a heavenly home. Origen, one of the early Church Fathers, taught that when a person died he or she first lived in a place called "Paradise" to be instructed properly before entering heaven. Then the saint, once instructed, ascended through a series of mansions or stations ("halting places") on his or her way to God. The mansions were stages that saints passed through on their way to glory according to Origen.[6] Death was the beginning of a journey to heaven that passed through many tarrying places along the way. Origen's interpretation flies in the face of what we know about the meaning of this word and other Scripture that promises us immediate entry into heaven (2 Corinthians 5:8). The Greek word means abiding places, abodes, rooms or dwelling places not stages of life.[7] The Latin word "mansio" and the old English word "mansion" meant a dwelling place, not a palatial residence as we use the word today. The Jews believed that heaven had many compartments where people lived.[8] These compartments corresponded to the degrees of reward earned through life on earth. The early Church Father, Irenaeus, citing the "Elders," used John 14:2 to suggest that the dwelling places in heaven corresponded to the thirty, sixty and hundredfold harvests in the Parable of the Sower (Matthew 13:23). Clement of Alexandria taught that the dwelling places in heaven were given to saints according to their service on earth.[9]

The best way to understand the word is to see heaven as a condominium complex with many rooms, suites or apartments. These are permanent residences, not temporary motels we pass through on our journey. Jesus is telling us that heaven is one house with many apartments. The only other place in the New Testament where this word is used is a few verses later in John 14:23. Jesus said, "If anyone loves Me, he will keep My word; and My Father will love him, and We will come to him and make our abode with him." This is clearly a permanent residence - a home - not a temporary tarrying place nor a stage in a journey.

The clause – "if it were not so, I would have told you" – can be translated as either a question or a statement. As a question, it reads, "If it were not so would I have told you that I go to prepare a place for you?" (ESV, NIV) As a statement, it reads, "If it were not so I would have told you, for I go to prepare a place for you." (NASB, KJV) There were no punctuation marks in the original manuscripts, so either translation is possible. I don't think we should understand the clause as a question because Jesus never told them before that He was going to prepare a place for them so the question would be meaningless. I think it is best to understand the clause as introduced by "because" making the preceding clause parenthetical. I connect the final clause – "because I go to prepare a place for you" – with the first clause – "in My Father's house are many dwelling places" – making the middle clause a parenthesis. There are many rooms in heaven because He is going to prepare them for us.

> In My Father's house, there are many rooms (but if not, I
> would have told you) because I am going to prepare a
> place for you.

Jesus reassures us that there is room in heaven for us or He would have warned us not to expect a room in heaven. He left earth to prepare a place for us in heaven. The word "place" meant a room to live, stay or sit.[10] The word "to prepare" was commonly used for preparations made for someone coming to visit.[11] Jesus is preparing our rooms for our homecoming much like a parent prepares the room of a child coming home from college. Our assurance is that Jesus would have warned us not to expect a homecoming if this was not true. Jesus goes on to say that if this were not so, I obviously would have warned you before I left. I am going *to prepare a place for you.* This is my purpose for leaving. My immediate question is, "What's taking so long?" The God who spoke the world into existence in six days does not need 2000 years to build my condominium does He? Of course not. So, what is taking so long?

The question misses the whole point of the passage I think. When Jesus says, "I go to prepare a place for you," He is not saying "I am returning to my Father's house so that after I get there I can begin to prepare your houses for you." The expression about Jesus going in the Gospel of John is almost a technical expression referring to the death, burial and resurrection of Jesus Christ. In other words, His going is the very means by which he prepares a place for us in heaven. His delay in returning is not because my condo isn't quite ready yet. It was ready the moment He left this earth. His delay in returning for me is to allow me to get ready for my condo! As Augustine nicely put it: "Jesus is preparing a place for his followers, not the least by preparing his followers for the place."

The language Jesus uses is relational language. Our house is the 'Father's" house – a family residence – a home. It is our permanent home like no home we ever had on earth. The going of Jesus was necessary to prepare for our arrival. Jesus welcomes us to His home when our work on earth is done. He is preparing the home by preparing us for life in His home.

HE'S COMING BACK!

Jesus made an important promise to us on His last night before the crucifixion. He said, "If I go and prepare a place for you, I will come again and receive you to myself" (John 14:3). This wonderful promise has comforted believers through many trials throughout history. What exactly did Jesus mean by His promise? Christians have understood this promise in a number of ways. 1) Jesus promises a spiritual coming at every trial, but when did He ever leave them spiritually? 2) Jesus promises to come to them in the resurrection, but how does He receive them to Himself at the Resurrection? 3) Jesus promises to come to them in the coming of the Holy Spirit on the Day of Pentecost, but how is this a coming "again" and how does He receive them to Himself at that time? 4) Jesus promises to come to believers – including us – when we die, but the Bible usually presents death as our going to Him (Phil. 1:23; 2 Cor. 5:8). None of these views satisfactorily explains what Jesus promises.

Jesus promises us that He will come again to earth from heaven. Christ's return is the hope of every Christian and the correct understanding of His promise for the following reasons. 1) The use of "again" points back to a first coming. The first coming was bodily not spiritually and on earth not in heaven, so the second coming must be the same. 2) The coming and receiving are grammatically parallel to the going and preparing. If "I go" then "I will come again"! He is leaving them bodily not spiritually, so the coming must be bodily not spiritually.

63

"If I prepare a place for you" then "I will receive you to myself." The prepared place is heaven so the reception must be in heaven. 3) Jesus speaks elsewhere of coming again with reference to His bodily return (John 14:28; 21:22).

The hope of the future is the return of Christ. His return is personal. He does not say, "I will send my angel to get you." He says, "*I will come again,*" showing us how much He values us. No angelic emissary will meet us. Jesus Himself is coming back to lead us into His heavenly welcome reception. He welcomes us into the intimacy of His home forever, the perfect culmination of our friendship with Jesus. Jesus will come back for us *that where I am there you may be also.* Here is the simplest expression of heaven in the Bible. Heaven is where Jesus lives. Whatever we experience here on earth ends in the arms of our Lord when He welcomes us home. We are waiting for His welcome. Death interrupts the wait. If earth is the waiting room for heaven, then death is the side door out of that waiting room. Jesus is there to welcome us to be with Him. It is the language of intimacy.

The phone call came from her husband, Rich, an elder in our church. Yes, the cancer was back, and she was in the hospital. Two years earlier, Terry von Salza Brown had gone to the doctor because she was feeling tired. The diagnosis shocked us all – acute lymphoblastic leukemia. Her busy and productive life was instantly transformed into a battle against death. For two years she underwent heavy doses of chemotherapy followed by a maintenance regimen of medications. The process was exhausting, but the prognosis seemed good. The medical staff told her that the opening blast of chemo was the best hope for life because if leukemia returned there was not much they could do. All the reports were good. The two-year battle would be complete in a couple of months. It seemed like the horrific process had been successful … until that day. The cancer was back. There were few options. When I met with Terry in the hospital, she said, "Pastor, the two years were almost over. I could see the light at the end of the tunnel. Now I know the light is Jesus. I will see Him soon." The next week I closed our worship service at church with this letter from Terry to our church family.

To my dear and much-loved church family, after many blood tests and a bone marrow biopsy, we have been told that my leukemia has relapsed. There are a few options available to me, and I have chosen the moderate one that I can do locally and buy some time to get my affairs in order. Sometime early this week I will be admitted to Maine Med and will start induction chemo for ALL, staying there until I am well enough to come home. I may be able to do continuing chemo on an outpatient basis or may have to be admitted for that. We will just have to see how it goes. When the chemo becomes ineffective, I will get hospice care until Jesus greets me in Heaven. I am so thankful He lives so that I can too! Knowing where I am going after death makes the journey a bit gentler.

Over the next months, we walked with Terry and Rich, along with their daughter, Katie, through the painful process. We wept with them and rejoiced with them. We gathered in their home for praise and prayer times, and many helped wherever they could. A rotation of women from the church stayed with her at night while Rich worked. The times were sweet and precious as we ushered her into her home with Jesus. She was a great example to us all of what it means to trust Jesus and today she is enjoying her welcome into her heavenly home.[12]

THE THOMAS SYNDROME

There is an old explanation of the difference between the four classes, freshmen, sophomores, juniors, and seniors. Freshmen are those who don't know and don't know that they don't know. Sophomores are those who don't know but know that they don't know. Juniors are students who know but don't know what they know. Seniors are supposed to be those who know and know that they know! If that is the case, then we would have to classify the disciples in John 14 as sophomores in the school of Christ. They are confused by the lessons, but at least they know that they are confused! They are lost, but at least they know it!

Where are you going? How do we get there? Thomas asks our questions too. Jesus said, "You know the way where I am going" (v.4), but Thomas is lost. He understands that destination determines direction so he wants to know where Jesus is going and how they are to follow Him to

65

that location. Those are pragmatic questions. He expects the leader to lead the way, and he is ready to follow in his footsteps. Except that he misses the whole point. He is only a sophomore after all!

Jesus' point in verse 4 is not the destination but the route He will travel to arrive at the destination.[13] Jesus is saying something like this. "I have been teaching you for some time now that I go to the Father's house by way of the cross. I have told you often that I must be betrayed, die and rise again. This is the path I must travel to return to my Father's house. You already know this so now I want to prepare you for these events with some important lessons which will help you after I am gone." The way of the cross is the only way that He can return to the Father and still fulfill the Father's will.

Now the way that Christ travels to the Father and the way that we travel to the Father are two different ways. Thomas does not understand this distinction in verse 5. Jesus is not talking about the same way in verse 4 that He is talking about in verse 6. Thomas asks a question which causes Jesus to pause in His teaching. He stops talking about His way to the Father and starts to talk about the way the disciples must travel to the Father. His way is not our way at all! He is our way! The point here is not that Jesus is the trailblazer who leads the way, and we follow in His path, the way Thomas is thinking. He is not so much our guide to the Father as He is the path itself. We cannot follow in His footsteps. His way is the way of the cross. He atones for our sins. He pays the price for our salvation on the cross. We can never atone for our sins by following His example. Those who try are lost.

Hugo Grotius was a man who lived hundreds of years ago, but his influence is still felt today. Grotius proposed a view of the atonement which is called "The Moral Influence" view. He argued that Jesus did not die in our place, but He died to show us how to die. We are saved by following His example. He died merely to influence us to live and die like He lived and died. It is the Thomas syndrome. People rigorously abuse themselves; follow all sorts of rules and regulations; religiously subscribe to certain rituals all in the pursuit of God's favor. Such people are very religious, very pious but happily lost. They claim to follow Christ's example, but Christ is more than our example. He is our way. Christ's way is the cross. Our way is Christ. He gets to the Father by way of the cross. We get to the Father by the way of Christ (v. 6).

Jesus is saying the cross is my way, but I am your way! Christ makes a triple claim in this verse which is the foundation for the Christian faith. It is also the most offensive of all statements to the modern mind because it is so exclusive. Lots of people today want to follow Christ, but the Christ they want to follow is a figment of their imagination. He is reconstructed by revisionist historians who want to re-invent Christ for the modern mind. He is either a nice, soft, cuddly person who gives us lots of warm "fuzzies," or else he is a revolutionary, political radical who challenges the establishment. Neither is the Christ of John 14:6.

The striking element in this verse is the repetition of the definite article "the" with each of the nouns. The Greeks generally used one definite article for all the nouns which were connected by "and." They did not like to be wordy, so they grouped them all together under one article. Here the article is deliberately repeated all three times. Jesus is saying that He is the real, genuine, exclusive way in contrast with all other ways. He is the real, genuine, exclusive truth in contrast to all other truths. He is the real, genuine, exclusive life in contrast to all other lives. Put that way the statement is the claim of a religious looney unless it is the statement of the Lord of Lords! Jesus says, "I am the personal way and the ultimate truth and the forever life." Jesus does not merely teach us the way. He does not just show us the way or point out the way. He is not just our guide. We do not get to heaven by some impersonal force or philosophical principle. We are saved by a person who is in Himself the very way to God.

I was in O'Hare Airport in Chicago on a return trip home. I had to change planes from a commuter flight from Fort Wayne Indiana to a long-distance flight bound for Portland, Maine. I knew my destination was home. I even knew the flight numbers and times. My problem was that I only had thirty-five minutes to change planes, and I had to walk from one concourse to another. Now I was very happy for the T.V. monitors which told me what gate to go to. I was happy for the signs which pointed out the direction I needed to walk. I would have liked it even better if someone had picked me up in one of those little carts at one gate and took me through the airport to the other gate. Jesus is not just the sign which points the way. He is the cart we ride, the escalator we walk on and the plane we fly to get home to the Father.

Jesus is the ultimate truth. Jesus is not saying simply that He communicates or speaks the truth. He is saying that He is the truth. He embodies truth. He, Himself, in His very person is the truth par excellence, the ultimate truth which supersedes all that has come before or will come after. John began his book about Jesus this way. In John 1:14 he said, "The Word became flesh, and dwelt among us, and we saw His glory, glory as of the only begotten from the Father, full of grace and *truth*." Then in John 1:17 he wrote, "For the law was given through Moses, grace and *truth* were realized through Jesus Christ." It is not so much that the writings of Moses are not true as that Jesus is the ultimate revelation of truth from God to man.

Jesus is life itself. Jesus is not merely saying that He is the one who demonstrates life for us. He doesn't simply show us how to live. He is life itself. He is the source of life, the giver of life. He is the very antithesis of death, the very opposite of termination. He is life that has no end. He, Himself, is and gives life without end. He is the forever life. That is His claim. Jesus said at the tomb of Lazarus, "I am the resurrection and the life; he who believes in Me will live even if He dies, and everyone who lives and believes in Me will never die" (Jn. 11:25-26). The Apostle John later writes about Jesus Christ in 1 John 5:20, "This is the true God and eternal life." Jesus is saying that I am the way even though Roman and Jewish courts call me a heretic and a menace. I am the truth even though lying witnesses condemn me to die. I am the life even though you will soon see my battered body thrown into a cave to decompose. I am all those things, and furthermore, no one comes to the Father but through me!

5-378-724-7478

Did you ever consider how narrow-minded the telephone company is? Years ago before cell phones made pay phones obsolete I was trying to call my wife long distance, so I had to call collect. I dialed 0 and then the number, only I transposed one number out of ten. Then I said my name into the voice mail system. Do you know that whoever answered the phone had the audacity to refuse my collect phone call! Why? The number is exclusive. One digit off, and there is no connection. We have a direct line to the Father, but it comes only through Jesus Christ. 5-378-724-7478 is Jesus Christ in Nynex language! One digit off and you will never reach the Father. One digit off and you will never get to heaven. Christianity is that exclusive.

When my daughter, Katie, was about three or four years old we went Christmas shopping together at the Maine Mall. It was one of the scariest moments of my life. I was looking for a gift for my wife in the ladies' department, but Katie was bored. She was playing hiding games in the racks. The next thing I knew she was gone. I looked everywhere. With my heart in my throat, I quickly called security. They came and took the information and left to look for her. Almost immediately, I heard my name over the loudspeaker telling me to come to the Jewelry counter. I rushed over there to find Katie sitting calmly on a stool, licking a candy bar and chatting with the salesclerks, smiling and happy. She had wandered out of the store into the mall. Then she entered another store and found her way back to the first store. She had walked up to the counter and told them my name and asked them to find me. She had even shoplifted the candy bar! We paid for the candy bar and immediately left for home. I never liked shopping anyway! Just like her, many people are lost in the malls of this world and don't even know it. They are busy licking the candy bars of life oblivious to the consequences of their actions. Happy but lost. Jesus says, "I am the way, the truth, and the life. No one comes to the Father but by me." Christianity is exclusively personal and unapologetically relational.

6
SLOW LEARNERS!

John 14:7-11

One of J. I. Packer's close friends was a biblical scholar who was denied opportunities to advance in academia because he had disagreed with church leaders about doctrine. Packer had mentioned the lack of career advancement to his friend who responded with these words, "But it doesn't matter for I've known God and they haven't." He writes: "Not many of us, I think, would ever naturally say that we have known God. The words imply a definiteness and matter-of-factness of experience to which most of us if we are honest, have to admit that we are still strangers. We … say that we know God … but would it occur to us to say, without hesitation … that we have known God? I doubt it, for I suspect that with most of us experience of God has never become so vivid as that."[1]

How can we know God?

Jesus tells us in verse 7, "If you had known Me, you would have known My Father also." Verse 7 is predicated on verse 6 however: "No one comes to the Father but by me!" And verse 6 is predicated on verse 2: "In my Father's house are many dwelling places." And verse 2 is predicated on verse 1 so that the issue is stated boldly in verse 1. The Father is God, and Jesus lays claim to deity here when He says, "Believe in God (the Father); believe also in me!" Trust me with the same faith that you trust God! Why? Verse 7 gives us the answer: knowing Jesus means knowing God!

The conditional sentence implies that the disciples have not known Jesus and so have not known God. Certainly it is true that they knew Jesus on one level. They walked with Him, talked with Him, worked with Him and listened to Him. On the other hand, they did not yet know Him and so did not know the Father because to know Jesus is to know the Father.

John 14:7 can be translated in two ways because of a textual problem. 1) "If you had known me, you would have known my Father also" (ESV). 2) "If you really knew me, you will know my Father as well" (NIV). The first version is a rebuke and the second is a promise. Is Jesus rebuking them for not knowing Him as they should have known him or is Jesus promising them that they will know the Father because they already know the Son? I take it to be a rebuke. "If you had known me, you would have known my Father also." There are two reasons for this conclusion. 1) Jesus made the same statement in John 8:19 to the Jews in the temple. They did not know Jesus so they could not know His Father. 2) This translation is consistent with the rebuke Jesus gives to Philip in John 14:9. Philip immediately proved he did not really know Jesus by his question (v.8), so Jesus rebuked him for his lack of knowledge.[2]

This kind of knowledge involves ongoing results. To know Christ means that you know Him in such a way that the knowledge changes how you live and function. Like knowing your wife or husband in the fullest sense of the word changes how you relate to everyone else. It changes the choices you make in life. So knowing Christ changes how you live. It is experiential knowledge, not academic knowledge. Experiential knowledge is the only way to know God. Only knowing God experientially allows us to look back on life and say that we have known God.

Many people know *about* Jesus Christ. Therefore, many people know *about* God. They are religious, but they do not know God because they do not know Jesus in a life-changing way. Jesus goes on to say that *from now on* they know the Father and have seen the Father. From this point on something has happened to the disciples. They knew Jesus and the Father on one level before. Jesus is essentially saying that from this point on you recognize the Father because you realize now that you see

Him in Me. The disciples had to realize that knowledge of Jesus in this life changing sense is, in fact, knowledge of God. Until we understand that truth, we cannot know God. Jesus is the way, the truth, and the life. But He is more than even that. He is God in the flesh. Until we accept Jesus as God, we cannot know God!

PATHWAYS TO GOD

Are there many different pathways to knowing God? Yes, and no! Because knowing God is experiential and relational, we can experience God in many ways, but we must start with Jesus. Gary Thomas, in his book *Sacred Pathways: Discover Your Soul's Path to God*, suggests nine distinct pathways to knowing God. He is talking about relational knowledge. He writes: "What is a 'sacred pathway'? Put very simply; it describes the way we relate to God, how we draw near to Him. Do we have just one pathway? Not necessarily. Most of us, however, will naturally have a certain predisposition for relating to God, which is our predominant temperament."[3] His research leads him to identify the following nine pathways to knowing God relationally.

1. Naturalists: Loving God Outdoors
2. Sensates: Loving God with the Senses
3. Traditionalists: Loving God through Ritual and Symbol
4. Ascetics: Loving God in Solitude and Simplicity
5. Activists: Loving God through Confrontation
6. Caregivers: Loving God by Loving Others
7. Enthusiasts: Loving God with Mystery and Celebration
8. Contemplatives: Loving God through Adoration
9. Intellectuals: Loving God with the Mind[4]

I confess to loving God first with my mind. I am analytical. The exegetical study of God's Word thrills me. I love to dig deep into history, grammar, and theology to know God. Right doctrine is very important to me, and I cannot relate to God well in environments where doctrine is unimportant. I am also a naturalist and contemplative. Paddling my kayak on a pristine lake in Maine while the sun sets over the mountains can lead me to depths of worship not known in any other experience. The mist rising on a cool morning over a mountain lake produces in me a euphoria of adoration as I contemplate the glory of God in His creation.

However, all nine pathways have the same starting point. We may relate to God in different ways for we are different people, but we all start from the same point. If not, as Thomas points out, our worship becomes idolatry.[5] If we trace each path back to its origin, each starts with the person of Jesus. We must start with Jesus to know God. There is no other way to know God.

Philip raised the question many wrestle with in John 14:8. Essentially he is saying to Jesus on this last night before He was crucified: "Show me God! That's all. It will be sufficient for me to see God for myself. I will be satisfied if I can just see God." Many people echo that feeling today. "I would believe in God if I could just see Him for myself. All He has to do is prove Himself to me. Just show me and I will believe." People understand the basic concept that if God really exists then it would be impossible to know such a God unless He chose to reveal Himself to us. As the familiar saying goes: "Through God alone can God be known!" But the challenge is further qualified: "God, if you want me to believe in you, just prove yourself to me and I will believe."

The sad truth is that the enemies of Christ, some of His most bitter opponents, recognized what He claimed before the apostles did. The apostles were slow learners. They struggled with the depth of what he was saying, but the enemies saw it immediately. Back in John 10:33 they said to Jesus, "We seek to stone you for blasphemy *because you, a mere man, claim to be God.*" He was crucified for His claim that men could see God when they saw Him. His claim was and is blasphemy – or else it is true.

WHO DO YOU THINK YOU ARE – GOD?

Jacob Neusner is one of the foremost authorities on Judaism in the modern world. He has written over 500 books on Judaism throughout his teaching career in the university world. He is more than just an expert on Rabbinic Judaism – he is a devout Jew himself. In his book entitled *A Rabbi Talks with Jesus*, he takes a look at Jesus' teaching in the Gospel of Matthew. His method is to imagine that he, himself, is a faithful Jew living with his family in Galilee at the time when Jesus taught there. He imagines himself holding long conversations with Jesus using Jesus' answers from the book of Matthew.

The first century Neusner is greatly disturbed by Jesus' claims because Jesus claims for Himself the right to adapt and modify God's law. He is the authority over the Torah. He is bothered by how Jesus, the Rabbi, shifts the emphasis from "us" as a Jewish community to "I" as the personal authority. He writes: "At issue is the figure of Jesus, not the teachings at all. ... In the end, the master, Jesus, makes a demand that only God makes." So Neusner wants to ask Jesus, "Who do you think you are – God?" In the end, Neusner parts company with Jesus the Rabbi. Jesus leaves for Jerusalem, and the cross, with his little band of followers, and Neusner chooses to go home to his village and his family. He cannot accept the personal claims of Jesus.[6]

Philip cried out 2,000 years ago, "Show me God and I will believe." Jacob Neusner writes 2,000 years later, "Who do you think you are – God?" Jesus' answer haunts the modern mind. "YES! When you have seen me, you have seen the Father because the Son and the Father are both co-equally God." Until you accept Jesus' answer, you cannot be a Christian. There is the intellectual stumbling block which has challenged the world for 2,000 years. Jesus goes on in verse 9 to tell us that when we know Christ, we will know God.

"Show me God," Philip cried. Jesus replies, in effect, "O Philip, you are such a slow learner. Have I spent so much time among all of you and you still do not realize who I am?" The first "you" is plural, meaning that Jesus is addressing all of the disciples even as He speaks to Philip. The statement is shockingly simple yet infinitely profound. "From now on you know Him (God) and you have seen Him" (John 14:7). "You know God now," Jesus claims "You may not know that you know God, but you do." "You all have seen God," Jesus continues, "and you continue to see God."[7] Jesus expands His thought in response to Philip's question. "The one who has seen me has seen the Father" (John 14:9). It is not that they will see God. They have seen God – in Jesus. Jesus is not saying that He and the Father are the same person. He has just said in verse 6 that people "come to the Father" through Him so they must be two different persons who are both equally God. Jesus is not saying that He represents the Father or is the Father's ambassador. You cannot know someone through knowing someone who knows him. Jesus is saying that you actually know the Father when you know me. When you see me, you have actually seen the invisible Father. It is a staggering claim.

SEEING GOD

Easter Sunday dawns and the women go to the tomb. They see the stone rolled away and run back to tell the disciples that the body is gone. Peter and John run together to the tomb, but John is younger and gets there first. He looks into the tomb but does not go in. He "sees" the linen wrappings (John 20:5). The simplest word for "see" is used here. It means that he physically observed the facts. Peter comes running along, and he barges right past John into the tomb. He "sees" the grave clothes too (John 20:6). But this is a different Greek word for "see." It means to examine or "puzzle over" the facts. Then John enters the tomb and he "sees" (John 20:8). The third Greek word for "see" is used here. It means to understand with the eyes of faith, and it is the word used in John 14:9. The word used here refers to spiritual perception.[8] We see when we believe, and then we know!

John uses the word for what the Son in His preexistence saw when He was with the Father in eternity past (John 3:11, 32; 6:46; 8:38).[9] No one else has seen the Father, until now, Jesus asserts! The Bible teaches that God is invisible (Col. 1:15; 1 Tim. 1:17). Moses "saw" God in the Old Testament but it was a theophany – a manifestation of God (Ex. 33:13, 18). Jesus now claims that the disciples have seen God in a way that Moses never did precisely because they have seen Jesus. He claims that when you see Jesus, you have seen the invisible God!

The "seeing" Jesus speaks about here has ongoing, life changing results. He is talking about understanding or insight. The word means more than simple sight. It means insight based on careful reflection. When we understand or comprehend Jesus, then this changes our lives forever. Until we understand Jesus, we cannot ever understand God the Father. We see Jesus through the eyes of faith, not intellect. We accept Jesus' claims by faith, and so we come to understand Him. Then, and then only, do we begin to comprehend God. It is not intellectual prowess which helps us understand God. It is faith to trust Jesus. We see through the eyes of faith.

Many years ago a member of our church gave me a gift from his woodworking shop which I still keep on my desk in the office. It is a set of small blocks of wood cut in various shapes and mounted on a flat panel standing in a grooved base all carefully stained and finished. The blocks of wood form spaces between them that make the letters for "JESUS." It is an optical illusion that plays tricks with the mind. He brought it to a church meeting one night, and we set it on the conference table in the midst of a group of twenty of our church leaders. Some had no problem seeing the name "JESUS", but I could not see no matter how hard I tried. We went on to conduct church business for some time when I happened to glance at the artwork. Suddenly I could see it! I don't know what happened, but I could see it. I blurted out to the whole group in the middle of some discussion of church business, "I can see Jesus!" The key is to look at the spaces and not the raised blocks of wood. The mind must think differently to see differently. Even now I have to train my mind to look at the spaces to see Jesus. Faith does this in our lives. Faith sees Jesus in the spaces. When we can see Jesus in the spaces of life, then we can make sense of what God is doing. Jesus reveals God to us. We must trust Jesus to know God.

WHO DOES WHAT AND HOW?

God is one, and God is three. How God is three is different than how God is one. Millard Erickson writes: "The threeness and the oneness of God are not in the same respect."[10] Analogies are only partially acceptable because God is unique. There is no other being like Him in the universe so we cannot argue from analogy very well. God is one (Deut. 6:4), but the one is the oneness of "we" (John 17:22). He is one in substance, being or essence according to the classic definition. He is three in terms of person or personality. The word trinity is actually a poor word to describe God. The word trinity emphasizes the three over the one and often borders on tri-theism. The best word to describe God is tri-unity. He is three in one. Perhaps a simple mathematical formula will help explain the difference.

$$1+1+1 = 3 \text{ This is tri-theism.}$$
$$1 \times 1 \times 1 = 1 \text{ This is tri-unity.}$$

The Father is one. The Son is one, and the Spirit is one. Each "one" does not add anything to the other. Each one is fully God in Himself, and yet the result of all three is still one. The unity of the Trinity teaches tri-unity. We must affirm both sides of an apparently contradictory idea even when we can't fully understand it. Jesus, in John 14:10-11, is

77

attempting to teach us how the triune God works in this world. In these verses, of course, He is not addressing the role of the Holy Spirit, which He will do shortly in this chapter. He is trying to help us understand how the Father and the Son work together in this tri-unity. As such, we are delving here into the mysteries of the Godhead itself. As someone has said, "Try to explain it, and you'll lose your mind; but try to deny it, and you'll lose your soul."[11]

God was not lonely in eternity past. He was and is complete in Himself. God exists eternally as the perfect friendship of three! Wayne Grudem writes: "If there is no Trinity, then there were no interpersonal relationships within the being of God before creation, and, without personal relationships, it is difficult to see how God could be genuinely personal or be without the need for a creation to relate to."[12] God, to be God, needs nothing outside Himself. God, to be relational, needs no other person outside Himself. God, in Himself, is the perfect model of friendship, and He invites us to enjoy full "intimacy with the Almighty."[13]

Trust is the foundation for transparency, and transparency leads to intimacy. Within the friendship of the Almighty Three, there is perfect trust and transparency, so there is perfect intimacy. Jesus invites us to enjoy that same intimacy with Him and therefore with God. When Jesus invites us into His friendship, He invites us into the friendship of the triune God. Klaus Issler writes: "God is an eternally existing society of three persons – Father, Son, and Holy Spirit – who love each other maximally and who constitute the one Christian God. Furthermore, God invites his children to experience a close friendship relationship within the enduring divine friendship within the Trinity."[14] Trusting Jesus is the doorway into that friendship, and transparency leads to the intimacy God models for us.

The Father and the Son are so perfectly related to each other that even though they are different personalities, everything either one does and says is exactly what the other is doing and saying. They are perfectly united in everything. Every word of the Son proves the work of the Father (v. 10). Every work of the Father proves the word of the Son (v. 11). As J.I. Packer notes: "The one God ("he") is also, and equally, "they," and "they" are always together and always cooperating, with the Father initiating, the Son complying, and the Spirit executing the will of both, which is His will also. This is the truth about God that was revealed through the words and works of Jesus."[15]

ONENESS AND INTIMACY

Jesus asks, "Do you not believe that I am in the Father, and the Father is in Me?" The form of the question he puts before the disciples shows us that he expects a "yes" answer. Jesus assumes that his followers will believe his words even if they don't always understand the meaning. A disciple might say: "Do you mean that you and the Father are in moral and ethical harmony with each other? Perhaps you mean that you are one in purpose? This is merely an expression of agreement together, right?" So Jesus goes on to say, "The words that I say to you I do not speak on My own initiative, but the Father abiding in Me does His works." Jesus does not say what we expect Him to say at this point. He does not say that His words are the words of the Father. He says that His words are the works of the Father. So every word of the Son is the work of the Father. What Jesus says reveals the character of the Father. The words of Jesus cannot be separated from the works of the Father.

Jesus also emphasizes His dependence on the Father in this verse. This dependence, or subordination, of Jesus to the Father gave rise to much argument in the early church. The argument of many in the first few centuries went something like this. If Jesus is dependent on the Father, then He must be subordinate to the Father. If Jesus is subordinate to the Father, then He must be inferior to the Father in some way. He must be either an expression or manifestation of the Father, or else he must be a being created by the Father to do the Father's will.

Orthodox Christianity since the church fathers has established some clear boundaries outside of which is heresy. We cannot say, on the one hand, that the Father, Son, and Holy Spirit are merely expressions or ways in which God presents Himself to humans. This teaching is called Modalism and was rejected as heresy by the early church councils. We see modalism in a modern form in organizations like "the Jesus only" branch of Pentecostalism. Nor can we say that the Father is God, and Jesus is a subordinate extension or creation of God. This teaching was called Arianism and was also rejected as heresy by the early church. We see Arianism alive today in such organizations as Unitarianism or Jehovah's Witnesses. What Jesus does is fully the action of God. He is not, somehow, less God and His actions less than God's actions. His dependence does not imply inferiority to the Father in any way. The subordination is a functional or operational subordination within the Godhead – a way of relating to each other while being equal in being.[16]

Jesus goes on to explain in verse 11 that every work of the Father proves the word of the Son. The union of the Father and the Son is proved by Jesus' words and the Father's works (John 14:10). Jesus proves that He is in the Father because He does not speak on His own initiative. He does not speak "by means of Himself." The Father proves that Jesus does not speak on His own initiative by the works God does through Jesus. The works verify the words (John 5:19-20). The Father is living in Jesus (John 14:10), and the Father's works verify the words of Jesus.[17]

Jesus is calling for them to accept Him by faith. Remember He is expanding the theme He began in verse 1 where he said, *Believe in God, believe also in me.* In verse 1, He was speaking of faith in Him personally. Here in verse 11, He calls them to believe a proposition. People often say that Christianity is a belief in a person not a doctrine but that is not true. Christianity is, in reality, both belief in a person and belief in a theological proposition. When Jesus says here, "Believe Me that," He is not saying, "believe in me as a person. Have faith in me personally." We need to do that, but He is saying grammatically that we must believe the proposition which He is about to make: "I am in the Father and the Father in Me." He is saying that they are one in essence or being.[18]

Why must we believe that? We must believe Jesus' words about His union with the Father because the mutual indwelling of the Father and the Son is the foundation for the mutual indwelling of Jesus and His followers (John 14:20). We are in Jesus, and Jesus is in us. Jesus is in the Father, and the Father is in Jesus. The Father sends the Spirit of Truth to be in us (John 14:17). The Tri-Unity of God is the model for our unity in Jesus, so the Tri-Unity of God is an essential teaching of our faith. The basis of our union with Jesus is His union with the Father. We must believe His union with the Father to experience our union with Jesus. The intimacy we enjoy with Jesus is grounded in the intimacy He enjoys with the Father. John Piper puts it this way: "Within the triune Godhead (Father, Son, and Holy Spirit), God has been uppermost in his own affections for all eternity. This belongs to his very nature, for he has begotten and loved the Son from all eternity. Therefore, God has been supremely and eternally happy in the fellowship of the Trinity."[19]

"If you won't believe that we are one in essence or being then at least believe that we are one in function," Jesus goes on to say. "At least believe because of the works which you have seen." Why? If you can at least believe that we are one in what we do, then you can begin to believe that we are one in who we are.

Oneness in doing proves oneness in being.
Oneness in function proves oneness of essence.

The word *works* which is used here refers to the miracles and signs which Jesus performed and which these disciples had witnessed. Who did the works? Jesus! His argument here is that these works were the works of the Father. So everything that Jesus did was actually, and exactly, what the Father did. The dependence of Jesus in this verse does not teach inferiority at all. The dependence of Jesus is a claim to perfect oneness with the Father in all that is said and done. This oneness teaches the tri-unity of God.

> Therefore, Jesus answered and was saying to them, "Truly, truly, I say to you, the Son can do nothing of Himself, unless it is something He sees the Father doing; for whatever the Father does, these things the Son also does in like manner. For the Father loves the Son, and shows Him all things that He Himself is doing; and the Father will show Him greater works than these, so that you will marvel. For just as the Father raises the dead and gives them life, even so the Son also gives life to whom He wishes. (John 5:19-21)

The Son does nothing by Himself, but then, Jesus says, the Father does nothing by Himself either. "Whatever the Father does, these things the Son also does!" There is subordination in the Godhead, but it is the subordination of perfect oneness. Everything that the Father says and does is exactly what the Son says and does. And everything that the Son says and does is exactly what the Father says and does. Every word of the Son is the work of the Father, and every work of the Father is the word of the Son! Jesus is dependent on the Father, but his dependence is so perfect, so complete that whatever He does is exactly what the Father does and whatever He says is exactly what Father says.

The Son perfectly reveals the Father because the Son perfectly obeys the Father. The perfect obedience is the only way to perfect disclosure. If the Son chose to act on His own in any way, then we could never tell whether the Son's actions were his or his father's. The only way to know the Father is by the perfect obedience of the Son in all he does.[20] God is one in essence so that whatever any person within that tri-unity does or says it is perfectly and exactly what the other says and does. And whatever anyone of the persons in that tri-unity says and does it adds nothing to the oneness. They are still one.

ALL OUT OF LOVE

The unity rises out of the love. The Father shows the Son what He is doing out of love for the Son. The Son obeys the Father out of love for the Father. We think of obedience mostly in terms of a servant relationship, but there is an obedience that arises from a relationship of friendship. Jesus will continue to develop this theme as it relates to our friendship with him (John 15:15). The key to friendship obedience is knowledge or, what we might call, transparency. The Father shows the Son his heart and mind out of love, and the Son does the will of the Father out of love. D.A. Carson writes:

> Jesus is so uniquely and unqualifiedly the Son of God that the Father shows him all he does, out of sheer love for him, and the Son, however dependent on his Father, does everything the Father does…This marvelous self-disclosure of the Father in the Son turns, ultimately, not on God's love for us, but on the Father's love for his unique Son. It is because the Father loves the Son that this pattern of divine self-disclosure pertains…The relationship between the Father and the Son is the standard for all love relationships.[21]

Jesus lays the foundation for his later teaching on our friendship with him by teaching us first about his friendship with the Father. He is disclosing to us the information we need to enter into a deeper intimacy with him. He is transparent with us so that we will trust him and become transparent with him. If we are to understand our intimacy with Jesus, we must first understand his intimacy with the Father. If we are to grasp our friendship with Jesus, we must first grasp his friendship with the Father. The friendship of the Godhead was one of absolute trust and utter transparency. Our friendship with Jesus must be built on the same foundation of trust and transparency.

I have a small book containing a collection of Puritan prayers that I keep in my office and read from time to time to keep my heart in tune with Jesus. One of those prayers is entitled "Vain Service."

> Forgive me for serving thee in sinful ways –
> > by glorying in my own strength,
> > by forcing myself to minister through necessity,
> > by accepting the applause of others,
> > by trusting in assumed grace and spiritual affection,
> > by a faith that rests upon my hold on Christ,
> > > not on him alone,
> > by having another foundation to stand upon
> > > beside thee;
> > > for thus I make flesh my arm.
>
> Help me to see
> > that it is faith stirred by grace that does the deed,
> > that faith brings a man nearer to thee,
> > > raising him above mere man,
> > that thou dost act upon the soul
> > > when thus elevated and lifted out of itself,
> > that faith centres in thee as God all sufficient,
> > > Father, Son, Holy Spirit,
> > as God efficient,
> > > mediately, as in thy commands and promises,
> > > immediately, in all the hidden power
> > > > that faith sees and knows to be in thee,
> > > abundantly, with omnipotent effect,
> > > > in the revelation of thy will.
> > If I have not such faith, I am nothing.[22]

7

THE MYSTERY OF PRAYER IN THE PRESENCE OF POWER

John 14:12-17

The way of Jesus is the path of power. Jesus wants us to see what we can be in His power, so He makes two promises to His friends. We will do greater works than Jesus (14:12), and He will do whatever we ask of Him (14:13-14). The promise of prayer taps into the promise of power raising extraordinary expectations, yet unanswered prayers haunt our reality. The promises are shocking. Easily minimized. Explained away. Ignored. Prayer remains a mystery we can't wrap our heads around. Why does God seem to answer some prayers and not others? If God promises that we can tap into His power, why do we feel so impotent - so ordinary?

The young couple sat anxiously together in the conference room in Malaga, Spain. They had just arrived by ferry from Tangier, Morocco on their way to their family home in Germany. I had only recently been traveling in Morocco with one of our missionaries encouraging and supporting kingdom workers like these two. God had called them to serve Him in this Islamic country, and they had faithfully carried out His calling.

Complications had developed in the pregnancy. The medical care was inadequate, and they were rushing home to get proper medical attention. Were they too late? I joined several others in a circle around this young couple. We prayed fervently. We asked God to intervene by his power and protect this unborn child. I heard later that the baby died in the womb. Why? We prayed. We sought God's power by the mystery of prayer, but God didn't save the baby.

Philip Yancey, in his book on prayer, tells about a forty-one-year-old woman dealing with breast cancer that had spread to her lungs and liver. Hundreds were praying for her healing. She wrestled with God in prayer herself. She taught an elementary class in a Christian school and gave an assignment to her students one day during the ordeal. "If you met Jesus walking down the street, what would you ask Him?" Most of the students asked questions about heaven or what life was like for Him while growing up. Two questions haunted her. "Why won't you heal my Mom?" "Why doesn't my dad find a job?" They were both written by her son. She knew the handwriting! Another letter Yancey received came from two parents who had prayed for God's protection for their emotionally disturbed son. One day their daughter called to tell them that their son, her brother, had committed suicide at age twenty-two. They listed the promises Jesus made in these verses and then cried out, "Lord, we prayed regularly for all three of our children - didn't you hear our prayers?"[1]

THE PROMISE OF POWER

The friends of Jesus will do the works of Jesus, and they will do greater works than He did because He is doing the works through them. I don't want to explain the promise away. I don't want to make excuses for weak results. Jesus made this promise, so Jesus is either a liar or it is true, and yet, the mystery remains. The promises are tied directly to the previous verses which spoke about the perfect unity of the Father and the Son. Whatever the Son does, the Father does. And whatever the Father does, the Son does. When we become friends of Jesus, we enter into a spiritual union with the Father too so that what God does, we do, and what we do, God does! (John 15:23-28) Prayer connects us with the mystery of the Trinity. No wonder we struggle to grasp the mystery of prayer.

These were the miraculous works of Jesus: He healed the sick, gave sight to the blind, fed the 5,000, and raised the dead! They are sensational works of incredible power. Jesus says that His friends will do those works too! And do them they did. Peter and John healed the lame man. Peter raised Dorcas from the dead. Paul healed the sick and cast out demons in the name of Christ. It is hard to believe in works more sensational than those recorded in the Bible. Yet Jesus says that his followers will do greater works than these. How can that be?

I do not believe that Jesus is telling us we will do more sensational works than these, but that the works that we do are greater in three ways. They are greater in privilege, scope, and value. We will do works that are greater in privilege! Jesus initiated the kingdom age; we participate in it. This does not mean that we are greater than He is but that we have a greater privilege than He did. Jesus in Matthew 11:11 used the same analogy regarding John the Baptist. He said, "I tell you the truth, among those born of women there has not risen one greater than John the Baptist; yet He who is least in the kingdom of Heaven is greater than he." Why? Because John never had the privilege of participating in the results of the kingdom of heaven. We do!

The explanation of greater privilege is a bit of a "let down." It is true, but explaining the promise this way feels like a sleight of hand trick that minimizes the promise by clever explanation. Jesus is talking about much more. We will do works that are greater in scope than He did. We do works that are greater in quantity but not greater in quality. Now, I think, we are getting closer to His meaning. After Jesus' ministry on this earth, how many lives had he changed? He spent three years teaching and preaching. He died and rose again but at His ascension there were barely more than 500 believers in the entire world (1 Cor. 15:6)! But on the Day of Pentecost, Peter preached one sermon and 3,000 people believed. One event, one sermon by one follower and the follower reached six times the people that Jesus reached in three years of preaching! And that was just the beginning of the works that His followers would perform in His name. The church grew from a tiny enclave of believers in the city of Jerusalem to a global army of believers transforming the world.

Still, Jesus is not just talking about more works, He is talking about the relative value of the works. Jesus is not just talking about greater quantity, Jesus is talking about works that are greater in value. The essence of what Jesus is saying is that He values the spiritual works which His followers will do over the physical miracles that He did while on earth. Jesus changed very few spiritual lives during His three years on earth even though He performed many sensational miracles. His followers perform very few miracles, but many are converted. Leon Morris, one commentator, points out: "What Jesus means we may see in the narratives of Acts. There are few miracles of healing, but the emphasis is on the mighty works of conversion."[2] Jesus places a far higher value on souls saved than on bodies healed. Jesus places a higher value on people who are spiritually converted than on people who are physically resurrected. Jesus places a higher value on the spiritual and eternal matters of life and death than on the physical and temporal matters of life and death. And so should we! A life saved spiritually is a far greater work than a life saved physically. Here is the heart of a Christian value system.

The greater works are conditioned upon our faith. Jesus said that only those who believe would do these greater works. He is not talking about the amount of my faith but the object of my faith. We have a false Christianity alive today which emphasizes a "name it and claim it" theology! It is said that we do not see the greater works of God today because we do not have enough faith. This doctrine is very damaging. It places all the burden on us. It amounts to faith in faith, not in God. People are saying by this that we do greater works than Jesus because we have greater faith than Jesus. Since we cannot have greater faith than Jesus, the theology is false. It is not the amount of faith but the object of our faith that counts. A small amount of faith in a great God is greater than a large amount of faith in a false god. Honestly, I often see God do great things in spite of me, not because of me.

God does the work. We trust Him to do that work through us. So He does the greater works, and these greater works are conditioned upon our faith and His departure. Jesus must depart so that the Holy Spirit can be sent (Jn. 7:39; 16:7). It is the Holy Spirit who empowers us to do the works of God. We don't actually do these works in our own power but in His power. The Holy Spirit is the power behind the greater works which we will do. What was Pentecost, after all, if it was not the infusion of God's power to perform God's work?

Charles Haddon Spurgeon, one of the greatest preachers that England ever produced, died at 11:05 on Sunday evening, January 31, 1892, while he was in Mentone, France. A total of more than 100,000 people attended his many memorial services that were held at the Metropolitan Tabernacle where he had preached for so many years. Spurgeon had preached to at least twenty million people over the years he served in London, and he had received 14,691 people into the membership of the Metropolitan Tabernacle.[3] These are the greater works which Jesus predicted 2,000 years ago.

These greater works are not just numbers. The greater works are individuals who have been changed by the grace of Jesus Christ. "On October 7, 1857, Charles Spurgeon preached at the Crystal Palace to a congregation of 23,654 persons, perhaps the largest congregation ever addressed by a preacher in London up to that time. But a few days earlier, Spurgeon had gone to Crystal Palace to test out the acoustics. He stood on the platform and said, 'Behold, the Lamb of God, which taketh away the sin of the world' (John 1:29). A workman painting in one of the upper galleries heard those words and came under deep conviction. Later, he found salvation in Christ."[4] The greater works are not just numbers but sinners who come to Christ through us by the power of God.

THE PROMISE OF PRAYER

Jesus made two promises to us. He told us that we will do greater works than He did. Then He told us that He will do whatever we ask of Him (14:13-14). If it is possible to have a greater promise than Jesus made in verse 12, it is the promise He makes in verses 13-14. It is the promise of answered prayer. The most striking feature of this promise is the scope. Jesus is not merely saying that He will hear our prayers and from time to time He will answer our prayers. Jesus is not saying that prayer is good for us even if we don't get our requests. Jesus is not saying that the more people we have praying, the more likely He is to hear us. He says, "Whatever you ask, I will do." It is the kind of promise a friend makes to a friend! "I'm here for you. Whatever you ask of me I will do for you!" Philip Yancey writes, "Prayer is the currency of friendship."[5] We tap into God's power by prayer.

The promise is so important that Jesus repeated it three more times in the next two chapters (14:14; 16:23, 24). Prayer is vital to the Christian life. A Christian who is not praying is a contradiction in terms. Yet we struggle with unanswered prayer. Quite frankly, the reason more Christians don't pray more is because we don't see God answer our prayers. And we don't see God answer our prayers because we don't pray correctly. R.A. Torrey says in his book, *The Power of Prayer and the Prayer of Power*, "There are certain people who can pray in a certain way and who will get not merely some good thing, or something just as good as what they ask, or something even better than what they ask, but they will get the very thing that they ask."[6]

Just as there are two conditions with the promise of power so there are two conditions with the promise of prayer. If we do not see answered prayer, the reason most often deals with these two conditions. And neither one has anything to do with faith. The problem of unanswered prayer is not just a lack of faith. Lack of faith can be a problem, but it is not what Jesus addresses here. His promise is conditioned upon His name and His glory. Praying in His name and for His glory are the keys that unlock the promise of His power.

A CONVERSATION BETWEEN FRIENDS

The conditions are the fine print for the promise, but I have come to see that the fine print is actually the heart of prayer. The conditions are not just excuses to explain why Jesus doesn't do what we want Him to do. The conditions are the very essence of what prayer is all about. Prayer is relational conversation. The conditions – the fine print – define the relationship. When the conditions are met, our hearts are aligned with His heart, our minds are in tune with His mind, and the result is dangerous to our self-interests. Eugene Petersen cautions us:

> Be slow to pray. …When we pray we have a more than average chance of ending up in a place that we quite definitely never wanted to be … We want life on our conditions, not on God's conditions. Praying puts us at risk of getting involved in God's conditions. Be slow to pray. Praying most often doesn't get us what we want but what God wants, something quite at variance with what we conceive to be in our best interests. And when we realize what is going on, it is often too late to go back. Be slow to pray.[7]

Twice Jesus tells us to ask in His name. Sometimes people stress the form of the prayer. They say that we must pray to the Father in the name of the Son, but we cannot pray to the Son. This is silly. Jesus said, in verse 14, "If you ask *ME* anything in my name, I will do it." So we can pray directly to Jesus, or we can pray to the Father in His name, but we need no other person to act as an intermediary between God and us.[8]

Someone might say, "I do ask in Jesus' name. I always close my prayers in Jesus name, Amen." But this is not a magic formula. Praying in Jesus' name means praying in harmony with His will. It is relational language. Unanswered prayer often comes because we are praying in our own names as if God owes us an answer instead of Jesus! We are not treating Jesus as a friend but as a slave. Our lives are out of harmony with Him. We harbor grudges or we lie or cheat. We are not in harmony with Him so we cannot claim His promise. Asking in Jesus' name means keeping Jesus' commandments. Jesus ties the two conditions together when He says, "If you ask Me anything in My name, I will do it. If you love Me, you will keep My commandments" (14:14-15).[9] The promise makes perfect sense when the relationship is right. If I make a request which is in harmony with the desires of Jesus, then, of course, He will give me my request. It is His desire too! The key is that I must be so in tune with Him relationally that I know and trust what He wants. It is as if I can read His mind, know what He wants and pray His prayer. Short of that level of harmony, I must pray with humility.

Ray McCauley was a white, Pentecostal preacher in South Africa in the 1990s during the final days of apartheid. Nelson Mandela and Bishop Tutu reached out to Ray for help in the growing crisis. Ray joined them as they spoke to the crowds in many tension filled situations. He would try and calm the white soldiers down in the face of 100,000 black protestors while Mandela and Tutu spoke to the chanting crowds. Emotions ran high. Shortly before the elections, McCauley found himself standing before the king of the Zulus. Mandela had learned that the South African government had been paying Zulu men to kill blacks in the townships while negotiating for peace with Mandela. The Zulu King was calling for a boycott of the country's first free elections, so McCauley and Mandela went to meet with him. The king sat on a throne covered with leopard skins and all around him stood powerful warriors. Ray spoke to him. "O King, you are a great king, but surely even you would wish to kneel before the King of Kings." The King of Zulus got down off his throne and kneeled as Ray prayed for peace, unity and the Kingdom of God. After the prayer meeting, the king appealed to the Zulu people to stop fighting. The elections were held with no violence. Ray said, "I'll never doubt the power of prayer again. Go figure – each one of those groups thought God was on their side. And yet in the midst of crisis, each one was willing to bow down, to yield before the God they thought they served."[10]

There is a second condition which is even more important if that is possible. Our request must be conditioned upon His glory. The purpose of our request must be that the Father is glorified in the Son. If we do not know that God would receive greater glory by answering our request, then we cannot claim the promise. You see, most often we pray for our own benefit and so He does not give us our request. We pray selfishly for God to fix our problems rather than for God to glorify Himself. I like what Ralph Keiper said, "God will never waste a blessing or a kindness on a careless, selfish saint."[11] Why should God waste His blessing on us if we are going to blow it or misuse it for ourselves? The goal of prayer is not to fulfill our needs but to glorify God. Why? Because that is the goal of Jesus, our friend. If we love Jesus, we will seek God's glory. Jesus loves the Father, so He does what the Father wants (14:31). He brings glory to the Father (17:4-5), so if we love Jesus, we will pray in a way that will glorify God.

Ralph Keiper was a wonderful Bible teacher whom I heard many years ago, but he had very poor vision. What we can see at 100 feet, he could only see at ten feet. When he was a theological student, he was upset by this limitation. He complained to God about his affliction. He figured that God could do something about it if He really wanted. He knew He was faithful to God, and He could see no reason why God should not answer His prayer. One Saturday afternoon he was studying his theological textbooks when the Holy Spirit began to speak to Him in the privacy of His mind. "What is the chief end of man?" "To glorify God, and to enjoy Him forever," Ralph replied! The Holy Spirit responded, "Do you wish to glorify God?" "Of course!" the young student assured Him. "If you had a choice, what would you rather do, glorify God or have perfect vision?" That was a tough one. Ralph Keiper struggled with that question for a long time, but the H.S. would not let him off the hook. It was a bitter struggle. Finally, he responded, "There is only one answer, and that choice is to glorify God." The H.S. continued His probing into his heart. "Do you really believe that God's glory is more important than your vision?" At last, Ralph surrendered. "My vision, or lack of it, is not worthy to be compared to the glory of God!" The H.S. continued, "Do you really wish to glorify God?" "Yes, I do!" "If you do, why worry about the method which God chooses for you to glorify Him?"[12]

Do you see the way the Lord works with us? He will do whatever we ask of him when we are in harmony with Him, and we seek His glory more than our benefit. The Father is in the Son. The Son is in the Father (John 14:10-11). To pray to one is to pray to the other. We pray to either Father or Son in Jesus' name. Prayer is not a magic formula that unlocks the power of God to fulfill our wants. Prayer is "love-talk" – the whispers of intimate conversation. Our requests which Jesus promises to answer reflect that intimacy. Prayer flows out of our intimate union with both Father and Son. Answers to our prayers flow out of the intimate union of the Father with the Son. Their intimacy with each other in purpose grounds our intimacy with them in prayer. It is the intimacy of friendship.

Prayer is best understood as a function of friendship. Asking and receiving is not a vending machine process. Asking and receiving is a conversation between friends.[13] Jesus makes two promises to His friends in these verses. They are powerful and grand promises – the kind of promises that friends make. My biggest problems in life are directly related to His biggest promises because I forget the context of friendship. First, my vision of what Jesus wants to do is too small! Second, my expectation of what Jesus can do is too selfish.

OUR FOREVER FRIEND

Our four-year-old daughter, Kari, was walking out from the elementary school after she went with my wife, Janie, to pick up her older sister, Katie. She always talked quite loud which was sometimes embarrassing. She said to Janie, "Mom, we aren't alone." Her words echoed down the hall of the public school. "After Jesus went to heaven, He sent His Holy Spirit to live inside of us and be our leader." She's right!

Our intimacy with Jesus is grounded in the intimacy of the Trinity. We catch a glimpse of this spiritual intimacy in John 14:16 where Jesus promises us, *"I will ask the Father, and He will give you another Helper."* The Father's gift of a Helper for us comes at the request of the Son on our behalf. Jesus' request to the Father rises from an intimate conversation about us with the Father.[14] Jesus promises the disciples that shortly He will have an intimate conversation with the Father. The topic of this conversation will be them! I take it that Jesus continues to have intimate conversations with the Father about us. The result of these

93

intimate conversations is that we continue to enjoy the help we need with the problems we face in this life.

If we are obedient to the Lord (John 14:15), then Jesus promises that we will enjoy the presence of "another Comforter or Helper." The word *another* is very important. Jesus is the first comforter, but He is leaving the physical presence of his followers so He will send another helper who is different but not antithetical to the first helper. The new helper is an additional helper. There are two Greek words for "another" used in Scripture. The first word for "another" tends to distinguish two subjects. The second word for "another" tends to add two subjects. The second word is the word used here. Jesus requests more help, or additional help, for us. So the Holy Spirit is an additional helper for us. We cannot look around and see Jesus, but we have another person of His very nature and essence to guide us through life. Christ makes this promise to His followers.

This word "comforter or helper" is the translation of the Greek word, "Paraclete." The Greek word Paraclete is very difficult to define with one English word. No single English word seems to do justice to this word Paraclete. The word Paraclete is made up of two Greek words meaning "one who is called alongside." It is related to a Greek verb which means to encourage or comfort.[15] The word Paraclete was used for a friend of an accused person, not his hired attorney. The friend was more than just a helper. He was called alongside to speak about a person's character and provide personal support for his friend in need.[16] He was first a friend. He was a "pleader" on behalf of his friend. I like the thought that the Holy Spirit, as our Paraclete, is our "legal friend".[17] He is our helper in a legal sense, but he is more than a hired helper and more than a legal advocate. The Paraclete is a true friend who pleads for us and stands with us in our times of need. We have two friends in high places. Jesus is our first Paraclete. He is now in heaven. The Holy Spirit is our friend on earth. He is with us, and in us, here and now. They both vouch for us when we have needs so that we find peace in their friendship. We have two friends who stand with us through our struggles in life - one friend in heaven and one friend on earth! With friends like these, we are never alone and never at a loss.

The word is often translated "comforter" in our English Bibles, but we shouldn't think only of a person who consoles us. The Holy Spirit is a person not a "Linus Blanket" in our lives. If we only think of him as a "comforter" like we think of that down quilt we wrap up in to make ourselves feel comfortable when we are miserable, then we have missed the whole point. Yes, the Holy Spirit sometimes wraps us up in His love but more importantly He encourages us to live. Donald Grey Barnhouse called the Holy Spirit, God's "ramrod down your backbone to make you stand for truth."[18] He gives us the strength when we are down. He exhorts us to get up and fight when the enemy has beaten us to a pulp. He gives us the power to make it another day when we don't know how or where to turn.

"What happens when a dozen professional educators say one thing and two parents disagree with our assessment?" The teacher was speaking to the Assistant Superintendent of the school system where our first-grade daughter was a student. We were seated in a large conference room with a dozen educators including the psychological examiner and an administrator who had given their reports about Katie, our special needs daughter. The setting was intended to intimidate us as parents, and, after several hours, the situation was tense. They wanted her placed in a contained classroom, and we wanted her in another elementary school where she could be mainstreamed in a regular classroom with an aide. It was the professionals versus the parents in an era when mainstreaming special needs children was not widely practiced. We turned to our advocate, and he suggested we take a break so we could talk. The state provided a legal advocate for parents in those days to help them navigate the jumble of policies and provisions for special education. Our legal advocate told us how to handle the matter. We went back in and told them we weren't budging from our request and why. The Assistant Superintendent told the teacher that the legal advocate was correct. We had the right to do what we were asking them to do. End of the matter. Our legal advocate was not a lawyer. He was simply a "friend," called alongside us to help us in the matter. The Holy Spirit is our legal friend just like that man. He helps us deal with overwhelming and intimidating situations and gives us the resources to handle the difficult situations we face in life.

Christ's purpose in sending this comforter is to give us a friend forever. We never have to worry that the Holy Spirit will leave us. We have an eternal friendship with Him. He runs right alongside us through the race of life! When we are at our lowest point, He is right there with us.

95

He is our comforter, our helper, our encourager and our defender. He is our divine support person – our legal advocate!

We hear a lot about the need to have support people in our lives today. These are people who are "replenishers." You can go to them and know that they will give you the encouragement to keep going. Everyone needs replenishers in their lives. Everyone needs support people. We have two! The Holy Spirit is another Paraclete just like Jesus. In 1 John 2:1 we read: "If anyone sins, we have an advocate with the Father, Jesus Christ, the righteous." That word "advocate" is the same Greek word. It is the word "paraclete." So we have two advocates, one in heaven and one on earth.

When we have sinned, blown it, really made a mess of life, and we are miserable with guilt, that is when the devil goes to work on us. He gets in there and starts to accuse us. "What makes you think you are a Christian? Look at yourself. You are the worst excuse for a Christian I've ever seen. God couldn't possibly see anything deserving in you." At that point, we must remember that we have two "pleaders" standing up for us. Jesus Christ, God's son is our advocate in heaven. The Holy Spirit is our advocate right here with us. And the judge is our Father Himself! How can we lose the case?

At the same time, the Spirit will neither excuse nor ignore what needs to change in our lives. He is our legal friend and will always speak the truth to our souls. Our greatest advocate is the Spirit of Truth (14:17). The Holy Spirit communicates the truth and nothing but the truth. Encouragement is a false encouragement if it is only lies or flattery. Comfort is no comfort unless it is the truth. The greatest friends are those who can tell us the truth. Real friends communicate truth even if it hurts. The Holy Spirit is always that kind of friend. The only way to know the Spirit is to love Jesus and show your love by following His commands (14:15), which is why the world is incapable of knowing the Spirit. If we commit ourselves to follow Christ we enjoy a special relationship with the Holy Spirit (14:17).

Jesus told His disciples that they already knew this friend "because He abides with you and will be in you" (14:17). The promise was future for the disciples but present for us. A change was coming that we experience today. We enjoy a more intimate experience with the Holy Spirit than believers in the Old Testament experienced.[19] The prepositions teach us about the changing role of the Spirit. A change came with the

96

departure of Jesus, and the Spirit is no longer just *with* believers, He is now *in* believers.[20] The Spirit had formerly been alongside them but now will be inside them. This will be the new role of the Spirit, unknown and not experienced before this time.

The preposition "in" is the most intimate of the prepositions. It is a favorite word used by Jesus to explain our new intimacy with God in this chapter, so we should understand it in its full force. Jesus has just told them that He has been with them (14:9) so they should have known the Father because Jesus is in the Father and the Father is in Jesus (14:11). He tells us to ask our requests in His name (14:13-14). Jesus culminates the lesson in intimacy in verse 20 by saying, "I am in the Father, and you are in Me, and I am in you" (14:20). The Trinity is our foundation for intimacy. We can enjoy a deeper intimacy with God because our friend, the Holy Spirit, lives inside us. We enjoy the intimacy of our friend named Jesus, who lives in perfect intimacy with the Father. We are wrapped in an intimate embrace with the Godhead because our hearts are joined as one with all three persons of the Godhead. It is a friendship deeper than any words and stronger than the strongest bonds.

Back in John 7:39 Jesus "spoke of the Spirit, whom those who believed in Him were to receive; for the Spirit was not yet given, because Jesus was not yet glorified." In other words, Jesus says that the Holy Spirit will be given to the disciples in a different way than before only after Jesus leaves this earth. The Holy Spirit has always been active in this world from creation onward. He empowered people in the Old Testament to do God's work, and He convicted people of their sin. But the Old Testament references all refer to temporary power. The Holy Spirit does not permanently indwell anyone in the Old Testament. That permanent indwelling begins with the church after Jesus leaves this world. At that point, the Holy Spirit takes up His residence in the church which is the body of Christ composed of all who follow Jesus Christ.

We enjoy a special relationship with the Holy Spirit, unlike the relationship which Abraham, Moses or David ever experienced. Jesus can now speak of the Holy Spirit as being both with us and in us. It is not that He is with the church as a whole and in us as individuals. He is at the same time external to us and yet lives within us. We must keep that balance, or we slide into theological error. He is externally transcendent! He is outside of us. We cannot reduce the Holy Spirit to some internal conscience or impression. He is all that God is and stands above and

97

beyond all that we are. He is a person and, as a person stands separate from us as people. He is internally immanent. He lives inside of us. We cannot reduce the Holy Spirit to some spiritual force which influences the world. He is a person who chooses to live within us so we can know him and hurt him and have a relationship with Him even when we are otherwise totally alone.

Corrie ten Boom has been an inspiration to many over the years. She lived through a Nazi concentration camp as a young person and grew to minister to people all over the world. Joni Eareckson Tada, likewise, is an inspiration to all of us. She became a quadriplegic as a result of a diving accident at seventeen and went on to establish a global disability ministry. Joni visited Corrie at her home in California after a series of strokes had incapacitated Corrie. Her home had become a center of prayer and Joni visited her there shortly before her death. Pam, Corrie's helper, wheeled her out of her bedroom to sit with Joni. Joni did most of the talking since the strokes had limited Corrie's speech significantly. When it came time to leave, Corrie indicated that she wanted to pray by grabbing Joni's paralyzed hand with her good hand and holding them up. They bowed their heads in prayer and Corrie ten Boom began to pray. She spoke partly in Dutch, English and words garbled by her impairments, but she prayed fervently and with power. The Holy Spirit was the only one who could understand her mangled words. Joni writes:

> Don't try to diagram the path of those prayers in the Spirit or wrap a precise theological definition around them. Just know God knows our every thought, and He has no difficulty sorting out English from Dutch from some deep well of spiritual language that could never be translated this side of heaven. ... Corrie's apparent gibberish – Spirit aided as it was – may have stopped angels in their tracks as it came before the Father. But there is so much more to this mystery of prayer beyond even these wonders. And it shouldn't surprise us that rubies of surpassing value may be hard-won through suffering.[21]

8

ORPHANS NO LONGER

John 14:18-24

We can feel lost in a crowd, alone in the midst of many. Loneliness happens when we feel disconnected from the group or abandoned by friends. We have a need to belong – to be part of something bigger than ourselves and to be joined with someone greater than our limitations. Joseph Addison, an early 18th-century English writer and politician, had what he called his "3 Grand Essentials" for a meaningful life. To live meaningfully, he said, we must have "something to do, someone to love and something to hope for."[1]

Hope is essential for a meaningful life. Where am I going in life? There must be more to life than this! We often go through life with no idea where we are going. We are very, very busy. We work and play hard. Something is missing. We are on the go so much that our cars are becoming more like a combination of office and home with electronic entertainment, telephones, and computers. We think that we know where we are going in life. We have everything under control. We are immune from the problems we read about in the paper. Then the crisis hits us – sickness, death, job loss! Suddenly, we are lost. We have no hope and nowhere to turn for hope.

The disciples thought that they understood where they were going. They had hope. They had plans. They were following Jesus. Suddenly

Jesus was talking about abandoning them, about dying! His words were very troubling. They needed a new focus in life. Like them, we need a hope that is not focused on our ambitions, our jobs, our hobbies or even our families. There must be more to life than this!

RESURRECTION HOPE

The word "leave" means to "forsake" or "abandon" (John 14:18). Jesus is saying that he is about to die, but he will not forsake them. He will not leave them like babies without parents. He says, "I will come to you." There are three ways that people have interpreted His promise.

1. The first way that this promise is understood is that Jesus is talking about His return to this earth. We have to go all the way back to John 14:3 to find a reference to Christ's return in this passage. There He said, "If I go and prepare a place for you, I will come again, and receive you to Myself." However, in that passage he specifically used the expression, *come again*, and He does not use the word *again* here.

2. The second way that people have understood this verse is to take it as a reference to the Holy Spirit. In other words, Jesus Christ will come to them in the person of the Holy Spirit. He has just delivered the promise of the Holy Spirit in verses 16-17. However, verse 19 explains the point He is making by using the word "behold" (see) twice. When he speaks of the world not "seeing" Jesus He is obviously speaking about seeing Jesus physically. So it is most natural to assume that when He comes, the believers will see Him in the same sense that the world does not see him. Jesus is talking about seeing Him physically in contrast to the world's inability to see Him physically.

3. So it is best to take this, not as a reference to the invisible presence of the Holy Spirit, but to His physical resurrection from the dead. Jesus is talking about His resurrection in John 16:23 when he says: *A little while and you will no longer behold Me; and again a little while and you will see Me.* A little while, namely tomorrow, and you won't see me anymore because I am going to die. From that point on the world will not be able to see me, but I am rising again. Three days later I will rise bodily from that grave, and you will see me because I will come to you. Jesus says that he will not

forsake them and leave them as orphans. He will come to them after the resurrection, and they will see him again.

All of that leads up to His great promise at the end of verse 19 when He says: "Because I live, you shall live also!" His promise means resurrection hope for us. Our resurrection is bound up in, grounded on and established in the truth, the reality, the fact of His physical resurrection. If Jesus did not rise physically from the grave, then we have no hope of resurrection either. Easter reminds us annually that Jesus Christ did rise from the grave. He kept His promise when He said, "I will come to you." So we can believe that He will keep His promise that we will rise from the dead too!

I stood at the graveside of Chet, one of our Trustees and longtime members. I stood there with family and friends as I have stood with many others over the years, grieving the loss yet rejoicing in the hope. Many graveyards in rural Maine are not open in the winter so the body is stored until the spring when the burial can be scheduled. The burial stimulates the grieving process all over again months later. The night before, his wife, Frances, had said how hard this was for her. It was like going through the death all over again. We both knew we had hope. I could stand at that graveside and offer hope because of the resurrection of Jesus Christ. There is more to life than this. There is life beyond the grave. His promise gives resurrection hope. There is no hope without faith in the resurrection of Jesus. The person who doesn't know Jesus doesn't have hope.

She threw herself on the grave marker wailing in grief. There was no consoling her. She was young, perhaps in her late twenties. I didn't know her or the young man we had just buried. The funeral home director had asked me to do a graveside service for a young man who had been killed in Boston. The death was suspicious. The police considered it a homicide, but the family wanted to have some closure to the death while the investigation proceeded. I met them at the cemetery and led them in a brief committal service. As I backed away from the grave to give the family and friends some space to grieve, the woman erupted in agony. She was his girlfriend I found out and could not fathom his death. No one knew what to do. I went to her and knelt beside her on the ground. I prayed with her, but I could not offer her a promise that her boyfriend was in heaven so I pointed her to the friend who can be closer than any other friend and invited her to trust Jesus. We stayed on the ground for a long time after prayer with my arm around her until I could gently help her rise and give her into the hands of those around her. No hope! Lost!

Where am I going? Is there more to life than this? We know the answers to those questions when we know Jesus. I am going to rise again and live forever with my Lord. Resurrection hope is the kind of hope that will get us through our deepest losses in life. There is real security in Christ that we will find nowhere else. I was teaching a baptismal class with nine children ages 8-10 years of age. We were talking about what it means to trust Christ as our Savior. I was telling them that we will go to Heaven to be with Him even after we die. One little boy, his brow all furrowed in deep thought, said, "what if we get amnesia and forget that we accepted Him?" To which I replied, "That's a problem for us but aren't you glad that God never gets amnesia!"

In that day – in the day of His resurrection – the disciples would understand what they could only begin to grasp before (John 14:20). We see it now from the other side of the grave. Because Jesus rose from the dead, we can understand that Christ is in the Father, and we are in Christ, so Christ is in us. Just like the bird is in the air and yet the air is in the bird, there is a unity – oneness which we share with God in Jesus Christ. Our deepest intimacy with God comes from this mutual indwelling.[2] Jesus is in the Father. Their mutual indwelling is the foundational indwelling for our benefit. We are in Jesus, and Jesus is in us. The Son and the Spirit are in us who are in the Son, who is in the Father. The theological term for this concept is "perichoresis."

> This is the teaching that the life of each of the persons flows through each of the others, so each sustains each of the others, and each has direct access to the consciousness of others. Thus, the human organism serves as a good illustration of the Triune God. For example, the brain, heart, and lungs of a given individual all sustain and supply each other, and each is dependent on the other. Conjoined twins, sharing one heart, and liver, also illustrate this intercommunion.[3]

It is a position of impenetrable security like our most precious documents placed inside a fire box that is, in turn, placed inside a bank vault! The order is significant. We are in Christ and only then is Christ in us. We place our faith in Him, and He takes up residence in us. The security of the believer is bound up in our identity in Christ. Who am I? I am a Christ-ian. I am a little Christ. It is also a position of deepest, life-giving, life-sustaining intimacy. Jesus is in us, and we are in Jesus like a fish is in water, and water is in the fish. This total and mutual immersion of life in life forms a spiritual connection deeper than the most intimate human bond can ever hope to achieve.

Here, in this verse, we find the basis for the extended metaphor of the "Vine and Branches" (John 15). Jesus explains our deep connection with Him in the analogy of the vine and branches. A cleft graft uniting a fruit-bearing shoot with the stock of a vine is a linkage of life inside life. The stock is split, and the branch is sliced so that the branch fits deep into – and matches up with – the stock. The life of the stock flows into the branch. We are in Jesus, and Jesus is in us – life in life. His life flows in us who are living in Him.

THIRD LEVEL FRIENDSHIP

The philosopher, Aristotle, classified friendship on three levels in his treatise, *Nicomachean Ethics*. We find the first level of friendship in common interests. We share in common pleasures or activities like members of a sewing circle or a group that gathers to watch football. Many of our friends fit this first level of friendship. The second level involves friendships founded on certain benefits gained from the relationship. Business partners, colleagues in a university, or partners in a church ministry are all examples of this kind of friendship. Friendships of common interests and friendships of mutual benefit are examples of what we often experience in life. The third level of friendship according to Aristotle is "friendship for its own sake, a friendship of character, for the sake of the friend himself or herself."[4] This category forms the deepest bonds and the strongest ties.

Jesus invites us to enter the third level of friendship with him, but, all too often, we turn His friendship into a friendship of usefulness or benefit. We follow Jesus for what Jesus can do for us. A shallow friendship results because we use Jesus for our benefit. Intimacy starts with friendship for friendship sake. He waits for us to open the door and welcome him into our lives not simply for our benefit but for the sake of deep friendship.

Those whom I love, I reprove and discipline; therefore, be zealous and repent. Behold I stand at the door and knock; if anyone hears my voice and opens the door, I will come in to him and will dine with him, and he with Me. He who overcomes, I will grant to him to sit down with Me on My throne, as I also overcame and sat down with My Father on His throne. (Revelation 3:19-21)

These verses are not talking about conversion but communion. They are talking about people who have already placed their faith in Christ and are invited to enjoy His friendship more deeply. Jesus is talking about those whom He loves and rebukes. When we repent of our sin, then we can enjoy His friendship. Jesus invites us to enjoy the intimacy of His love by opening the door of our hearts to Him. He goes on to say in verse 21 that all the overcomers will get a special treat. The overcomers are not a special class of believers. All true believers are overcomers. Jesus overcame in the day of His resurrection. In the day of our resurrection, we will overcome and sit down with Christ on His throne just as Christ overcame and sat down with His Father on His throne.

Our security is found in our friendship with Jesus. A good friend of mine was climbing the corporate ladder. He was doing well in his career. Then he lost his job. For a year, he was unemployed except for odd jobs and contracts which he could pick up on his own. I met with him during that year on a regular basis for prayer and encouragement. He told me that he learned so much about the Lord, and His priorities changed significantly. He confessed that he had focused his identity in his career. When he lost that job, he found His real identity in Christ. Eventually, he took a new job in another state, but he learned lessons that year that he could not have learned any other way. God refocused his life and even now, as he works for a company and is doing very well, he knows that life is bound up not in his career but in the Lord. Sometimes we have to lose what doesn't matter to find what does.

When you boil the Christian life down to its simplest element, it is love. Christianity at its core is a relationship with Jesus Christ. We live to love Him and be loved by Him. Living in love with Jesus is our purpose. Friendship with God is a primary focus of the Christian life. Why am I here? I am not here just to do a job. We often reduce the Christian life to duty and obligation as if being a good Christian is merely following some rules and performing some duties. Christianity is much more than duty and obligation. A husband can do his duty to his wife and never enjoy a love relationship. He can bring home a paycheck, mow the lawn and wash the dishes because it is his obligation. A wife can vacuum the house, wash the clothes and bring home a paycheck because she feels it is her duty. But this is not a relationship of love. It is a relationship of mere duty unless the duty is an expression of deep love. The obedience that expresses love leads to a deeper experience of love. When I do the dishes for my wife out of love, the love we share is deepened.

We love to be loved. It is the nature of love. So Jesus goes on to say that the one who loves Him *shall be loved by my Father and I will love Him.* It is not that we have to earn His love by our obedience at all. We cannot earn God's love. In fact, Scripture teaches us that he loved us first and that our love is in response to His love. He is the love initiator. We respond to His love in obedience, and the reward of loving obedience is more love. Christ's love precedes our love and motivates us to keep His commands. Then His love follows our love and rewards us for keeping those commands. So the whole relationship is bathed in love from start to finish.

FULL DISCLOSURE

How can we know Jesus? We can know Jesus only to the extent that He discloses Himself to us just like in any intimate relationship. Intimacy requires self-disclosure, and self-disclosure only takes place in the context of a committed and trustworthy love. Apart from a commitment to love, there will be limited self-disclosure, so the depth of our friendship depends on the depth of our commitment. (John 14:21) Obedience to Jesus is the evidence of our love for Jesus. It is not enough to have His commands. We must keep them. The "having" and the "keeping" are ongoing actions that prove an ongoing love. My friendship with Jesus does not depend on what others think about me or how successful I am in ministry. My identity does not come from my ministry. My identity comes from my identification with Him. The level of intimacy I enjoy with Jesus depends on my obedience to Him as the proof of my love for Him.

Jesus promises to disclose Himself to those who love Him as demonstrated by our obedience to Him. The word "disclose" is in the future tense. Jesus promised to disclose Himself to the disciples in a way that He had not yet disclosed Himself although serving together for the past three years on earth. The word means to "reveal" and emphasizes a self-revealing or self-disclosure. It was a word used in the Greek translation of Exodus 33:13 in the context of a theophany – a self-revelation of God. Jesus promised full disclosure of Himself but only to those who love Him.

Judas (not the traitor) was shocked (John 14:22). He expected a visible and public revelation of Jesus as God. He could not grasp a self-disclosure that was personal, private and intimate. How could Jesus reveal Himself to those who loved and obeyed Him in a way that He did not reveal Himself to the world? Isn't full messianic disclosure public? Judas certainly expected that it was. He did not grasp the point Jesus was making about the intimacy of true friendship and the self-disclosure that takes place between friends.

The self-disclosure Jesus promised was a spiritual, personal and private illumination in the heart of a true disciple. Jesus said, "I will disclose Myself to him." The word was used figuratively in the Jewish wisdom literature of something that took place in the soul of a person.[5] Jesus promised to disclose Himself to those who love Him in the intimacy of friendship. Intimacy is the language of the Spirit with our spirits (John 14:26; 16:14-15). It is relational language. The greater our love for Jesus, the more He discloses Himself to us and the deeper our friendship grows. We will see God in our lives when we experience God in our love. And we will never need to be lonely again! "Behold I stand at the door and knock; if anyone hears my voice and opens the door, I will come in to him and will dine with him, and he with Me." Jesus invites us into intimacy with Him. All we have to do is open the door by the obedience that arises from love and accepts His friendship to enjoy His full disclosure.

Trust leads to transparency. When we open the door of our inner lives to Jesus, we trust Him to see our inner realities – warts and all! He already sees them, of course, but He rewards our transparency with His self-disclosure so we can enter a deeper level of friendship with Him. When we try to hide our secrets from Him, we lose out on our friendship with Him. Emory Griffin writes: "Self-disclosure usually draws us closer to those who listen. To my mind, this is the greatest effect of transparency. ... Breadth and depth of self-revelation is still the most reliable indication of the level of friendship."[6] He calls this mutual self-disclosure a "form of kenosis – self-emptying."[7] Mutual transparency is a necessary condition for true friendship. Matthew Kelly writes: "Intimacy is mutual self-revelation. It is two people constantly discovering and rediscovering each other."[8] The epitome of the Christian life is our ongoing discovery and rediscovery of Jesus and all He is as we open ourselves up to Him with all we are. "Behold I stand at the door and knock; if anyone hears my voice and opens the door, I will come in to him and will dine with him, and he with Me" (Revelation 3:20).

A HOME FOR GOD

It is an incontrovertible fact that some Christians seem to experience a much closer intimacy with God than others. They appear to enjoy a reverent familiarity with Him that is foreign to us. Is it a matter of favoritism or caprice on the part of God? Or do such people qualify in some way for that desirable intimacy?[9]

There is a vast difference between serving Jesus and loving Jesus. Many of us are so busy serving God that we have lost the joy of loving God. We will find Jesus when we learn to love Jesus. We will never see Jesus as long as we fail to love him. The biggest and grandest cathedrals in all the world are nothing if they are not a home for God! The most spectacular works that we do are nothing if our hearts are not his home. Jesus promises that God will make His home with us when we learn to cherish Jesus (John 14:23).

Ludwig van Beethoven lived in Bonn, Germany, and his home has been restored as a museum. In one room is a piano that he used to create many of his greatest musical compositions. The piano, valued at more than $50 million, stands behind a rope that protects it from the thousands of visitors who enter the museum each year. One year a group of students from Vassar College was touring the museum. One of the students couldn't resist her desire to play the piano. Convincing the guard to let her play the piano with a generous bribe, she sat down at the keyboard and played a section of the Moonlight Sonata. Her classmates applauded her performance although many were just fooling around. She turned to the guard as she stepped back behind the rope and said, "I suppose over the years all the great pianists that have come here have played the piano?" The guard replied, "No Miss. In fact, just two years ago I was standing in this very place when Paderewski visited the museum. He was accompanied by the director of the museum and the international press, who had all come in the hope he would play the piano. When he entered the room, he stood over there, where your friends are standing, and gazed at the piano in silent contemplation for almost fifteen minutes. The director of the museum invited him to play the piano, but with tears in his eyes, Paderewski declined, saying that he was not worthy even to touch it."[10]

We cherish what we respect. In the hustle and bustle of our lives, we become self-absorbed, focused on our goals, and we lose the ability to cherish Jesus for who He is. One of the casualties of our spiritual casualness is the loss of deep respect for the Lord – call it reverence! Respect for another is foundational for true and deep friendship. We cannot cherish what we do not respect. Our respect for the one we cherish opens the door to intimate friendship. We want to do what that person desires. We respect the person so much that we desire to do what he wants. We long to please the one we cherish.

Obedience is the key which unlocks the door of our hearts. Jesus stands knocking at the door. He wants to make his home with us. But we must decide to obey His word. We must decide to surrender to Him and do His will. Obedience is the key. Obedience is not the key to becoming a Christian. We become Christians by accepting God's love gift for us. Jesus died for us that we might have this love relationship with God. But we enjoy His love by obeying His word. We will never enjoy this intimate friendship without obedience because obedience expresses our respect. We obey the person we cherish.

Jesus said, "If anyone loves me, He will keep my word." It is singular, not plural. We do not keep His words but His word. His whole message must be kept. It is not enough for us to preserve that message and repeat it each Sunday morning. We must obey that word and live it all week long. Obedience proves our love and results in His love. When obedience unlocks the door, love walks through. Jesus continued, "And my Father will love him." We often say that God loves unconditionally, but there's another side to that coin. Love is a relational concept. Unconditional love is one-way love! Experiencing the benefits of God's love is always conditional. Jesus discloses Himself to those who cherish Him. The result is a deeply intimate friendship with Jesus, which not all Christians experience and even those that do will not experience all the time.

Dr. Eric Frykenberg was a bear of a man with a tender voice and a gentle spirit. He and his wife, Doris, spent a lifetime of service in India. My parents were missionaries to Pakistan, and he was in our home there. Later Dad invited him to speak in our church in Old Town, Maine when I was a teenager. He stayed with John and Jean Bond, my future in-laws, and my mother-in-law later told me that he would get so lost in talking with God that he would forget the time. She would go in to remind him that it was time to leave for church, and he would be immersed in prayer with his Bible open on his lap oblivious to all that was happening around him. His speaking style was unique and powerful. He would stand at the pulpit with his Bible open and begin speaking without notes in his strong Swedish brogue. His voice was quiet but powerful. He simply talked out the message that Jesus had lived into him. He would read a verse or a phrase and then talk about what Jesus had taught him. He would read another phrase or word and pause to talk some more. After an hour or so, he would close his Bible and say, "Well that's enough for tonight. We'll pick up here tomorrow night." The next night we would start where he left off as if no time had intervened. His words were so powerful yet intimate that I felt like he was giving me a glimpse into his private conversations with Jesus. Jesus, himself, seemed to be talking through Dr. Frykenberg because his words reflected such a deep friendship with the person he cherished more than any other person. I remember longing to have the kind of friendship with Jesus where my words were the spillover of His life in me.

Obedience unlocks the door of our hearts, love walks into our lives, and God becomes our roommate! Jesus says, "*We will come to him.*" It is plural. Both the Father and the Son choose to make their home with us. Jesus goes on to say; "we will make our abode with him." When we demonstrate our love in obedience, then God comes to live with us. The text literally says that God will make a room with me. The word "room" is the same word which is used back in John 14:2 where He says, "In my Father's house are many rooms." So He has prepared a room for us in the Father's house in heaven by his death on the cross for our sins, but, meanwhile, we prepare a room for Him in our lives on earth by obeying His word.

There is more here. The word for "with" which He uses here when He says "with him" is the first part of the word for Paraclete, which is the name of the Holy Spirit in verse 16. We translate it "helper or comforter." It means to be called alongside someone. Verse 17 says that

109

He is with us wherever we go. So the Holy Spirit is our Paraclete, called alongside us to help us through our lives. And both the Father and the Son are now said to take up a room with us. The triune God is our roommate for life.

ROOMMATES WITH JESUS

When I went off to college in Philadelphia, I learned the joy of having a roommate. My freshman year I had two roommates. The first one had arrived before I did and when I got there, he had filled up the entire closet and dresser with his clothes and belongings. He apologized and offered me a corner to put my things in. I knew this was a relationship that couldn't last. He was not there to study but to play. He loved to stay up until all hours of the night playing cards. I liked to go to bed. He liked parties. I liked peace. We lasted one semester together. The second semester, I had a new roommate. He was kind and considerate, mostly. He was not much for parties. But he still wasn't into his studies, and he had one annoying habit. Whenever he was upset, he played his radio turned to the hardest rock station he could find – loud! We lasted one semester.

I didn't have another roommate until my senior year in college. I got married! This roommate was different! We were roommates but not roommates like my college buddies. We were permanent roommates. We were making a home together. I could say that Janie lives here. It was not a one-semester arrangement to be endured. This was a relationship for life to be enjoyed. There is no comparison between a college roommate and a marriage roommate! I would never go back to that arrangement again.

That is where many Christians are living the Christian life. It is a religious arrangement. An arrangement for convenience. God wants to be more than our temporary dormitory roommate. God wants to make His home with us. He wants to go where we go, be what we are and enjoy what we enjoy. He wants to live with us, walk with us and talk with us. We can have this relationship with Him because He stands at the door of our lives and knocks. We open that door by obedient love. We cherish Him. As long as we cherish him, we will enjoy his love. Obedient love opens the door, but lack of love bars the door (14:24).

"He who does not love me, does not keep my words." It takes far more commitment to build a marriage with someone than it does to live

110

with a college roommate, but the rewards are far greater as well. In a marriage, I must keep the words of my wife, and she must keep my words for the relationship to grow and deepen. Many marriages start well. There is intimacy and joy, but then the little quarrels creep in and eat away at the love. Over time, many married couples become little more than college roommates. The same thing can happen in our spiritual lives. If obedience unlocks the door, then disobedience locks the door.

We stop keeping His words. Now I may be reading a little more into this than is justified but I find it significant that here "words" is plural and in verse 23 it is singular. We still keep his word, his message. We have not stopped believing in Christ. We still preserve the values of Christianity, but we have stopped obeying his words. We have allowed the little sins of life to eat away at our relationship with the Lord. We have allowed the little lies, the little slips of the tongue, the little failures to eat away at our spiritual relationship. We wake up one day and realize that we have reverted to being college roommates with the Lord because we stopped cherishing Him.

We have locked him out of our room. "Lord you can live in that part of life – the part that I do on Sunday but not this part of life. We have a two-bedroom apartment now, and you have that part, and I will live my life over here." We have found a way to separate God and life from each other. We compartmentalize our lives into the sacred and secular, and we lose the joy of His love. Jesus says, "Watch out. This is your Father speaking! The word which you hear is not mine, but the Father's who sent me." Once again, we see that whatever the Son says, the Father says. Whatever the Father says, the Son says. When we disobey Jesus, we are disobedient to God the Father. It is a warning to us to open our hearts to Him by obedience.

Many Christians would be willing to do all sorts of spectacular things for God. We would be willing to do great and grand things to know Him better, but we are not willing to straighten out the little and commonplace things through simple obedience. In the same way, many Christians see sin only in the big things of life. The real problem is with the little sins of life that pile up until they eat away at us. We stop cherishing Jesus, but when we learn to obey him in the little things of life and confess our disobedience to him in the ordinary everyday experiences of life, then He reveals himself to us. We will see Him as He is. Our friendship becomes transparently intimate.

111

A student in one of my Bible College classes (we'll call him Jim) was sharing about this lesson in class many years ago. The students had a big paper to turn into me, and he was struggling to get it done. He tried and tried. He spent many hours on the paper, but nothing would come. He just couldn't seem to get it together. He seemed blocked and felt estranged from the Lord. He began to examine his life. He wondered if there was something blocking his relationship with the Lord and hindering his work on this paper. He was in Sunday school class, and the teacher was talking about the passage that speaks of obeying your master in the work world. It suddenly hit him. It was his boss at work. He hated him. He didn't like what he said and how he wanted it done. He never refused to obey him, but he would make sure it didn't get done quite right. He would do it his way. He criticized him to his friends. Every time he saw him, he just got mad inside. He knew this was not right, so he took it to the Lord in prayer. He asked God's forgiveness for his attitude toward his boss. Jim felt free and began doing what the boss said out of respect for him and the Lord. He noticed that he could now work on his biblical project much easier. He enjoyed life much more. And he was happier at his job. A couple of weeks later, his boss came up to him and told him that he didn't know what had happened, but he appreciated his attitude. He was a lot easier to work with, and he just wanted him to know that. The student then told him about his bad attitude and how God had changed it for him. The man looked at him strangely, but Jim said that he took that opportunity to share his faith briefly with his boss.

Jesus wants to make his home with us. He wants to reveal Himself to us. He wants to walk and talk with us. He wants to enjoy us. The question is, do we want Him? Do we cherish Him? He stands knocking. Will we become transparent with Him so that He can be transparent with us? J. Oswald Sanders notes that, of all the disciples, John seemed to enjoy a deeper friendship with Jesus, reclining on the breast of Jesus at the final meal (John 13:23).

> Mutual love and confidence are the keys to intimacy. It would seem that admission to the inner circle of deepening intimacy with God is the outcome of deep desire. Only those who count such intimacy a prize worth sacrificing anything else for are likely to attain it. If other intimacies are more desirable to us, we will not gain entry to that

circle. The place on Jesus' breast is still vacant, and open to any who are willing to pay the price of deepening intimacy. We are now, and we will be in the future, only as intimate with God as we really choose to be.[11]

9

THE PARACLETE'S PEACE

John 14:25-31

Saturday, May 11, 1996, ValuJet flight 592 bound from Miami to Atlanta crashed killing all 110 passengers on board some of whom were traveling home to celebrate Mother's Day. The DC 9 nose-dived into the Everglades minutes after take-off. Speculation immediately centered on a fire in the cargo area, and the accounts were later confirmed by investigators. An inexperienced shipping clerk placed canisters called oxygen generators with highly reactive chemicals improperly marked as empty in the cargo hold. These canisters exploded, igniting an intense fire that caused the crash. One of my college students asked for prayer in class that week because he was flying out the next Monday for Florida on board a ValuJet and the tickets were non-refundable![1] A few days later on Wednesday, twelve fires were set in a single night in a single neighborhood in Biddeford, Maine leaving five families homeless. Gerard Roberge said: "It makes you scared. You don't know if they're going to come back to finish what they started." Brenda Parker said: "My daughter was so scared by the fire. She took her favorite doll and hid it away and covered it all up. She told me she was afraid and didn't want anything to happen to her."[2]

Fear! What do you do when you are alone and afraid? Where do you turn for help? The disciples felt fear overwhelming them. They were like little children, alone in the dark, scared and helpless. Jesus is leaving them. Jesus says: "But you are not alone. You do not need to fear because I will never leave you alone." Jesus goes on to identify two gifts which God gives to help us when we are alone and afraid.

THE GIFT OF THE HOLY SPIRIT

The Holy Spirit is called a "Helper" in verse 26. He is a person, not an impersonal force. When I am alone, an impersonal force is little comfort. Far too many Christians never come to appreciate the Holy Spirit as a real person who thinks and feels; a person to whom you can talk and who can communicate with you. Many Christians do not ever experience the full reality of His comfort because they do not see the Holy Spirit as a person. The sooner we understand that the Holy Spirit is a real person who is there to help us through those times of fear the sooner we will experience peace in our lives.

The Greek word "paraclete" means "someone who is called alongside us" to help and encourage us in our struggles. We are never alone in the Christian life. He is a person who is called alongside us to do three things according to this verse. He is called alongside us to represent Jesus; to teach us, and to remind us of what Jesus has taught. Jesus says that the Father will send the Holy Spirit *in my name*. The Holy Spirit comes alongside us with the authority of Jesus. He comes in the place of Jesus as an ambassador represents the President of the U.S. The Holy Spirit is commissioned by the Father in the name of the Son. The Son also sends him in the name of the Father (15:26)! Once again we have the triune God influencing our lives.

The Holy Spirit is our helper to represent all that God is to us in our lives. He is the one who makes God real in our everyday experience. Sometimes Christians say to me that God feels so distant. He doesn't seem real. I was trying to comfort my daughter with her fears one night when she was very young, and I said, "Now you know that God is right here with you, so you don't have to be afraid." She said, "But I can't see him, and I can see you. Please stay with me."

David Seamands, in his book *Healing for Damaged Emotions*, writes about a man who was preparing for open-heart surgery. The recovery

116

room nurse came to see him the day before the surgery. She told him to hold her hand while she explained what was going to happen. He would be disconnected from his heart while he was kept alive by a machine during the operation. When it was over, he would go to the recovery room where he would be awake but immobile for up to six hours. He would be conscious but not able to move, speak or even open his eyes. He would know what was happening around him but be unable to move. She said, "During those six hours I will be at your side, and I will hold your hand exactly as I am doing now. I will stay with you until you are fully recovered. Although you may feel absolutely helpless, when you feel my hand, you will know that I will not leave you." It happened just as she said but holding on to the hand of that nurse made all the difference in his times of fear.[3] The Holy Spirit is commissioned by Jesus to hold our hand in the midst of our fear. He stays with us in the darkness. He is our helper sent by Jesus himself.

The Holy Spirit is also called alongside us to teach us. Jesus is very emphatic here when He says, "That one shall teach you all things." We do not rely on the Holy Spirit to teach us geography or algebra, physics or biology. He is not teaching us the mating habits of the salamander! The "all things" here is limited by its context. He teaches us all things pertaining to spiritual life – life with Jesus. We cannot survive spiritually without His teaching, and we cannot understand God's will without the Spirit's instruction. Paul wrote: "Now we have received, not the spirit of the world, but the Spirit who is from God, that we might know the things freely given to us by God, which things we also speak, not in words taught by human wisdom, but in those taught by the Spirit." (1 Cor. 2:12-13) Elisabeth Elliott wrote:

> Acceptance of the will of God is always a simple thing, though for us who are yet far from sainthood it is often not an easy thing. Our lives are still complicated, our aims mixed, our vision clouded. ... I would like to do nothing but what I was made to do. I am sure this is what God intends. How shall I know what that is except in quietness? How listen if I am full of talk? I must cease the rehearsal of personal wants and feelings, willingly release things that seem important but in fact have nothing to do with my true goal. The itch to know and to have and to be anything

117

other than what God intends me to know, to have, and to be must go.[4]

We are dense sometimes to the Spirit's teaching because we are so self-absorbed that we fail to listen. We do not welcome His word. It is not brilliant intellect which makes the difference. It is listening and learning from the Spirit. It is a teachable heart. The Holy Spirit is called alongside us to represent Jesus; to teach us all things and to remind us what Jesus has taught.

The disciples did not understand "Palm Sunday!" Jesus and his disciples had been enjoying a quiet stay with Lazarus in the village of Bethany near Jerusalem. Mary had taken a pound of expensive perfume and anointed Jesus, and the sweet smell of worship filled the whole house. Judas alone objected to the extravagant gesture of love. All the others enjoyed these intimate moments with Jesus. The crowds soon intruded on their intimacy. The Feast of Passover was upon them. The next day Jesus and his disciples began to work their way around the Mount of Olives toward the city of Jerusalem. The sight of the city from the eastern hillside was breathtaking. The temple stood resplendent on the hill across the valley from where they walked the quiet path with Jesus. Suddenly, the shouts of the crowd interrupted their conversations. The people surged across the Kidron Valley and up the hillside toward them. People everywhere were waving palm branches and shouting, "Hosanna! Blessed is He who comes in the name of the Lord" and calling him "King of Israel." Jesus mounted a young donkey and rode into the city in triumph. John records his observation:

> These things His disciples did not understand at the first; but when Jesus was glorified, then they remembered that these things were written of Him, and that they had done these things to Him (John 12:16).

Here is an example of the Holy Spirit's work. The disciples did not understand what Palm Sunday was all about until after Jesus had ascended to the Father. Why? Because after the ascension, the Holy Spirit went to work to remind them of all these things. The four Gospels are the written record of the Holy Spirit's reminding the disciples of all those little details which they had forgotten or had not previously understood.

The Holy Spirit is still at work today in our lives just as He was in the disciples' lives. He still makes God real to us. He still teaches us what we need to know for our spiritual health. He is still reminding us of those things that Jesus did and taught. How does He do all of this in our lives today?

The Holy Spirit teaches us:

> * Through the Bible
> * Through God's people
> * Through our circumstances

The methods are not mutually exclusive of course. The Spirit weaves His lessons through the full curriculum He has planned for us. The illuminating work of the Spirit draws from our study of Scripture to apply the truths to our lives in the moments we most need them. Walt Russell explains what it felt like when his 18-month old son, Christopher, died suddenly in his sleep. He said that as he stood at the graveside, it may have been the "most despairing, skeptical, and faithless moment" of his life. Into that "faithless moment," the Spirit breathed a memory of 1 Thessalonians 4:13-18 – a passage he had studied many times. The words comforted him in his sorrow. He writes that the force of the Spirit's illuminating work "relates to our welcoming of the truths of Scripture rather than our understanding of them."[5]

We must study the Bible to learn what He wants to teach us. The Holy Spirit will never violate what the Bible says. The only way that He can remind us of what Jesus did and taught is if we have studied His record in the Bible. He teaches us through other people. He does this through pastors, through friends, through teachers and others that He brings into our lives to help us. And the Holy Spirit teaches us through our circumstances. The man flat on his back in the hospital with a heart attack is in the school of the Spirit. The woman who has just lost her job and is struggling to make sense of life is in the Academy of the Spirit. God teaches us through our circumstances on the job and in the home.

The question is: are we listening? Do we have teachable spirits? God chooses to work with soft hearts. I taught men and women in a Bible College for many years. Every semester I would assign grades to each student. Some people passed, and some flunked. Some received A's and some received C's. There is nothing spiritual about grades. They are the circumstances of life. The Holy Spirit is teaching people to have soft and teachable hearts as they progress through four years of Bible College. The grades of a professor are merely one of the circumstances God uses to teach His lessons. I watched students come and go and I could predict with fair accuracy who would make it in ministry and who would not. It had nothing to do with the grades themselves. I have watched A students fail miserably in ministry. I have watched C students succeed wonderfully in ministry. I have watched with a sinking heart some very talented people sit in my office and make excuses. They are not serving the Lord today. I have watched others who failed a test sit with a tender heart seeking to learn from the experience. They are in ministry today.

What is the difference? The difference is the soft heart. The difference is the teachable spirit. Do we listen to what the Holy Spirit is trying to teach us through His Word, through other people and their evaluations and our circumstances? If we do, we will learn His lessons and accomplish His work. If not, we will go from one failure to another never learning.

THE GIFT OF PERSONAL PEACE

The gift of the Holy Spirit (v. 26) and the gift of personal peace (v. 27) are directly related to one another. In other words, how we respond to the Spirit's teaching is directly related to how we experience Christ's peace in our lives. If we are not listening to Him, we will not understand His peace. Christ's peace is not the absence or suppression of our feelings. It is not peace that ignores our emotions because the last part of the verse ties his peace directly to our emotions, our fear, and our anxiety. This peace is not just intellectual or rational logic. It has to do with subjective feelings and personal experiences.

We often perceive peace as the absence of conflict, chaos, and disorder. Jesus presents peace as the presence of harmony, wholeness, and order. Biblical peace is not the absence of negative emotions. Christ's peace is the presence of personal convictions leading to a sense of well-being. Peace reflects the Old Testament teaching of "shalom." Biblical peace is an assurance of order in the midst of disorder, wholeness in the midst of chaos, and well-being in the midst of conflict because we know all matters are in our Father's hands.

Christ's peace is the assurance or conviction that our circumstances are in God's hands. Peace is a Christian brother sharing with me the assurance that his steps are in God's hands when I visit him in the hospital as he faces open heart surgery. Peace is the Christian mother, whose son has just been arrested and put in jail, saying to me through her tears, "Pastor, God has him just where he needs to be!" Christ's peace is the sense that "It is well with my soul" when nothing is well with my situation. That peace is not a peace which you can find anywhere in this world. It is supernatural. It comes from Christ Himself through the ministry of the Holy Spirit in our lives.

To be at peace with my God and to be at peace with myself are the two dimensions which Christ talks about in this verse. Jesus leaves us peace and gives us His peace. The two verbs help us understand the peace we have in life. The first is reconciliation and the second is serenity. We experience reconciliation when we are at peace with God. Jesus said, "Peace I leave with you." The word *leave* indicates a bequest or a legacy.[6] Reconciliation is the peace He left behind for us. It is His last will and testament to us. He left us peace with God. It is the peace of reconciliation. God is no longer angry with us, and we are no longer fighting God. We are at peace with God.

A bequest is what someone else has earned in life and left for us to enjoy. We can be at peace with God because Jesus earned that peace by His death on the cross. We do not have to earn peace with God. We can have that peace simply by accepting it from Him. Jesus already bought that peace and left it for us to enjoy – reconciliation with God.

Serenity is to be at peace with myself and my situation. Jesus added, "My peace I give to you." Serenity is the peace Jesus experienced. It is not the peace of reconciliation with the Father for Jesus never had to experience reconciliation. He never was an enemy of God like us. "My peace," Jesus says. Jesus gives us His peace whenever we need it in life.[7] It is not so much the peace we can have with others. It is personal peace. It is internal peace. This peace does not ignore conflict or problems. It is a peace that transcends those problems by faith in Christ. Christ's peace is the peace which He experienced in life Himself. Peace is the serenity, the tranquility, that He experienced in front of the howling mob at His crucifixion. He was at peace with Himself, and He gives that peace to us.

121

Wholeness in the midst of chaos, order in the midst of disorder, and harmony in the midst of conflict are His personal gifts to us.

He does not give us peace like the world gives us peace. The world tries to give us peace with a bigger paycheck, better circumstances or personal affirmation. The world wants us to "feel good about ourselves" but this is not the way to experience Christ's peace. We will enjoy serenity only when we accept responsibility for our sin and turn it over into His hands. Sin is the barrier to peace even with ourselves. So much of our bitterness and resentment in life comes from our selfishness, our pride, and our ambition. We can never experience His peace until we deal with those sin issues in our lives.

Reconciliation and serenity come hand in hand. To be at peace with myself, I must be at peace with my God. "Let not your heart be troubled, nor let it be afraid" (v. 27), Jesus goes on to say. He started this whole chapter with similar words (14:1). The word for "troubled" means to be angry, upset and anxious. It means to be filled with turmoil; to have all those emotions tumbling around inside of us. The word for "fear" means to be timid or cowardly. Jesus is saying that we need to be confident, not cowardly!

Why? How? We can be confident because we have the promise of His Spirit and the promise of His peace. If we will listen to His Spirit and accept His peace, then we will enjoy His confidence. We will not be afraid. We have many fears. Our worries are real. We have the fear of death, the fear of failure, the fear of rejection, and the fear of embarrassment. We have the fear of sickness and the fear of losing someone we love. There is the mother whose two-year-old died on the playground and the families of 500 people who died in the tornado in Bangladesh. Who can explain the live infant lying in his dead mother's lap after that tornado? There is John, who must face his vice president tomorrow because of a $100,000 mistake knowing that he could lose his job. There is the teenager who looks vacantly out the window and says, "Life is the pits, and then you die." There is the young mom staring down the driveway as her former husband leaves with the three children for the weekend knowing that she is all alone – again. To all of us, Jesus says, "Don't let the fear cripple your life. You can have my peace and my helper. In me, you can still say, 'It is well with my soul,' even if it is not well with your circumstances. Come and rest in me."

LOVE AND FAITH

Worry, like water, is a powerful force. A thin stream of water can slowly carve a large channel through sand and even rock. Worry is like that. Worry starts small but cuts deep into the soul. One writer said: "Worry is a thin stream of fear trickling through the mind. If encouraged, it cuts a channel into which all other thoughts are drained."[8] I've certainly experienced those worries that lead to sleepless nights. After a while, you can think of nothing else. Worry consumes your mind like a black hole, sucking every thought into the abyss.

Jesus says, "Trust me because I do what is best for you!" We don't stop worrying because He guarantees to deliver what we want. Jesus is a friend, not a magic genie. We stop worrying when we learn to trust Him. Trusting Jesus is the ultimate antidote for worry. We stop worrying because He will do what is best for us. He knows what we need better than we do. Our real self-interest lies in putting Jesus' interest first. The disciples were upset by the news He had told them. They were confused and worried. They didn't want Him to go away and return at some later time. They wanted Him to stay with them right then. They wanted to hang onto Him. So Jesus delivers a mild rebuke here (v. 28). "If you were really loving me on an ongoing basis you would be delighted with this news that I am going away. The fact that you are upset proves that you don't really love me."[9]

Why should they be happy that He is leaving them at this crucial juncture of their lives? "Lord, it seems like you are leaving us when we need you most. How can this be in our best interest? How can we be happy about this?" Jesus answers them by making a theologically profound statement. He says that they should be happy because He is going to the Father and then He adds, "For the Father is greater than I." The Arians in the 2nd and 3rd centuries of church history argued that this verse proved that Jesus was not fully God because He said that the Father, meaning God, was greater than He was. But this is a ludicrous argument to make. If I were to stand up in all seriousness and say, "God is greater than I am" you would think me terribly arrogant. As if there was any question that God was greater than I am! In fact, the statement is an implied claim to deity because He is actually suggesting that in some sense the Father is not greater than He is.

The context governs the comparison of greatness. He is explaining why they should be happy that He is going back to the Father. They should be happy about that because the Father is currently greater than He is! He is not saying that the Father is more God than He is. He is saying the Father is greater in glory than He is because right now He is humbled by His incarnation. He left His glory to become a man but the Father retained His glory. Jesus in John 17:5 will say "And now, glorify Thou Me together with Thyself, Father, with the glory which I had with Thee before the world was." Jesus is returning to claim that glory back again after He dies and rises from the dead.

Jesus' argument runs something like this. I am leaving to return to the Father and my glorious position as Ruler of this universe. If you loved me, you would be happy that I am returning to my rightful position. It is in our interest that He return because that means that He has redeemed us, He reigns as King over His kingdom and He gives us His Spirit's power. We get all of that if He goes back to the Father. Instead of selfish enjoyment of His personal presence, the disciples would receive so much more by letting Him go. Consider what they would miss out on if He didn't go! No redemption, salvation or eternal life. No kingdom and no Spirit power. The disciples could only see what they were missing if He went. They could not see that the immediate pain of the loss was worth it for the joy that lay ahead.

We have the same problem today. We are like little children who have a problem with delayed gratification. Everything is immediate. Like little children, we cry out, "I can't wait." We don't realize that our self-interest lies in putting His interest first. Whatever troubles us, God sends it for our good.

The ironic truth is that if we are interested in ourselves, we will put Him first. What He does is always in our best interest. Joseph, after his brothers sold him into slavery, said, "What you did you meant for evil but God meant it for good" (Genesis 50:20). Paul wrote in Romans 8:28, "All things work together for good to them that love the Lord." He did not say that all things are good. All things are not good in themselves, but everything that God brings into our lives is for our good. It is in our best interest.

Instead, we have a shallow and shortsighted selfishness which cannot see beyond our immediate circumstances, wants and wishes. We can see only the here and now, but Christ holds the future in the palm of

His hands. He can say, "Trust me because I know what the future holds" (v. 29). Jesus says, "Look, I have said to you in the past, and I continue to predict these events to you now so that when they happen you will learn to trust me." Jesus predicted His death, burial and resurrection repeatedly in the gospels. How could He do that so perfectly if He did not control the events that were about to take place? The death of Christ on the cross was not an accident or defeat. Jesus went willingly to the cross. He chose to die. In fact, He set it up. He told Judas to get on with it. He deliberately made Himself available where He knew Judas would find Him. He told His followers not to defend Him. In the Garden, when the soldiers come to arrest Him, He turns to His disciples and says, "Don't you know that I could call twelve legions of angels to defend me if I wanted?" In front of Pilate, He says, "You would have no power over me unless it were given you from above." Jesus was in full control of His own death, so our faith rests in His control.

We can make all the plans we want. We can pursue our goals and objectives in life but in the end, we cannot predict what will happen tomorrow! We are inept at controlling what will come to pass. Our faith rests in his control! We have to believe that nothing happens to us which is not allowed by God for our good. If we pursue our shallow self-interests, we will miss out on all the good God has for us. He knows what the future holds. We do not. All we can do is trust Him and put Him first, and the result will be best for us.

I had the privilege of attending a conference on bioethics where Joni Eareckson Tada spoke about the lessons she has learned through a lifetime of trusting God as a quadriplegic. She told the story of her experience in the hospital in the months after the tragic diving accident that paralyzed her from the neck down. She was depressed. The days were dark and the nights darker. She wanted to die. In her suicidal state, she used to shake her head violently back and forth trying to break her neck and end her life. A friend named Steve Estes helped guide her through those dark days with these words. He said, "Trusting God has nothing to do with trustful feelings." Trust is a choice, an act of the will. We choose to trust our friend Jesus that He will always do what is best for us. The feelings follow the trust.

THE SPIDER'S WEB

Evil abounds in this world. Terrorists in Paris and hooded decapitators in Syria are real, driven by Satan, the master of evil. But we don't need to worry because even the devil is predictable to Jesus! Jesus says, trust me because I know what the devil plans (v. 30). The ruler or prince of this world is the devil himself. He has power. He has great power over this world system, but He is not all-powerful. His power is even now under the control of Christ. He cannot do whatever he wants to do. What he does, he does by permission!

Jesus says, "I will not be talking much longer to you because the days of darkness are coming when the devil will have his way by permission of the Father. Don't be afraid. The devil has nothing in me." Jesus is saying, "I know what the devil is about to do. I know every move that he will make before he makes it, and furthermore, he has no foothold in my life by which to defeat me." Here is an important key to understanding how the devil works. Jesus uses a double negative to emphasize, "In me he does not have *nothing*! He has no claim on me. He has no foothold or handhold in my life. The devil has nothing that he can hold over my head."

Sin and guilt are the greatest weapons the devil has over us. When we have sinned or failed in the past, then the devil is going to use that failure every chance that he can get. He is going to drive us with guilt. He is going to work us over with our sin. He is going to hold it over our heads and make us miserable. This is how the devil operates. Sin gives him a foothold in our lives. Sin allows him to grab onto something in us and destroy us with it.

Not Jesus!

Jesus is beyond Satan's domain. Jesus is sinless. Though Satan should search for eternity, he would find nothing to hold over Christ's head. There is nothing that He can grab onto.[10] The fact that Satan has nothing on Jesus is significant because when we come to Christ in faith then our sins are transferred to Him and His righteousness is transferred to us. There is nothing the devil can hold over our heads which is not covered by the blood of Christ. As long as I repent and confess that sin to the Lord and stand cleansed in His righteousness, then there is nothing,

126

absolutely nothing, that the devil can lay claim to in my life. My friend, Jesus, guarantees it!

The author of Hebrews wrote:

> For we do not have a high priest who cannot sympathize with our weaknesses, but one who has been tempted in all things as we are, yet without sin. Let us, therefore, draw near with confidence to the throne of grace that we may receive mercy and may find grace to help in time of need. (4:15-16)

Our confidence rests on His perfection![11] That is why John wrote in 1 John 4:4, "You are from God, little children, and have overcome them; because greater is He who is in you than He who is in the world." We can have such confidence because of His perfection, not ours.

We have a natural tendency to see salvation only in terms of our benefit. God loved us and Jesus died for us so that we can have eternal life with Him. Very true. But it is hardly the only reason that Jesus came to this earth. Jesus gives us another reason for the cross in verse 31 – so that the world may know that I love the Father! The cross reveals how much the Son loved the Father in the unity of the Godhead. Jesus chose to die not only because He loved us but because He loved the Father. Our salvation is the by-product of His love. The cross-work of Christ proves to the world, as wicked and sinful as it is, the love relationship that the Father, Son, and Holy Spirit have together. Even the most evil people in this world must acknowledge someday that the Son loved the Father so much that He did what the Father said even to the point of the cross.

We learn more about this love relationship within the Godhead because we see here that the Father commands and the Son obeys. The Father sends, and the Son goes. So Jesus demonstrated exactly what He calls us to demonstrate. He had said, "If you love me keep my commandments." He loved the Father, so He did what the Father wanted. Jesus did what He calls us to do. Trust me because I do what the Father wants!

This verse explains the expression back in verse 28 where Jesus said, "The Father is greater than I." The Father is greater in position and authority but not in essence. He is no more God than Jesus, but Jesus is positionally subordinate to the Father. "Absolute equality is harmonious with relative inequality."[12] Subordination does not imply inferiority. At one time I was both pastor of a church and an associate professor at a Bible College. The President of the college was a member of the church where I was a pastor. So I was over him at church and under him at the college, but we were both equally sons of God. It is all positional. In one role, I must exercise oversight, and in the other role, he must exercise oversight, but we are equal before the Lord.

The Godhead functions this way. The Father gives the orders, and the Son executes the mission. The Son demonstrates his love for the Father by fulfilling the Father's will. This is why we can trust Him. He and the Father are united in perfect love so that what the Son does is exactly what the Father wants. We never need to worry that there is conflict in the Godhead.

Trust, in its essence, is not a feeling, but the decision to trust results in feelings of peace. The choice of our trust unwraps the gift of God's peace. We look around at our circumstances in despair. We see no way out of our prison. Then God shows up in some seemingly inconsequential way. We see a glimmer of His power – a glimpse of His control. We choose to trust. New feelings, long buried, rise in our hearts. Peace emerges to blanket our souls with His love.

Nien Cheng, the exiled widow who passed away in Washington, D.C. in 2009, was a victim of China's "Cultural Revolution" under Chairman Mao. Her husband was the general manager of the Shanghai office for Shell International Petroleum Company, and, after his death from cancer, she became an advisor to management for the company, living in relative comfort with her daughter until the Red Guards came to take her away. She was admitted into the "No. 1 Detention House" and held in solitary confinement for many weeks. Depressed by the long weeks of isolation and worried about her daughter, she was often so choked with emotion she could hardly even breathe or swallow food.

In the early afternoon one day, she looked up at the single window to see a tiny spider climbing from one bar to another. The spider, no bigger than a pea, crawled to the top of one bar and swung down to the bottom of the next, spinning her silken thread from bar to bar. There was no hesitation, no hurry. The spider knew exactly what to do as it confidently weaved its web, strand by strand. The result was a thing of beauty in an ugly place. The spider moved to the center of the web and settled down in peace. Day after day, the spider became her companion, lifting her spirits by drawing her to consider the God she could trust.

> I had just watched an architectural feat by an extremely skilled artist, and my mind was full of questions. Who had taught the spider how to make a web? Could it really have acquired the skill through evolution, or did God create the spider and endow it with the ability to make a web so that it could catch food and perpetuate its species? ... For the moment, I knew I had just witnessed something that was extraordinarily beautiful and uplifting. Whether God had made the spider or not, I thanked Him for what I had just seen. A miracle of life had been shown to me. It helped me to see that God was in control. Mao Zedong and his Revolutionaries seemed much less menacing. I felt a renewal of hope and confidence.[13]

Jesus says to us, "Arise, let us go from here." It is time to face the enemy. Let's move ahead. Trust me. I'm in control.

THE IMPORTANCE OF PERSEVERANCE

10

THE GARDEN OF HIS DELIGHT

John 15:1-4

It was dark out now. The narrow winding streets of the city which had, only a few hours before, been filled with teeming crowds of people, were mostly empty. Jesus led his disciples down the outside stairway from the upper room and along the back streets toward the temple complex. They walked in silence, each filled with his own thoughts and questions about the night ahead. Each wondering about the strange talk of the master so rich and yet so melancholy. Jesus stopped next to a wall covered with one of the grape vines which were everywhere in the city. John watched as Jesus gently fingered the vine and then turned to the bewildered disciples and said, "I am the true vine, and my Father is the vinedresser."

The words were tinged with irony. The grape vine was the ancient symbol of the nation of Israel. Israel had been God's vine. Had not the Prophet Isaiah quoted God as saying, "I had planted you (Israel) like a choice vine of sound and reliable stock. How then did you turn against me into a corrupt, wild vine?" (Is. 5:2) Instead of producing good grapes Israel had rebelled against God and produced sour grapes. Jesus now claims to be the true, genuine, authentic vine as opposed to the false vine of Israel. In Jesus is life and His life is meant to grow fruit.

The purpose is the produce! Will we produce good grapes or sour grapes? The life Jesus gives us is intended to produce fruit in us. If there is no fruit then, perhaps, there is no life! "I am the true vine, and my Father is the vinedresser." The Father is at work to produce His fruit in us. It takes careful, painstaking, time-consuming work to produce good grapes. God is at work in us to produce good grapes, not sour grapes. A humble, faithful, godly character takes a lifetime to develop. The gardener is in no hurry. He is growing us for eternity. C.H. Spurgeon, the great Baptist preacher, reportedly once said, "By perseverance the snail reached the ark." By perseverance, the gardener cultivates His fruit in us.

The extended metaphor of the vine and the branches in John 15 deals with fruit bearing through abiding in Christ. The word "fruit" is used eight times in verses 1-16. The word "abide" is used 11 times in verses 1-16. To "abide" means to remain or continue. Branches produce fruit by remaining connected to the vine. The life flowing from Jesus (the Vine) produces the fruit in believers (the branches.). The Father is the gardener. Jesus is the vine and believers are the branches. The branches, Jesus says, are "in Me" (15:2). A branch is not a branch if it is not "in Me," Jesus says. He is speaking only about branches that are in union with Jesus. Every branch in the metaphor is connected to Christ. Jesus is not talking about branches from other vines. These branches are all from His vine. Therefore, all branches in this metaphor are genuine believers.

LEVELS OF FRUITLESSNESS

Jesus tells us how the Father works to produce His character in us. There are two levels of fruitlessness in the analogy of the vine and the branches (John 15:2). There are "no fruit" branches and "some fruit" branches, but both are still branches (Christians). God, the Father, is the gardener. He intends that all branches will bear "much fruit" so He cultivates the branches to make them fruitful. What does the gardener do to make us fruitful?

Level One, No Fruit Christians: "Every branch in Me that does not bear fruit, He takes away." Many translations understand the verb in the sense of take away, remove or cut off.[1] This interpretation would be a

134

judgmental action, and verse 6 is used to bolster the argument that this is an act of judgment by God. Some even view it as the "sin unto death" where God removes a person from this life (1 John 5:16). However, the passage is talking about people who are already in Christ. Jesus clearly says that the fruitless branches are "in me!" These are not branches that have no life. These are not branches which have never borne fruit. In fact, the Greek word for "does not bear fruit" speaks of the current situation.[2] He is talking about branches that are connected to Christ but who are not currently bearing fruit for one reason or another.

I think it is better to understand the verb in the sense of lift up which fits better with the sequence of "no fruit" and "some fruit" in this verse. It also conforms to the normal process of gardening. The branches of the vine grow heavy and trail across the ground. If left on the ground, they not only become fruitless but eventually rot. The gardener's first job is to lift up the branches so that they can become fruitful. God does this in our lives whenever we become fruitless because we are mired in the dirt of life. God's first action with fruitless Christians is not to condemn us but to assist us. He lifts us up from the dirtiness of the life into which we have fallen. When we become unproductive because of sin and rebellion, He gently lifts us up out of the muck we have fallen into so that we can enjoy His fresh air and sunshine. We begin to gain spiritual strength so that we can become productive Christians once again.

Level Two, Some Fruit Christians: "Every branch that bears fruit, He prunes it so that it may bear more fruit." The verb translated "prune" originally meant to clean, sweep or cleanse.[3] The noun form was used as a technical term in agriculture for the use of chemicals to get rid of parasites or fungus. The gardener cleanses the branch of impurities and cuts away the extra woody growths – the suckers – that will hinder the production of fruit. The gardener's goal is to help the branch produce more fruit. God, the spiritual gardener, takes both of these actions in our lives as needed. When we become mired in the dirt of life and stop producing fruit, God lifts us up so we can grow spiritually. When we are struggling to produce fruit because parasites are affecting our lives or distractions are impeding our growth, the gardener cleanses us with the insecticide of grace and cuts away the distractions in our lives. He will not let us continue as we are but will work to clean us up and prune us down. We may not like the process, but the product is God's luscious fruit.

The branches He prunes are those which are already producing fruit. The objective is to produce more fruit. So if God is pruning us, it is a sign that He knows we have been productive, but He wants to make us more productive. That can be a painful process. The order is significant here.[4] The Christian is first lifted up to worship the Lord and experience His grace and only then does the pruning take place. Only after we have experienced God's restoring grace does He begin to cut away those elements which are damaging our lives. The painful cutting takes place among those who are already producing some fruit so that they will produce more fruit for the master. If we try to reverse the order by lopping off the practices in our lives we deem unspiritual before we are drawn to the Father by His grace, we will end up in the hypocrisy of legalism.

The pain is not for punishment but for production. The suckers are cut away because they are sucking the life of the vine from the fruit. The parasites are washed away because they are infecting the branches diminishing the quality of the fruit. Any element in our lives which is sucking our spiritual vitality away from the production of good fruit must be eliminated. Any parasite which we have allowed to infiltrate our experience must be washed away if we are to become more productive Christians. Any element of our character which is inhibiting us from moving to the next level of productivity for the Lord must be dealt with, and, until He cuts it out of our lives, we can never reach the next level of productivity.

We may reach some level of productivity before we resist the lessons which God is trying to teach us. We fight the knife because it hurts. Maybe we become satisfied with our current productivity. Maybe pride takes root in our souls. Whatever the problem the Father will keep bringing us around to learn that lesson until we submit to His knife. Why? Because He wants to take us to the next level. He wants us to produce more, but we cannot produce more until we submit to the painful knife! Elisabeth Elliot wrote:

> Many in the world today endure great suffering that we in North America have never known. We have not been vouchsafed that privilege. Yet it seems to me that having something we don't want or wanting something we don't have, no matter how insignificant, is like learning the scales on the piano. They're a far cry from a fugue, but you can't

play the fugue if you haven't mastered the scales. Our Heavenly Father sets the lessons suited to our progress. All of His grace.[5]

When I was a freshman at Philadelphia College of Bible, I tried out for the baseball team. The coach, Dan Richner, selected virtually everyone who tried out for the team. I was not a very good player, so I didn't play very much. In fact, another freshman and I had a bet going to see who would play the least that season. He won but not because I was better. It was the last game of the season, and neither of us had played even one inning. When we were getting dressed in our uniforms before the game, he realized that he had forgotten the shirt to his uniform. When the coach called Gary to go into the game, the umpire would not let him play, so the coach had to put me in instead. I did get a trophy at the end of the year because our team won the conference championship.

The season would be a forgettable footnote in my life if not for an important spiritual lesson I learned the hard way. I was becoming very busy with school and other activities half way through the season, and I felt the increased pressure on my time. I decided that I should sacrifice baseball since it took up so much time for practice and trips and I never played anyway. I went to Coach Richner and told him that I was quitting the baseball team because I never played and I had more important things to do with my time. I will never forget his response. He looked at me and said, "That is fine if that is your decision, but I want you to remember something. It is easy to have enough character to be a star on the team, but do you have enough character to sit on the bench? The decision is your decision, David. I will know what your character is by whether or not you are at practice this afternoon." I left his office, but I finished the season and never missed a practice. Coach Richner had taught me a valuable life lesson – a character lesson in commitment and perseverance.

God strips us to use us. Jesus shapes us for His purpose. He remakes us to produce His fruit. The purpose is in the produce. The Father is at work to produce His fruit in us through the life of the Son flowing into us. Obstructions in our lives must be removed, and infections must be cleansed so that the sap can flow freely through us into the fruit of our lives.

Jesus stops at this point in His metaphor to interject a reassuring statement in verse 3. "You are already clean." The word *clean* is the noun form of the verb translated *prune* in verse 2. Cleansing is part of pruning. Jesus is making a reference back to something which He said earlier that very night in response to Peter, who didn't want Jesus to wash his feet. When Peter was told that he couldn't have any part with Jesus if he was not washed then he wanted Jesus to wash his whole body. But Jesus says that Peter is already clean and needs only to wash up for supper (John 13:10-11)

> Jesus said to him, "He who has bathed needs only to wash
> his feet, but is completely clean; and you are clean, but not
> all of you." For He knew the one who was betraying Him;
> for this reason, He said, "Not all of you are clean."

Jesus is saying that they were already saved people. They had already been washed except for Judas. They were already spiritually in union with Christ. What they needed was to wash their feet for supper. He is saying the same thing in chapter 15. Being in Christ is the sole source of life (John 15:3). You cannot have eternal life apart from Jesus Christ (John 14:6). John 15 is not about how to become a Christian or even the difference between Christians and non-Christians. John 15 is about communion with Christ not union with Him. They were already clean. They were already connected to the vine. He wanted them to be more fruitful. Being in Christ is the sole source of life but remaining in Christ is the sole source of fruitfulness (John 15:4).

COMMUNION REQUIRES CONNECTION

Jesus identifies two conditions – which are really one condition – necessary for fruit bearing in John 15:4. "Abide in Me, and I in you." Abiding is necessary for producing fruit. The branch is not capable of producing fruit by itself "unless it abides in the vine, so neither can you unless you abide in Me." Some form of the verb "abide" is used eleven times in this chapter. The word means to remain, stay or continue,[6] and it can have the sense of dwell or live together. For example, the word is used of Mary, who stayed or lived with her sister, Elizabeth, for three months (Luke 1:56).

Jesus states the first condition as a command, "Abide in Me."[7] The command that we remain in Christ implies that we are already in union with Christ otherwise how could we remain? Since it is a command for us to take action, it also implies that we can stop remaining in Christ. These two implications, taken together, show us that the verse is talking about our communion with Jesus not our union with Jesus. We are never commanded to be in union with Christ, but we are commanded to stay in communion with Christ. The source of life is being in Him. The source of fruitfulness is remaining in Him.

Jesus states the second condition as an addition to the first, "And I in you." The condition is a promise. Jesus is saying, "Abide in me and I promise to abide in you."[8] We can only take care of our part in the relationship. We cannot make Jesus remain in us. He promises to remain in us on the condition that we remain in Him, so the two conditions are really one condition. The result of this mutual remaining is fruit bearing.

The vine does not block its life flow into the branches, but the branches might block the life flow from the vine. Jesus does not disconnect from us. We disconnect from Him, and the result is fruitlessness. Personal, persistent and continuous intimacy with Jesus produces fruitfulness because He promises that His life will flow into us as we remain connected to Him. Our continuous communion with Jesus unleashes the power of His spiritual life flowing into us to produce fruit.

Abiding is the language of friendship. Friends stick together, stay connected. Aristotle said, "Wishing to be friends is quick work, but friendship is a slow-ripening fruit." Perseverance is a mark of true friendship. Persistence helps friends stay connected. We must stay in constant communion with the Lord if we are to produce fruit. We must enjoy His friendship if we are to be fruitful Christians because He alone produces the fruit. Just as the life-giving sap from the vine must flow out through the branches into the fruit so the life of Christ must flow through us and be demonstrated in our attitudes and actions.

"Stick with me," Jesus says. "Stay connected to me! Don't block me or avoid me." Jesus exhorts us to remain constantly in Him. So many times as a pastor I have watched Christians "unfriend" Jesus by drifting away through the distractions of busyness; the pursuit of worldly pleasures or the lure of sin. The Father must clean up the infections and cut away the distractions so we can abide in Jesus. Any attitude in our relationship which blocks the flow of His life-giving sap to the fruit must be eliminated. Any distraction which side-tracks the flow of His power away from the fruit must be pruned. Any sucker that saps our energy must be cut away.

Our gracious Father cleanses and prunes our lives in His love. He is not finished with us. The losses we feel here on earth draw us to depend more on Him. We let go of what we grasp so tightly to grab Him more intensely. The career we pursued so ambitiously may need to go. The position we held with pride may be taken away by His gentle hand prying our fingers free. The dream house we loved may be lost through financial pressures. The person we thought was irreplaceable in our lives may be replaced with Jesus himself. Any sin that breaks our connection with Him must be repaired by the renewed flow of His grace.

We camp each year on a lake in northwest Maine located a dozen miles off the main road. The spectacular view and the serenity of kayaking make the isolated location well worth the drive. No cell phone reception and limited electrical power are added bonuses. I consider the week to be a technology Sabbath. We can drive out to a scenic turnout in the mountains where we can access cell phone towers, but otherwise we are disconnected from the outside world. The first day I fight withdrawal as I am tempted to check my email or news feeds. After that, I enjoy the peace that comes from resetting my walk with the Lord through reading and reflection.

The campground offers generator power only during the day. At night, there is no electricity. One year our battery backup power on the camper didn't work rendering the small refrigerator worthless. I drove out to get a new battery at a store – a half day trek – but it failed to correct the problem. I drove out again and texted a friend who was coming up in a few days asking him to bring his voltage meter with him. He arrived, and we began testing the electrical lines eventually isolating a connection under the camper where two lines came together in a small box. He tested the continuity between the two terminals and discovered a break. There was a tiny reset button located on the side of the box which the owner's manual failed to mention. Hit the reset button. Continuity restored. Full power once again. It is the same with our spiritual lives. When the continuity is broken by the distractions of life, we need to hit the reset button and restore our communication with Jesus.

PRUNING AND INTIMACY

The heavenly gardener's pruning draws us into deeper intimacy with Jesus. Abiding in Him is the goal of the gardener. The rest of the chapter is an explanation of what Jesus means by abiding in Him. To abide in His love, for example, means to keep His commandments (John 15:10-11). When we keep His commandments, we experience His joy. Obedience is the key to abiding in Christ. Joy is the result! Joy comes from abiding in Him and abiding in Him means obeying His will. To obey His will, we must study His word; worship Him with our wills; share with Him our thoughts and listen to Him with our hearts. We must accept His cleansing, pruning work in our lives. The confluence of all these disciplines leads to abiding in Him.

My plan for my life may not be God's plan. I may think I know where I ought to be and what I ought to be doing, and God may want me somewhere else doing something else. If I fight Him at that point, then I stop remaining in Him. I become disobedient. I stop abiding. I stop the flow of His life. I stop the fruit. There is nobody more miserable in life than the disobedient Christian. God has a way of interrupting our lives and re-directing them for His will. He will hit the reset button! The process can be painful, but when we learn to accept the way He has designed us and the limitations which He has placed on us, then we will learn to enjoy life in Him. This is what it means to abide in Christ. God has certainly re-arranged my plans on several occasions, and I have sometimes fought Him bitterly. I saw myself a certain way, and I had certain ambitions in life. I didn't want to see myself differently. Yet God has me exactly where He wants me for now. The result is the most fulfilled and contented life possible even in the midst of problems and struggles.

Paul Brand is a world renowned missionary surgeon who has spent his entire life helping people with leprosy. He tells the story of "Uncle Robbie." Uncle Robbie was a man from New Zealand who turned up unannounced at the leprosarium in Vellore, India where Brand spent most of his life. He simply told Paul Brand, "I have a little experience in shoemaking. I wonder if I could be of help to your leprosy patients. I'm retired now and don't need money. Just a bench and a few tools."

And so he went to work. Uncle Robbie lived alone in a guest room at the leprosarium. His wife had died several years earlier. He would spend hours painstakingly making a single pair of shoes which were custom fitted to each foot. Tenderly he would work with each foot to make a shoe which would gently protect the stress points of each deformed foot. Over time, his story came out. He was an orthopedic surgeon. In fact, he had become chief of all Orthopedics in New Zealand at one time. Then he had to give up surgery, his great joy in life because his fingers began trembling. So he learned the art of making shoes and came to the leprosarium to help those in need. He spent four years in Vellore and trained a whole group of Indian shoemakers for the leprosarium.

Brand says that no one ever felt sorry for Uncle Robbie living alone, his joy and livelihood taken away from him. Brand says that Uncle Robbie was the most contented person he has ever known because he did his work for the glory of God alone![9]

11
ARE YOU ABIDING?

John 15:5-7

Sadhu Sundar Singh, a converted Sikh, is considered the St. Paul of India. I heard his name mentioned numerous times growing up in Pakistan. He had persecuted Christians intensely until Jesus met him in a "Damascus Road Experience" and transformed his life. He became a great evangelist for the Lord in India in the early 1900's. Sadhu Sundar Singh was last seen in 1929 on a trail through the high mountains leading into Tibet as he sought to bring the Gospel to the people of Tibet. He taught that the secret of the inner life with Jesus was not intellectual knowledge but relational knowledge. He often told the story of a scientist holding a bird in his hand and wondering about the secret of life. The scientist dissects the bird seeking to understand the meaning of life only to find that the life is lost, and his search has failed. He wrote in his classic work, *With and Without Christ*:

> Those who try to understand the inner life merely intellectually will meet a similar failure. The life for which they are looking will vanish in the analysis. ... Our ever growing soul and its capacities can be satisfied only in the infinite God. As water is restless until it reaches its level, so the soul has no peace until it rests in God.[1]

Relational knowledge is real knowledge. Abiding in Jesus is more about relational knowledge than intellectual knowledge. It is a dialogue between spirits. Jesus refers to the person "who abides in Me, and I in him" (v.5). Abiding is a mutual intimacy – a mating of the souls in the bond of love. We abide by sharing our inner lives with each other. Have you ever sought to open a relationship with another who refuses to let you enter his life? He retreats behind high castle walls and pulls up the drawbridge. There is little you can do to breach those walls of withdrawal. We do this sometimes with Jesus. We withdraw from Him. We do not remain – abide – in Him. The result is fruitlessness. Jesus invites us to abide in Him to live fruitfully for Him – full lives producing luscious results.

How do we measure success? What is the fruit of our lives? So often what we consider wasted effort is the very yardstick of real success because we have such an inverted value system. James Boswell, the famous English writer years, ago often mentioned a favorite childhood memory. It was the memory of a day he spent fishing with his father. Apparently, this one day had changed his life for the better. He talked about the many lessons which his father taught him on that one day. Many years later someone discovered an entry in his father's journal. Boswell's dad wrote: "Gone fishing today with my son; a day wasted."[2]

We measure success by our accomplishments and our accumulation. Jesus measures success by our communion and our character. The fruit comes from abiding. Character comes from communion. The fruit of our lives is the true measure of our success, but relational knowledge produces the fruit. Neither our analytical skills nor our vocational achievements produce the fruit that God wants to produce in us. Learning life's lessons comes from our relationship with our master. Abiding in Jesus grows fruit for the Father. "To produce my kind of fruit," Jesus says, "You need me!" The power for producing fruit comes from Christ because the life is in the vine. Jesus says, "Apart from Me you can do nothing" (v.5).

A SPIRITUAL PROGRESSION

There is a natural progression in these verses. The gardener begins with branches which are not bearing fruit (v.2). He lifts these branches up by His grace so that they begin to produce fruit. Next, there are branches producing some fruit, but the gardener wants them to produce more fruit (vs.2). These branches He prunes and cleanses. The gardener now has branches which have been lifted up, pruned and are ready to produce much fruit. The only purpose for the vine is fruit. A grape vine does not exist for its looks but for its fruit. The value of the branch is in the fruit. The word for branch in this passage literally refers to a vine twig. We are twigs for Christ, and the fruit is far more important than the twig!

Many people talk about fruit as if it were other people who come to Christ. However, nowhere in this passage is fruit identified with converts to Christianity. The twigs do not produce more twigs. Instead, the context of Chapters 14 and 15 talk about things like love, joy, peace, obedience, faithfulness, commitment, friendship, and service. These are all character issues. God is most interested in our character, and, if our character is godly, then the by-product will be converted lives. We don't measure success by the number of conversions. We measure success by godly character. Character is the fruit Jesus is speaking about here. It is the fruit that the Spirit of God produces in our lives.

The only way to produce this kind of fruit is by abiding in Christ. Apart from Him, we can accomplish nothing. There is no room for a "holier than thou" attitude on our part because He produces the fruit in us. Fruit is the natural product of the branches. Did you ever see a cluster of grapes struggling to get bigger? No! They just stay in the vine and let the life of the vine flow into the grapes. So Jesus says, "Stay in me! Please! Stick with me."

A few hours after admonishing his disciples to stay with Him, Jesus led them into the Garden of Gethsemane, a place of deepest intimacy. Jesus asked the disciples to sit there with him while he moved a slight distance away to pray. The garden today is not a large place. When I visited, I could have thrown a stone across the width of the garden. It was undoubtedly larger in the first century but still it was a place where they would not be far removed from Jesus. He invited Peter, James and John to come even closer to him as he prayed. Jesus agonized that night while the disciples fell asleep just yards away. The disciples were with Him but not truly with Him! Jesus returns to find them sleeping and says: "So you men could not keep watch with Me for one hour? Keep watching and praying that you may not enter into temptation; the spirit is willing, but the flesh is weak" (Mt. 26:40-41). Jesus wanted them to lean on Him not for His sake but for their sakes. It wasn't to support Him but to depend on Him so as to be prepared to avoid temptation. They didn't know it yet, but they would need Him before the night was out, and He was gone. He wanted them to experience His sufficient grace. So it is with us. The sufficiency of grace is found in our relationship with Jesus. Learning, leaning, trusting, sharing; these are the characteristics of abiding, and Jesus might have to knock away our human supports to teach us His sufficiency.

When Jesus talks about abiding in him, He is talking about our wills. The work of God in our lives connected us to Christ. Now we must maintain a close friendship with Christ by the decisions we make in life. Each decision is a choice between staying in close friendship with the Lord or following our plans. The choices we make on a daily basis affect our friendship. We can choose to worship Him, read our Bibles, pray, maintain healthy relationships with our wives or husbands and children, control our tongues and our tempers. All of these are choices we make to stay in Him. When we fail, then we quickly settle the issue with Him and with those we have wronged so that there is no blockage in our fellowship, and the life of the vine can flow out into the fruit of our lives. As someone has said: "Out of the will of God there is no such thing as success; in the will of God, there cannot be failure."

WARNING! WARNING!

The progression continues in verse 6. We have the ability to produce much fruit, so the responsibility is ours to stay in communion with Him. When we don't, problems develop. If we don't abide in Christ, we won't produce fruit. If we don't produce fruit, then the gardener will judge us as fruitless branches. This is a difficult verse any way you look at it. We must be careful to understand the warning that Jesus presents here. There are those who argue that Jesus is talking about an unbeliever here. He is talking about a "Judas Iscariot" kind of person. This person looks like a branch, talks like a branch, acts like a branch but is not a branch at all. He is a fake branch. I know many good scholars who argue for this position, but it seems to cleverly avoid the point. Jesus is dealing with real branches here. Every branch has life, or it would never have become a branch. The point has to do with fruit, not life.

Others argue that this verse is talking about a real believer who loses his salvation. Here is a branch that was alive once, but now is dead. The problem with this view is that it flies in the face of other Scriptures. If this verse is about a believer who loses his salvation, then it contradicts other promises which Jesus makes to His followers. For example, Jesus says that no man can "snatch (us) out of the Father's hand" (Jn. 10:28). Some say, "That is true. Nobody can take us away from Jesus, but we can decide to jump out of His hand." However, John 15:6 does not speak about jumping out of Christ's hand. The verse says that Christ casts us out. It is Christ, Himself, who throws us away and this is precisely what He promised that He would never do. He said, "All that the Father gives Me will come to Me, and the one who comes to Me I will certainly not cast out" (John 6:37). Therefore, this verse cannot be talking about a person who loses his salvation.

We must remember that this is all a figure of speech, a long metaphor. When you take figurative language and make it literal, then you are going to have problems. Jesus is not a literal vine. The father is not a literal gardener. We are not literal branches. The throwing away is not a literal throwing away, and the fire is not a literal fire. These are figures of speech to illustrate the judgment of God upon fruitless believers. Jesus says that the fruitless believer is *like a twig* so what happens to fruitless twigs is an illustration of what happens to fruitless Christians. Both fruitless twigs and fruitless Christians are judged for their uselessness and set aside as worthless to the master gardener. Fruitless branches are cast away not because of a lack of life but because of a lack of fruit.

There are five actions that happen to fruitless twigs in this verse. These five actions picture God's judgment of believers as a progressive judgment.

1. SET ASIDE: God stops using us in His work. He sets us aside when we come to the point of blocking His work in our lives. We become useless, and we hinder his purposes. Don't think that God would never do that. He would, and He does all the time. This is a serious warning to believers to stay in close communion with the Lord because He may just fire us from His employment.

2. DRIED UP: The word was used to describe the withering of trees and plants or the drying up of a river.[3] When we are set aside by the gardener, the discarding causes us to wither spiritually. We lose our vitality. We become brittle and bitter, and we break easily. Jesus said that if salt loses its potency, it is good for nothing but to be thrown out and

147

trampled (Mt. 5:13). Fruitless Christians may even be removed from life on earth (1 John 5:16).

3. GATHERED TOGETHER: Many struggle to identify who does the gathering, but it is a fruitless discussion. All three verbs have plural subjects, but the plural is an impersonal or editorial plural not to be identified with any particular subject.[4] The point is that there comes a time when believers are gathered together at the judgment seat of Christ, and we are evaluated for the lives we have lived and the fruit we have produced.

4. TESTED BY FIRE: The fire is a figure of speech for God's holy evaluation of our lives. The fire reveals the worthlessness of our fruitfulness (1 Cor. 3:13). It should make us tremble that we will one day face the Lord and give an account of how we have invested our lives for Him. Fruitfulness is finally measured at the judgment seat of Christ. We are tried by the fire of God's holiness, and only the fruit of our lives remains in the end. Since fruitfulness is the result of abiding, the quality of our abiding is measured by the quality of our fruit. We don't produce the fruit. He does. Our responsibility is to abide in Him and allow His life to grow fruit in our lives.

5. LEFT WITH NOTHING: Those branches which do not produce fruit because they did not abide in Him will be left with nothing. Fruitless Christians are left with nothing because they did not abide in Him and through that abiding produce fruit that possessed eternal value. The sum of their lives is burned up. This sense of loss is precisely the imagery for the judgment of Christians that Paul uses (1 Cor. 3:13-15). The fruitless Christian suffers loss, but he is saved *"as through fire"* (1 Cor. 3:15).

Abraham's nephew, Lot, pursued wealth and fame for himself and his family. He chose to live comfortably in the city of Sodom. He became so caught up in accomplishments and accumulation that he lost sight of God's purpose. In the end, he left the city of Sodom with his wife and two daughters. Everything he had worked so hard for disintegrated in a flash of God's fire. He even lost his wife to the desires of this world. Lot paid an awful price for his fruitlessness.

PROSPERITY VS. PRAYER

The temptation of success has long lured Christians to pursue prosperity at the expense of abiding in Christ. Adolph Hitler banked on the bait of success to push Christian leaders in pre-war Germany to trade the cross for the swastika. He sneered, "The Parsons will dig their own graves. They will betray their God to us. They will betray anything for the sake of their miserable jobs and incomes."[5] Hitler controlled the purse strings of Germany in the 1930s and so controlled Christians who readily traded the true cross for the broken cross and lost connection to the suffering Savior. Helmut Thielicke preached a sermon after the war to a church in Stuttgart in April of 1945. He reminded Christians that "the worship of success is generally the form of idol worship the devil cultivates most assiduously. ... We could observe in the first years after 1933 the almost suggestive compulsion that emanates from great successes and how under the influence of these successes even Christians stopped asking in whose name and at what price they were achieved. ... Success is the greatest narcotic of all."[6]

The pursuit of prosperity will soon lead us away from the intimacy of prayer. We cease to abide in Jesus, and we silence His words from abiding in us. Fruitlessness is the natural result of prayerlessness (John 15:7). Prayer becomes an anachronism in our world of achievement. Who needs prayer when we have what we want already? As time passes, we simply stop praying. If we pray at all, it is to manipulate God to help us accomplish our goals. Someone has said that "the object of most prayers is to wangle an advance on good intentions." We treat prayer in such odd ways in the church. Prayer becomes a duty or an obligation which we are supposed to perform, losing the sense that prayer is just conversation with God. Imagine me treating a conversation with my wife, Janie, as a duty. "Well, I guess we need to talk. It's my duty to take the next half an hour to converse with you!" What kind of a relationship will we have if I do that for very long? Perhaps prayer becomes a way to get "brownie points" with God. Prayer is our "lucky rabbit's foot." "If I spend 15 minutes in prayer every morning then I will have a successful day." Or maybe it is just a mechanical practice like punching the time clock at work. It is my "membership card" with God and the church – a way to pay my "union dues" to Jesus.

149

One mother told me about an experience with her daughter shortly after a church service where I had preached on what we ask God for in our lives. Her daughter was praying with her one night and said, "Our Heavenly Father, would you please make my Mom and Dad give me everything I want. Amen!" Jesus did say, "Ask whatever you wish and it will be done for you" (John 15:7) so she claimed those words for herself. She is not so different from the rest of us who treat prayer like rubbing the magic lamp until the genie pops out to fulfill our wishes.

Jesus does not talk about prayer that way at all. Prayer is the joyful means of staying in communion with Christ. The verse is a circle. We remain in Him. His words remain in us. We ask what we want. He gives us what we want. Christ says, "Stay in me and ask what you want." Augustine said, "Love God and do as you please." One of the ways that we abide in Christ and His words abide in us is through the conversation of prayer. My most meaningful prayer times are not planned and programmed but spontaneous talks with Jesus. They are the times when I am riding in the car or taking a walk, and I just pour out my heart to God. What I want changes as I abide in Him, and I abide in Him as I express what I want to Him. His words abide in me as I listen to His response. If you are staying in Him, you can ask what you want because what you want will come to line up with what He wants for you. Our values change as we abide in Him. Our friendship with Jesus transforms our wants. Just like any friendship, we come to want what our friend wants. He influences us to desire His desires.

Anne Steele (1717-1778) was one of the greatest female hymn writers of the 18th century. She was born into a family of "Dissenters" in Southern England. The daughter of a "Particular Baptist" pastor, she learned her spiritual lessons from a young age. Anne contracted the dreaded disease of malaria as a child. It was a common sickness for those living near the Wallop River and other marshy areas of England. She struggled the rest of her life with the lingering effects of the disease that often wasted her energy and left her painfully tired. She wrote, "Even this affliction, may I not call it a blessing from the happy effects which I hope it has produced? … How gentle, O my God, were the strokes of thy chastising hand."[7] She learned through suffering to surrender herself to the sovereign will of God for her life. One of her well-known hymns was entitled "Humble Reliance."

Whate'er thy providence denies,
I calmly would resign,
For thou art just, and good, and wise;
O bend my will to thine.

Whate'er thy sacred will ordains,
O give me strength to bear;
And let me know my Father reigns,
And trust his tender care.

If pain and sickness rend this frame,
And life almost depart,
Is not thy mercy still the same,
To cheer my drooping heart?

Thy sov'reign ways are all unknown
To my weak, erring sight;
Yet let my soul, adoring, own
That all thy ways are right.

My God, my Father, be thy name
My solace and my stay;
O wilt thou seal my humble claim,
And drive my fears away.[8]

R. Kent Hughes writes: "Think of it this way: our lives are like photographic plates, and prayer is like a time exposure to God. As we expose ourselves to God ... his image is imprinted more and more upon us."[9] We become like Him as we converse with Him. Heaven's values are the opposite of earth's values! When we abide in Christ and His words abide in us, we develop heaven's value system. We can ask whatever we want, and God will give it to us. He delights to give us the desires of His heart. Our friendship with Him produces fruit for Him through our prayers to Him even when we can't see what is happening because of our circumstances.

Philip Yancey tells the story of his friend who bicycled across China in 1984. His friend stayed with a couple who were both university professors. They told him their story of faith during the Cultural

Revolution. They had been blacklisted by the authorities because of their status. Red Guards watched them constantly and harassed their children if the parents showed any sign of religious interest. They did not want to put their children at risk, so they decided to remove all symbols of their faith from the home and to stop praying or talking about their faith in Christ even in the home. They knew that they were constantly watched even in the privacy of their family life. However, they could pray at night as they lay in bed together. They would hold hands and repeat the Lord's Prayer silently together. They would squeeze hands at the end of each line so that they could pray it silently, yet in unison. They would continue to hold hands for a time of silent prayer by each. They prayed much for the salvation of their children during those silent night prayers to a God they knew could still hear them no matter how dark the days might seem. Finally, the surveillance eased, and they sensed a greater freedom for faith. They decided to finally talk with their children after those long years of self-imposed silence. They feared that they might have lost the opportunity to influence their children to follow Christ because of the long silence about faith. Their children had grown up under a militantly atheist government, but within a year, all five children came to faith in Christ. "Our prayers were answered," they told Yancey's friend. "We had nothing to fear after all."[10]

12
FRUIT FOR THE GARDENER

John 15:8-11

Voyager 1 entered interstellar space in August of 2012 with Voyager 2 soon to follow. NASA launched the twin space crafts in 1977 with the mission to explore the outermost region of our solar system and beyond. A phonograph record in each Voyager carried a message from earth on a gold-plated copper disk with instructions in symbolic language on how to access the information. The "Golden Record" contains the sounds of earth including spoken greetings in many languages, a human heartbeat, and pictorial images of earth along with an eclectic mix of music. Annie Druyan, the wife of Carl Sagan, was the creative director of NASA's Voyager Interstellar Message (VIM) Project. She chose a beautiful but haunting piece of music entitled the "Cavatina Movement" from Beethoven's Opus 130 as a piece of music that would last millions of years in space. She said, "Part of what we wanted to capture in the Voyager message was this great longing we feel." The scientists from NASA wanted to express to the universe that humans are "creatures of longing."[1]

This cosmic yearning is not a yearning for what but for who! It is not what we have or do that brings fulfillment. It is who we know! We were made for God. We find our fulfillment in our Creator. We live, longing for the relationship we were created to enjoy. Many people today lead very busy lives but not full lives - lives of longing despite the achievements. Life is out of focus, fuzzy. Something is missing. We lack a sense of purpose leading to frustration and unhappiness. Jesus came to give us life more abundantly. He wants us to live lives of purpose and value. He made us to be significant, and we find our significance in His love. Jesus teaches us how to focus our lives so that they will be fruitful. We honor God by producing His fruit. We produce His fruit by living in Christ's love. When our longings are fulfilled in His love, we enjoy fulfilled lives. Our joy is full. Our yearnings are satisfied.

"The chief end of man is to glorify God and enjoy Him forever," reads the Westminster Catechism. Jesus said, "By this is my Father glorified." By what Jesus?[2] We glorify God in two ways: 1) by producing much fruit and 2) by being (or becoming) his disciples. Abiding in Christ is the means of producing fruit and being His disciple, bringing glory to the gardener. First, we honor our Father by producing His fruit – not just a little fruit but much fruit (John 15:8). The father wants an abundance of fruit, an overflowing of our lives with fruit. God is most honored when we are most fulfilled. We are most fulfilled by our relationship with Him. Our longings find fulfillment in our fruitfulness for Him – a fruitfulness that thrives on Jesus' life flowing abundantly through us in joyous union with Him. We enjoy Him most when we produce fruit for His enjoyment.

The Father prunes us for this purpose. He takes us through hard times not because we are totally unproductive but because He wants to take us to the next level of productivity. Suffering sanctifies us. I was talking to a fellow pastor who was going through some very difficult times in ministry. He said, "Dave, I know that God is pruning me right now, and I want Him to do that. I know that I have been fruitful in the past, but He wants me to be more fruitful so I am looking forward to what He will do with me in the future." That kind of attitude brings God glory and brings joy to us in the end.

We honor God when our character reflects His work. We honor God by being honest, truthful, gentle and faithful. We glorify God when we are kind to those who criticize us. We honor the Father when we obey what the Bible says even when it goes against our self-interest. We honor God when we love those who don't love us back. We honor God when we suffer physically or emotionally and still choose not to blame Him. After all, who gets the glory for the grapes – the twigs or the gardener? Whoever heard of complimenting the twigs for the wonderful produce! We compliment the master gardener for His skill in tending the vine and the branches so that they will produce the grapes. So our lives reflect His skill, His love, and His grace.

It is by producing this fruit for His glory that we be or become His disciples. Jesus is clearly speaking to those already his disciples so how could they glorify the gardener by becoming his disciples? Several translations supply the word "so" which is not in the text thereby turning the second clause into a result of the first clause. Many understand the fruit to be proof of discipleship. Bearing much fruit proves (or shows) that we are true disciples of Jesus. This verb means to be or become and is likely future in time indicating that we shall "be/become" His disciples.[3] Therefore, being a disciple is not a result of bearing fruit but rather a second way to glorify God. We glorify God by bearing much fruit and by being Jesus' disciples. Both are necessary to glorify God.

BELONGING FOR BECOMING

What does it mean to be/become a disciple?[4] Disciples are learners or pupils – students and followers of a teacher.[5] Learners are always learning and never learned. Disciples are continuously in process. Discipleship is a developmental process – a growing way of life – just as fruit growing on a branch is a process. Jesus is not talking about the point of origin but a continuing process. We have been pupils in the past. We are pupils now, and we will be pupils in the future. To return to the analogy of the vine and the branches, discipleship culminates at the end of life when the fruit of our lives is full and luscious thereby glorifying God, the master gardener. Furthermore, just like the twig does not produce good fruit by itself so we do not produce godly character by ourselves. The responsibility of the twig is to stay connected so that the life of the vine can produce the fruit. Our responsibility is to remain in Christ so that His life can produce God's fruit. Then He gets all the glory for the fruit – not us!

We experience Christ's love by abiding in Him (15:9-10). There is a comparison in these verses between Christ and us. We should have the same kind of relationship with Him that He has with the Father. Jesus begins with a declaration of His love for us and an exhortation to stay in that love relationship, as the Father loves the Son, so the Son loves us. The measure of Christ's love for me is the Father's love for Him. He loves me as much as the Father loves Him. The Trinity is such an incredible mystery but within that tri-unity of the Godhead is infinite love for one another. It is impossible for the Father to love the Son any more than He does. So it is impossible for Jesus to love us any more than He does. I often say to people who are struggling through deep waters of worry over a loved one, "Just remember, God loves your son or daughter, husband or wife even more than you do." And it is true! God accepts in Him, but His acceptance does not imply acceptance of our fruitlessness. He loves us as we are but He loves us too much to leave us where we are. Discipleship is a process of becoming what He wants us to be in the safety of belonging in His perfect love.

Jean Vanier, a former naval officer, began a global movement for the disabled in 1988 when he invited two men with Down's syndrome to leave the institution where they were cared for and live with him in his home. This simple act of welcome spawned a world-wide organization known as "L'Arche" which spans thirty-five countries with over 140 communities united by a shared vision of providing homes for the disabled – places of belonging for those who struggle to belong in this world. Jean Vanier, in a series of lectures at Harvard University, said:

> Living with men and women with mental disabilities has helped me to discover what it means to live in communion with someone. To be in communion means to be with someone and to discover we actually belong together. ... I want to add here a word about the danger of belonging. Belonging should always be for becoming. ... Of course, for Christians, the greatest becoming is entering into a deeper and more intimate relationship with Christ.[6]

Belonging does not eliminate becoming just as love does not preclude pain. The Father loved the Son infinitely, yet He allowed and even commanded the Son to die on the cross for our sins. In the same way, the Son can love us yet call us to suffer. We must beware of adopting a shallow view of God's love which promises only health and wealth. Such a love is not God's love. It is man's love. Enjoying God's love carries the price tag of commitment just as all true love does. J. Oswald Sanders wrote: "Both Scripture and experience teach that it is we, not God, who determine the degree of intimacy with Him that we enjoy. We are at this moment as close to God as we choose to be."[7]

OUR EMOTIONAL POSITIONING SYSTEM

Jesus goes on to say, "Stay in my love." The implication is that we might not stay in that love. He implies that we must actively remain in His love if we are to produce His fruit. You say, "I have a problem here. I thought God loved us unconditionally and that nothing can separate us from the love of Christ so how can He say that we must stay in that love? Now there seem to be conditions placed upon experiencing that love."

When we say this, we exhibit, once again, a shallow misconception of unconditional love. We must not think of love as one-dimensional. On one level God certainly loves us unconditionally. In fact, He loves the whole world unconditionally. He will never stop loving anyone no matter what they might do or how often they might reject Him. He loves those He sends to Hell! On a second level, God loves the Christian in a way that He does not love the non-Christian. We can never be separated from Christ's love on this level. This is the Romans 8 level of love. No matter what you or I do we will never be separated from His love for us.

On a third level, the deepest most intimate level, we can stop experiencing His love for us by our choices in life. We can hinder that love by our sin. He never stops loving us, but we stop experiencing that love because enjoying His love is conditional. Like a parent who says to his teenage daughter, Jesus says to us, "I have loved you and I always will, please stay in my love." Like a groom says to his bride, so Jesus says to us, "I have loved you from the time I first laid eyes on you, please stay in my love. Please do not wander from my love." Love guides our choices in life, and our choices keep us in love.

I find some help for understanding this circle of love and obedience from the world of the social sciences. A scientist named Antonio Damasio tested many people in his research to determine how brain damage affects decision making. Elliot was one of his most famous brain research subjects. Elliot was a successful and intelligent man who suffered damage to the frontal lobe of his brain from a tumor. After surgery, he began having great difficulty managing his life. He was easily distracted and couldn't make up his mind about even simple choices. He made foolish financial decisions that cost his family their savings. He divorced his wife and married another woman only to divorce her too. He seemed incapable of making good choices. Damasio ran many tests on Elliot and concluded that he had lost his emotional brain functions. He was emotionally flat, incapable of feeling, which led to his poor decision-making. David Brooks, commenting on the research writes: "It's an example of how lack of emotion leads to self-destructive and dangerous behavior. People who lack emotion don't lead well-planned lives in the manner of coolly rational Mr. Spocks. They lead foolish lives." Damasio developed a theory called the "somatic marker hypothesis." The point is that emotions (somatic markers) help us measure the value of things in life and guide us as we navigate life. Emotions are like a biasing device helping us make choices that lead toward what is best for us and away from what will hurt us. He called it an "Emotional Positioning System." It works much as a global positioning system works in our cars. Our emotions help us navigate the choices we make in life.[8]

Our love for Jesus is our emotional positioning system in life. We stay in His love by our obedience just as the Son stayed in the Father's love by His obedience. As the Son obeys the Father so we obey the Son (John 15:10). Back in John14:15 Jesus said, "If you love me, you will keep my commandments" now He says that if we keep His commandments, we abide in His love! Obedience is the key to abiding. It is not so much that obedience is an arbitrary condition for love as it is that love positions us for obedience, and obedience keeps us in His love. We can never experience intimacy with Him while living in disobedience because disobedience violates our emotional positioning system. We will never enjoy the fullness of His love unless we obey His word! It is not that He stops loving us but that a barrier is built up for experiencing that love, and until we deal with that barrier by repentance and confession we can never experience the love He has for us. On the other hand, if we allow our love for Jesus to guide the choices we make then our obedience is the outflow of our love. We stay in His love and enjoy the fullness of His love.

Once again, the standard for our obedience is the Son's obedience to the Father. Jesus obeyed the Father and so experienced the fullness of the Father's love. Jesus did not want to die. He said, "Father if it is your will, let this cup pass from me. Nevertheless, not my will but yours be done." Nevertheless, he obeyed because of His love for the Father and, because of His obedience, He experienced the joy of perfect love. When we obey Him out of love, then we come to experience the fullness of His love too. We remain in His love by being what He calls us to be and doing what He commands us to do no matter what the consequences. One thing that dominated our Lord is that He didn't care what the world or even the disciples thought. His guiding passion was His love for His Father. So we should be dominated by that same desire in all we do and say. Our love guides our choices; our choices keep us in love, so we experience the fullness of joy (John 15:11)!

THE JOY OF OBEDIENCE

Patti Awan was a young Sunday School teacher who had just given birth to a healthy son a few months earlier. It was the first child for her and her husband Javy so no one was surprised when she stood on that Sunday evening to share her testimony in the praise service, but the congregation grew quiet as she shared her story. Four years earlier she sat on the floor of her apartment in tears. The lab report proved she was pregnant. Patti professed faith in Christ, but she was living a double life. She still was using drugs and sleeping with a man from the downstairs apartment while going to church and working with the church youth group. The knowledge that she was pregnant exposed the hypocrisy of her double life. Patti decided the only answer was to get an abortion so no one in the church would ever know. A date was scheduled. Her boyfriend pushed her to keep that abortion date, but she was terrified. Her sister was enraged at her stupidity. Her parents were horrified. Her mother told her "If you don't get an abortion, I don't want to see you while you're pregnant. Your life will be ruined, and you will deserve it."

Staring out her bedroom window one night, Patti realized that she either believed in Jesus or she did not. If she believed in Jesus, then she couldn't get an abortion. She decided that night to follow Jesus. Her circumstances had not changed. She was still pregnant, abandoned by her family and rejected by her boyfriend but for the first time in her life, she says, she was "really peaceful," because she knew she was obedient. The love of Jesus changed her life and led her down the path of obedience. She confessed her double life to her church. Her obstetrician, impressed with her decision, chose not to charge her for her prenatal care and the delivery.

A Christian counseling center helped her give her baby up for adoption to a Christian couple. Patti shared in her testimony:

> And so that's why I praise God this evening. I thought in the depths of my despair that my life was ruined, but I knew I had to at least be obedient in taking responsibility for my sin. But today, because of that very despair and obedience, I have what I never thought I could – a godly husband and now a baby of our own. But what matters more than anything is that I have what I was searching for so desperately before – peace with God.[9]

Jesus said "These things I have spoken to you, that my joy may be in you, and that your joy may be made full." We enjoy our lives by following His will (15:11). Verse 11 is the climax of the whole section on abiding in the vine. Jesus says that all of these things which He has been speaking about in verses 1-10 have led up to this verse. His purpose in telling us all these things is that we might enjoy our lives to the fullest extent. Here is His purpose: "that my joy might be in you, and your joy might be full."

My joy looks back to verse 10.[10] This is the joy Jesus experienced not the joy Jesus produced. The Son and the Father experienced an inexhaustible joy in their love for one another from eternity past. God was not a lonely God before creation. He was complete in His own happiness. Jesus wants us to experience His joy. Jesus found His joy in obeying the Father. So our joy will be discovered in obeying the Son. Jesus poured out His love to the Father in prayer for us later that very night. He said, "Now I come to You, and these things I speak in the world so that they may have My joy made full in themselves" (John 17:13). Jesus knows we are not of this world system and that we will face the trials of this world that could lead us away from His love so He prays that the Father would protect us spiritually. He pleads with the Father, "Sanctify them in the truth; Your word is truth" (John 17:17). Our fullest joy in life as Patti Awan discovered comes when we follow His word and are sanctified by His truth. No longer living a double life, pretending to be what we aren't. Instead, we choose to surrender to His will. Only then will we know real joy – His joy – the joy He knows with the Father.

Many years later, John would write a letter sharing this same message: "so that you too may have fellowship with us; and indeed, our fellowship is with the Father, and with His Son Jesus Christ. These things we write, so that our joy may be made complete" (1 John. 1:3-4). Our joy in Christ is complete when we share His joy with others. John is talking about fellowship with the Father and with the Son. It is John 15 language. He is sharing the lessons learned on that night in the upper room with Jesus. He writes these things so that our joy, not your joy, may be complete or filled up. We fill up our joy as we share Christ with others. We fill up our joy as we witness to others. Our becoming full in Christ is only complete as we invite others into a life of belonging in His love. Jesus won't be satisfied until our cup of joy is filled to the brim and running over. Witnessing should be the natural overflow of our lives, not something artificial that we do as a duty. We should live our entire lives in such a way that we radiate His joy as our witness to others. A sour Christian is a contradiction in terms.

When I started the pastorate of Galilee Baptist Church, I was informed by the Financial Secretary that he would assign me a numbered offering envelope. However, he could not give me envelope #1 because he had already assigned the number to an older woman named Hazel McCrum and she was "#1 in his book!" I would have to settle for being #2 - a designation I was happy to accept! I have been #2 ever since. Hazel was a wonderful, godly woman in her 80's. She had served the Lord for many years, and her sweet spirit won my heart in the few years we shared together until she went to her Father in heaven. Hazel enjoyed passing on little stories for me to use in my sermons whenever she came across something good. One Sunday she passed on this little story. A father asked his little girl what she was drawing in her notebook. She told him she was drawing a picture of God. "But," said her father, "no one knows what God looks like." "I know it," the little girl replied brightly, "but they will when I finish this."

We are pictures of God to the world around us. How they see us is how they will see God. Do they see the joy in all of its fullness? I do not mean "backslapping, harty, har, har, pretend everything is wonderful Christianity." I mean genuine serenity and joy in who we are in Christ. No crusades. No defensiveness. Just open genuine contentment in Him that comes from abiding in His love. When people see that, they will know what real Christianity is all about.

161

Talent night had arrived at the Joni and Friends family retreat, and Cindy was the last person scheduled to perform. Her mother pushed Cindy on to the platform in her wheelchair and said that Cindy was going to sing "Amazing Grace" for the audience. She had been working hard on it all week. Everyone looked at each other wondering how this would work out since Cindy couldn't speak – let alone sing – because of her severe cerebral palsy. Her mother positioned the wheelchair on stage, turned and walked off the platform leaving Cindy all by herself. Cindy labored carefully with her hands until she pushed the button to start the computerized device on her chair. A monotone, computer voice began. "Amazing Grace, how sweet the sound, that saved a wretch like me." The computer voice droned on as Cindy turned to face the audience. With great effort, she mouthed the words in time with the song to the best of her ability. Her smile lit up the whole room that night. It was "Amazing Grace" as never sung before, filled with the joy of Jesus. Joni Eareckson Tada writes: I can't explain how, but somehow it rose up in that auditorium as a ringing hymn of praise to God. It was as though Cindy's song was backed by an eighty-piece orchestra. I can imagine the angels leaning over the edge in heaven, filled with wonder, to catch every word."[11] As Joni, herself likes to say; this was "joy hard won."

13
BEST FRIENDS FOREVER

John 15:12-17

Calvin, from Bill Watterson's comic strip "Calvin and Hobbes," is lying in bed, and he is scared. He says: "I can't sleep. I think nighttime is dark, so you can imagine your fears with less distraction. At nighttime, the world always seems so big and scary, and I always seem so small. I wish I could fall asleep so that it would be morning." The next frame finds him hiding under his covers still trying to get to sleep. Then he looks over at his stuffed tiger, Hobbes, in bed with him. "Look at Hobbes. He's asleep. Heh heh ... He sure looks funny when he sleeps. Tigers close their eyes so tight. I wonder what he's dreaming about. Good ol' Hobbes. What a friend." Then He lies down again and relaxes. "Things are never quite as scary when you've got a best friend," says Calvin. Then he smiles and goes to sleep.

Jesus calls us friends – no longer servants but friends! He has chosen us to be His friends and His friendship is not a friendship that comes and goes with the passing of time. His friendship is an eternal friendship. There is an eternity of love bound up in His friendship. He draws us by His sacrificial love as our Savior. He calls us by His sovereign love to serve Him, but He invites us by His persevering love to be His friends forever. He doesn't give up on us. Jesus seeks to pull us into a deeper, closer relationship with Him every day.

Emory Griffin, a professor of communication, writes about what he calls "the force field of relationships" in his book exploring friendship. Imagine intimacy as a steel ball on a sliding track being pulled by a great magnet. The track starts with "mere acquaintance and ends with "intimate friend." The force that pulls us is the same on either end of this sliding scale. The attraction draws us from acquaintance to casual friend to buddy or pal. There is a low cost to friendship on the acquaintance end of the scale, but as the friendship moves into "close confidant" and finally "intimate friend" we move sharply up the incline of the track. The path gets steeper, and the cost is higher. There is a high cost to closeness at this end of the scale. The magnet of Jesus' love must pull hard against the inertia of our other attractions to draw us into an intimate friendship with Him.[1] Many Christians, sadly, are far too willing to settle for being an acquaintance or casual friend of Jesus rather than paying the price to become an intimate friend.

One way Jesus draws us from servants to friends is through confiding with us His deepest secrets. He makes known to us what He learns from the Father (John 15:15). He changes us from slaves to friends by sharing with us the depths of His knowledge. Another way that Jesus draws us from servants into friends is by doing favors for us. One of the most powerful ways that a friend draws another into deeper friendship is by doing a favor for that friend, as Griffin points out in his research. The favor must not make us feel obligated to return the favor, or it loses its drawing power. We call this grace, of course, in biblical terms. Jesus offers His grace, sometimes in unexpected ways, to us drawing us ever deeper into His love. Since friendship is mutual, Jesus invites us to serve Him out of friendship, not duty. "There's a surprising twist to this business of doing favors – although we're drawn toward those who do nice things for us, we're even more attracted to those who let us do nice things for them."[2]

I think of this social principle, so well-known on the human level, and I see it in play in our relationship with Jesus as well. Jesus places conditions on our friendship with Him but, I think, the conditions are another way of inviting us to bond with Him by serving Him. As we do for Him, He draws us to Him. This kind of service, as we shall see, is not the service of a slave but the service of a friend. We serve him because we know Him. He is a servant, so we become servants. He sacrifices, so we sacrifice. We grow closer to Him as our friend as we grow more like Him in our lives. These patterns of similarity and service are ways that Jesus knits our hearts to Himself in friendship.

There are two sets of two conditions each in these verses. First, in verses 12-13, Jesus says, "You are my friends when you love as I love and when you give as I give." Second, in verses 14-15, Jesus says, "You are my friends when you do what I say and when you know what I mean." The conditions are the bands that tie us to Him in friendship. They are the price we must pay to experience the depths of intimacy with Jesus.

SACRIFICIAL LOVE

We are Jesus' friends, but this is not an exclusive friendship. I do not have the corner on friendship with Christ, and I cannot experience that friendship in isolation from other believers who also have that same friendship. I cannot adopt a hermit mentality and wishfully think, "O if I could spend my time with Jesus and not have to deal with church people just think how close I could come to Jesus. Such love and joy we would have together, just Jesus and me." Wrong! Our friendship would become obsessive, stunted, and sterile. Many think that they can experience friendship with Christ apart from the church, but they cannot. Yes, the church is made up of imperfect, annoying, selfish and demanding people ... just like us! But Jesus says "you will learn to experience my friendship when you love as I love (John 15:12)."

How can Jesus command that we love one another? How can love be commanded? Love is a feeling, an emotion. Love is something we cannot control or command, isn't it? I cannot decide to love someone I don't love or stop loving someone I love, can I? We live in a culture where emotions are our masters. We are a feeling oriented society, and our feelings dominate our thinking. Jesus would never command us to do something that we are incapable of doing. So we must have a misunderstanding of love which has been shaped by our popular culture.

The key to understanding the kind of love Jesus is talking about is to see the standard He sets in the second half of this verse. Jesus says that we are to love one another as He has loved us. He has shown us how to love. Jesus chose to love us even though we did not choose to love Him (vs.16)! His love for us was the overflow of His love for the Father.

165

Do you not believe that I am in the Father, and the Father is in Me? The words that I say to you I do not speak on My own initiative, but the Father abiding in Me does His works. (14:10).

So that the world may know that I love the Father, I do exactly as the Father commanded Me. (14:31).

If you keep My commandments, you will abide in My love; just as I have kept My Father's commandments and abide in His love. (15:10).

Out of His great love for the Father, He loved us. So out of our love for Christ, we love one another. It is incompatible with my love for Jesus to say that "I love the Lord, but I can't stand the church! I love the Lord, but she drives me crazy. I love the Lord, but I can't stand him!" Jesus does not give us that option. If we truly love Him, we will love those He loves.

Now, of course, there is a difference in capacity between the Lord and us. We do not have an infinite capacity for love like He does. We must prioritize our relationships. We cannot love the entire world equally like He does because we do not have an infinite capacity for love. We must choose to love one another in the limited relationships of our Christian fellowship. I do not mean that we deliberately exclude people. I mean that we choose to demonstrate love in those relationships we already have with one another. We do not seek to find other "one anothers" to love just because our current relationships are difficult. We don't dump the relationship and move on whenever the people get prickly. We start with those we know and seek to love one another as He loves us.

He is our model for sacrificial love. We must show our friendship with Jesus by sacrificing our relationship with the world for His sake. The world hates Jesus, so they will hate those who love Jesus. I will say more about this as we look at the second half of John 15. For now, we must understand that sacrificial love goes both ways. He sacrificed Himself for us, and we sacrifice ourselves for Him. Jesus calls us to live sacrificially for those He loves just as He loved us sacrificially.

Jesus says that we are His friends when we love as He loves and give as He gives. "Greater love has no one than this, that one lay down his life for his friends" (15:13). No cheap love is allowed here. We cannot be exclusive, selfish or manipulative with each other and expect to experience friendship with Christ. There are always going to be those Christians in our lives who send our blood pressure up. For each of us, they are a little different. I have a hard time loving whiny Christians, and manipulators drive me crazy. But the tough ones for me are the authoritarian legalists who want to tell me, and everyone else, how to think. Yet God calls me to love every one of them! The standard is the standard of self-sacrifice. One commentator writes, "The answer is to remember ... that Jesus himself loved His friends, his unlovely, whining, gossipy, arrogant, immature and silly friends, enough to die for them."[3]

Jesus is not talking in this verse about an atoning sacrifice on our part. We cannot die for the sins of anyone else. He is talking here about the heart of sacrifice which is so essential to our Christian relationships and which He modeled for us. Mother Teresa visited Washington, and the visit attracted the attention of media. She refused to spend her time with political leaders of the city, so they followed her into an impoverished inner city church. "What do you hope to accomplish here?" a reporter shouted. "The joy of loving and being loved," she smiled as she looked into the cameras. "That takes a lot of money doesn't it?" another reporter threw out the obvious question. Mother Teresa shook her head, "No, it takes a lot of sacrifice."[4]

Oseola McCarty, the washerwoman who died in 1999 at the age of 91, became famous for her selfless giving. She had done one thing all her life – laundry! She never married, spending her life washing clothes by hand for the wealthy families of Hattiesburg, Mississippi. Miss McCarty never went anywhere except to worship at her church, Friendship Baptist Church in Hattiesburg. She always said there was no place she wanted to go and nothing she wanted to buy. After buying her groceries each week, she put the rest of her money in a savings account. In 1995, at the age of 87, she retired. She decided to give away her life savings. "I'm giving it away so children won't have to work so hard like I did," she said. Oseola McCarty gave $150,000 to fund a scholarship at Southern Mississippi University to help those children get an education! News traveled fast and over 600 donors added $330,000 to the original scholarship. In the next few years, this humble washerwoman would shake hands with President Clinton, be honored at the United Nations, carry the Olympic torch through a section of Mississippi, and pull the switch to drop the ball in Times Square! When she died, her body lay in state in the rotunda of the

University's main building where thousands paid their respects. She understood the truth that Jesus taught. We enjoy our greatest pleasure when we give as Jesus gave. A reporter from People magazine once asked her why she didn't spend the money on herself. She pointed out the pleasure that comes from giving and said, "I am spending it on myself."[5] The way to be Jesus' friend is to be a friend to others. The way to experience Jesus' love is to love others.

Jesus lays out a second set of two conditions. Jesus is saying that you are my friends when you do what I say and when you know what I mean (15:14-15). Of course, this is not a friendship of equals! Friends are usually friends by mutual choice. Jesus says in verse 16, "You did not choose me, but I chose you," making the friendship reciprocal but not mutual. And friends are usually friends by mutual agreement to submit to each other. Yet Jesus says: "You are my friends when you do what I say," making the friendship a matter of obedience.

THE OBEDIENCE OF FRIENDS

We don't commonly associate obedience with friendship. We associate affection with friendship and obedience with slavery. A friend is not ordered to obey like a servant. There is no duty among friends, we think. The essence of friendship is voluntary action. Friends can choose how to act while still being accepted as friends. Jesus says, "You are My friends if you do what I command you" (John 15:14).[6]

Doesn't this condition turn us into servants not friends? Jesus goes on to explain that He calls us friends and not servants because a servant doesn't know the mind of the Master, but Jesus discloses to us "all things" that He has heard from His Father (15:15). The obedience of affection rises out of the self-disclosure of friendship. A friend shares the heart behind the command. Our knowledge changes the nature of our obedience. There is an obedience out of love that is an act of voluntary affection. Such obedience is a choice which explains the conditionality of our friendship with Jesus. In His love, He risks making known His deepest desires to us, and in our love, we choose to obey His commands. When we choose to obey out of love we enjoy the affection of friendship that comes from His self-disclosure

D.A. Carson illustrates the difference by the example of a Colonel and a private in the army. The Colonel tells the private to get the jeep and take him to Headquarters. If the private responds by saying that he will only get the jeep if the Colonel gives him permission to use it while the Colonel is in his meeting at Headquarters, he is asking for KP! He is a servant, not a friend. Imagine, however, that the Colonel has been a friend to the private's family for many years and says to him, "Get the jeep and take me to Headquarters for a meeting. I'll be there for the afternoon in a meeting with the General. You are welcome to use the jeep to do what you want. There is a great little restaurant in town that I like but be back to pick me up at 1800 hours." The private still must obey, but now he is obeying out of respect and affection. The additional information changed the nature of the order.[7]

Jesus carefully qualified this friendship. We are friends of His if we do what He says, but He does not reciprocate and say that He is our friend because He does what we say! We dare not have a friendship with Christ which diminishes the distinction between the King and His subjects. Jesus invites us into a friendship, but it is not a friendship of equals.

When my daughter, Kari, was four years old, she and I could be friends, but it was not a friendship of equals. One day I was in my study when I heard such a screaming and crying that I ran over to the window to see what was happening. I thought someone was dying. There in the driveway was a harmless little grass snake sunning itself. Kari was terrified, and my wife came running to ask me to take care of it. My wife hates snakes! I pointed out that the snake would just quietly go away if they left it alone to which she replied. "I don't want it to go away! I want it dead!" So I got a shovel, killed the snake and dumped it in the woods. Kari was thrilled. She looked up at me and said, "O Daddy, you're so great!" I was her hero, at least for that moment. We could have a friendship. We could play with her dollhouse or tea set all we wanted. I enjoyed that friendship, but it was not a friendship of equals. In even greater measure we must remember the distinction between us in our friendship with Jesus.

There is a conditional nature to our friendship with Jesus. Our friendship is based upon obedience to a superior who invites us to serve Him out of knowledge, not duty. We don't get to do whatever we want and still enjoy His friendship. We have to follow His orders to enjoy His love, but we follow His orders because of love. What are Christ's orders? Well, He has just said, "This is my commandment that you love one another." What happens when we love one another? We enjoy His friendship, and we experience His joy. It all fits together. He abides in the

Father's love by obeying the Father, and we abide in His love by obeying Him. The result is perfect, full complete joy in life. Jesus came to give us a full, abundant, exciting life, not a dull and dreary life. Here is how to have that kind of life – obey what he says in His book!

HANGING OUT WITH JESUS

However, Jesus does not stop here because this would give us an incomplete view of friendship. He quickly adds that He does not call us slaves or servants. The relationship He is talking about is more than just a master/servant relationship. Certainly on one level we are slaves of the Master, but we are not only slaves. We are friends. For many years in my Christian life, I did not think of Christ as my friend. He was my Lord and my Master. My relationship was based upon duty and obligation. I was fortunate to have parents who did not teach me to have a relationship of fear, but I know some who grew up in religious environments where the guiding principle of their relationship with God was fear. I have learned that the Lord wants more than this for us. He chooses us to be His friends not just His servants. He says that you are my friends when you know what I mean (15:15) – when you understand my desires!

I remember in high school my best friend and I did everything together. He and I didn't have to have some special activity to do. We often just "hung out" together. I was there when he got his pilot's license, and I went to his Civil Air Patrol ceremony. I was there when he was jilted by his girlfriend and threw the ring far into the woods in disgust. I listened to his passions and interests, and he listened to mine. In college, four friends and I traveled in a singing group together for a year and a half. We shared our hopes and dreams with each other. They all participated in my wedding. They drove all night to arrive Saturday morning. I knew they had arrived when a bucket of cold water was thrown over the top of the shower and peals of laughter rang out!

Friends talk to one another. They share secrets. They communicate. Friends tell one another what they know, and they learn to understand one another. There is no such thing as a one-way friendship. Jesus says that we are more than just servants – although we are servants – we are friends because He has chosen to tell us the Father's secrets. What He knows from His relationship with the Father in the eternally Triune Godhead, He lets us in on! He shares that knowledge with us.

Griffin writes: "Extensive research has identified a whole cluster of goodies that typify close friendship: enjoyment, acceptance, trust, respect, mutual assistance, confiding, understanding, and spontaneity."[8] We experience those same relational "goodies" with Jesus as we come to know Him. Jesus shares with us, His friends, the important details about Himself and about us – details which are necessary for us to have a right relationship with God and with each other. Jesus wants us to know what He means. He wants us to understand Him and ourselves. He wants to share with us and talk with us and confide with us through prayer and Bible study. As we spend time with Him, we learn to understand Him through prayer and the reading of His self-disclosure to us in the Bible. Here is the knowledge we need to understand what He means. He explains Himself in Scripture. Why? He doesn't have to explain Himself. He is, after all, the creator of the universe who does not owe us an explanation for anything. He wants to explain Himself to us so that we can be His friends so that we can obey out of knowledge, not duty.

I grew up practicing an evangelical "quiet time" twice a day. I was rigid and legalistic about this discipline. If I didn't keep my morning and evening devotional appointments with God, I thought that God would reprimand me in some way – my day would disintegrate, things would go wrong. I did not enjoy a friendship with Jesus. My relationship was more of a business arrangement built on scheduled appointments with my "boss." The discipline has some value, of course, but a scheduled friendship is a shallow friendship. Appointment prayer limits our relationship. It is not the friendship Jesus wants us to enjoy with Him. "Pray without ceasing," Paul wrote in 1 Thessalonians 5:17. Prayer is the conversation of friends, ongoing, spontaneous and enjoyable as we talk with Jesus about the everyday experiences of life. We need to "hang out" with Jesus more. Spontaneity characterizes friendship.

> We can use the phrase 'wasting time with God' to justify these special occasions – especially if we are a fairly driven kind of person. This kind of "wasting" is of high value in God's economy. Having no agenda is all right; in fact, it is preferred. Anything we do that truly nurtures our soul and relationship with God is worth the effort and time. Some believers have become so accustomed to a busy pace of

life that being alone for any length of time will initially involve discomfort and withdrawal pains.[9]

Many years ago I turned my car into a personal retreat center. I turned off the radio and refused to listen to audio recordings. I spent a fair amount of my day driving, and the car was the perfect place to "hang out" with God. Nobody could interrupt me, at least until I had a cell phone! When I wake up in the morning, I often take a few minutes while I lie in bed to talk with God. It is a great way to start the day. The same is true when I wake up in the night. If I read something interesting, I share it with Jesus. An email with a prayer request leads me to stop and talk with Him. Lunch can be a time to share life with Jesus. We all can find these times to "hang out" with God in the midst of our busy lives. The waiting room at a doctor's office can be a time to commune with God. Waiting in the parking lot to pick up a child from school can be a time to talk with Jesus. It is what friends do!

CHOSEN BY JESUS

Friendship is commonly mutual. Friends usually choose each other but not so with Jesus. Jesus says, "You did not choose Me but I chose you" (John 15:16). The doctrine here is the doctrine of election – a scary theological term to many! We live in a world which worships before the idol of free will as if we are free to do as we please. The truth is that we are never as free as we think we are. I read somewhere about one young man who went with his fiancée to meet with her minister to sign some pre-wedding papers. While filling out the last form, the young man read aloud a few of the questions. When he got to the last one, he read: "Are you entering this marriage of your own will?" He looked over at his fiancée. "Put down 'Yes'," she said.

It is the same spiritually. His choice drives our choice. We think that we have chosen God and in the end, we find out that He has chosen us. Election is a wonderfully humbling and encouraging doctrine of the Scriptures which we tend to misunderstand and misuse. Of course, men are responsible to repent of their sins and to believe in Jesus Christ, but that is not the end of the discussion. No person will ever be able to stand in heaven while their neighbor spends eternity in hell and congratulate themselves that they made the right choice. No one will ever be able to say,

"I was smart enough to believe, so I deserve heaven as my reward." We will sing forever around the throne words like these:

> I sought the Lord, and afterward I knew
> He moved my soul to seek Him, seeking me;
> It was not I that found, O Savior true:
> No, I was found of Thee.[10]

I cannot answer all the intellectual questions about unconditional election - nor would I even try! Instead of focusing on the question, "What happens to those people God does not choose?" Jesus focuses on "What happens to those people God does choose?" Jesus has just called us friends (John 15:14-15). Now He tells us that He chose us for friendship (John 15:16). Friendship is the purpose behind His election. His election is not so much an election to eternal life but an election to forever friendship. Jesus chose, by his distinguishing grace, to invite us to be His friends. The Greek word here means to "call out" someone. The construction means to call out that person for yourself, for your own benefit or personal interest.[11] Jesus is saying that we did not call out for Christ out of our own personal interest. He called us out – He chose us – for His personal interest. It is emphatic. "I myself, personally, have chosen you for myself." Here is the comforting mystery of election, a mystery so profound we will never fully comprehend it, but a mystery so comforting we will always appreciate it. Jesus chose us to be His friends.

Before we were Christians, we heard about the good news of salvation in Jesus Christ, and we decided of our own "free will" to place our faith in Jesus Christ. We made a decision to believe. Then we find out after we had made that decision that He selected us before we even knew about this matter called Christianity. He had chosen us before we were born. In fact, He elected us before the world was even created to be His friends (Ephesians 1:4). What is more, He did not choose us because we were more desirable than anyone else. He did not even choose us for our own benefit. We think of salvation as designed for our benefit, but here we learn that He chose us for His own purpose. He chose us for Himself! Every Christian is a called out one whether he is a janitor or a CEO. Every Christian is specifically chosen by Jesus for friendship.

We come to another loaded theological term – ordination! Jesus says, "I appointed (ordained) you that you would go and bear fruit, and that your fruit would remain, so that whatever you ask of the Father in My name, he may give it to you." All Christians, not just an elite few, are ordained by Jesus Christ for a purpose. Every one of us is appointed by Him. He appoints us for production. We are ordained to produce fruit for the Master. Every Christian life is designed to be significant. There are no insignificant Christians!

Jesus' statement of purpose has two parts. The first part has to do with fruit and the second with prayer. But both parts are related to production and I think that we often miss the connection between prayer and fruit. Jesus says that we are to "go and bear fruit." We can't just be static in this process. We must be active participants in the fruit production. The fruit Jesus is speaking about here is primarily our character although we cannot say it has nothing to do with new converts or other people. The truth is that we have only very limited control over what other people do, but we have great control over our own decisions. We are ordained by Jesus Christ to produce character worthy of His name, but we are to be actively involved in that process. We cannot just sit back and wait for God to do something. We must be diligent to produce the fruit He seeks by the power He provides.

> His divine power has granted to us everything pertaining to life and godliness, through the true knowledge of Him who called us by His own glory and excellence ... for this very reason also, applying all diligence, in your faith supply moral excellence, and in your moral excellence, knowledge, and in your knowledge, self-control, and in your self-control, perseverance, and in your perseverance, godliness, and in your godliness, brotherly kindness, and in your brotherly kindness, love. For if these qualities are yours and are increasing, they render you neither useless nor unfruitful in the true knowledge of our Lord Jesus Christ. (2 Peter 1:3, 5-8)

This fruit is intended to last (John 15:16). Jesus says "that your fruit should remain." Is it just here today and gone tomorrow or does the fruit of our lives have lasting value? The only way to find out about lasting value is to see that fruit – our character – tested through the course of time. Christ's question to us is "Does our fruit have lasting value?"

Our question to Christ is "How do we grow fruit that lasts?" Here is the vital connection to prayer. Jesus says, that whatever we ask of the Father in His name, He will give it to us. We must not take this promise out of its context though. The promise is directly related to fruit production. Every Christian, who is not regularly and consistently praying, is going to be a fruitless Christian. We cannot produce fruit for the master without talking to the master and seeking His direction and His guidance. Prayerlessness produces fruitlessness. Prayer is one of the ways we grow fruit because it is one of the primary ways that we stay in the vine!

THE TEFLON OF INTIMACY

Prayer is a conversation between friends. Asking a friend for something honors the friend. It is an expression of trust. My request risks allowing a friend to see my need. The deeper the request, the greater the risk and the more I must trust my friend. Like a knife slicing through the layers of an onion, my request is a form of self-disclosure. The deeper the knife penetrates, the greater the risk. Griffin writes, "My inner layers are so tightly wrapped that the blade can't overcome the resistance unless it's coated with a nonstick layer of Teflon. Trust is the Teflon of intimacy."[12]

Trust helps us understand the condition for His promise. We are to pray "in Jesus' name." This does not mean that we tack onto the end of our prayers "in Jesus' name, amen" as if it is some magical incantation. Praying in Jesus' name means that we pray in accord with His character and His plan. He will always be delighted to give us whatever we ask as long as it is in accord with His character and His plan. Praying "in Jesus' name" is our expression of trust and our invitation to Jesus to penetrate the layers of our souls. We trust him with our need knowing that He will always do what is best for us. A true friend may not always do what we ask. We risk that reality because we trust the friend. We know that a close friend will always do what is best for us. We trust Him.

I once heard Dr. Howard Hendricks tell the story about when he was single and available. One mother was trying her best to match him with her daughter. She said to him one day, "Howard, I just want you to know that I'm praying that you'll be my son-in-law." Then he paused and asked, "Have you ever thanked God for unanswered prayer?" We should because we pray in Jesus' name.

All of this brings us to verse 17 which is the culmination of this whole section explaining the vine and the branches. How do we know that we love Jesus? We know we love Jesus when we love one another. The teaching on friendship with Jesus is bracketed by the command to love one another (John 15:12, 17) and the conclusion of life in the vine. The degree to which I love Jesus is measured by the degree to which I love other Christians. I can never have a close friendship with Jesus if my relationship with other Christians is fractured. *If I won't love Jesus' friends, I can't be Jesus' friend!*

Jesus understood this principle, which is why he repeats this command so often that we could almost become irritated with His redundancy. It is so vital to life in the vine that we dare not forget its importance. Jesus talks much about the triune Godhead in these chapters. He speaks about how the three persons in the trinity love one another and how each fulfills His role because of that love. The Trinity is the perfect model for the perfect friendship. Love unites them so much that they each perform their responsibilities to perfection for the sake of the other (John 14:10-11, 26, 31).

In the same way, we are to love one another in our love for Him. The only way this triangle of love will happen is if we abide in the vine and allow the fruit of the Spirit to be produced in our lives by our commitment to follow Christ. Loving one another is the natural byproduct of our love for the Lord (15:10, 12-13). We will never learn to love one another until we understand the secrets of John 15 living. Experiencing Christ's love in all of its fullness qualifies us to love others with all our hearts.

His love means that we do not love people based on what they look like but based upon who they are in Christ. If they are friends of Christ's, then they are friends of ours even if we don't like it! Amy Carmichael wrote, "If monotony tries me, and I cannot stand drudgery; if stupid people fret me and little ruffles set me on edge; if I make much of the trifles of life, then I know nothing of Calvary love."[13] The irony of our friendship with Jesus is that we experience intimacy with Him through intimacy with other Christians. We know His love by sharing His love. In a very real sense, the degree to which we experience friendship with each other is the degree to which we experience friendship with Jesus. Friendship with Jesus is deepened through our fellowship with the community of His friends.

176

There is a wonderful convergence of teachings, a culmination of ideas, as Jesus draws His themes together in these verses: remaining in Him – knowing His will – bearing fruit for Him – obeying His word – sacrificing ourselves in love – praying in His name. Persevering in all these matters leads us to experience the depths of spiritual intimacy. We prove our perseverance in the battle with this world system that Jesus addresses in the next verses. Our friendship with Jesus is refined by the fires of spiritual battle.

There are two scenes from the movie, Lord of the Rings: The Return of the King, which capture the spirit of this passage – if we don't push the analogy too far theologically. The first scene finds the small army of Aragorn before the black gates of the Dark Lord Sauron challenging him to battle. The hordes of Mordor stream out from the gates of Isengard to encircle the tiny army of loyal fighters. It is obvious that good stands no reasonable chance against evil at that moment. Just before the battle begins, Gimli says to Legolas, "I never thought I'd die fighting side by side with an elf." Legolas looks down at the bushy-bearded dwarf and replies, "What about side by side with a friend?" Gimli turns slightly, "Aye. I could do that."

The second scene is called "The Coronation of Aragorn." The crowds have gathered to celebrate the crowning of their king. Aragorn walks among the people with his bride. The cheering crowds part for his passage until he faces the four friends who formed The Fellowship of the Ring with him. Frodo, Sam, Merry, and Pippin are hobbits. They are considered inconsequential in the world of humans. The four hobbits bow before King Aragorn, who stops his slow procession and motions for them to rise. "My friends. You bow to no one." The entire crowd cheers and bows before the four friends who risked their lives to save Middle-earth.[14]

No longer servants but friends forged by the bonds of battle!

14
A FAULT LINE WITH THE WORLD

John 15:18-25

Matthew Murray had spent about half an hour inside the Youth with a Mission training center in Arvada, a suburb of Denver talking with students when he asked if he could stay overnight. Tiffany Johnson was called to the front desk to explain to him that he could not stay overnight at the training center without arranging that in advance. Matthew pulled out a gun and said, "Then this is what I've got for you" and began shooting. He left the building and the door automatically locked behind him so he couldn't get back inside. He later killed two people at New Life Church in Colorado Springs. Holly, another YWAM trainee, began performing CPR on Tiffany, and she regained consciousness. Tiffany asked, "Is it bad?" Holly, with her boyfriend Dan standing nearby, replied that it was bad. Tiffany looked at them both and said, "We do this for Jesus, right guys? We do this for Jesus."[1]

Christianity is simple but never simplistic. We often present the great truths of grace, salvation and forgiveness simplistically. We share the great advantages and privileges of our faith without acknowledging the cost of being a Christian. Jesus warns us to count that cost because, just as

Christ's friends are the Christian's friends, so Christ's enemies are the Christian's enemies.

Opposition defines allegiance. Pressure forces choices. The result of abiding in Jesus is that we are not abiding in the world. The contrast is sharply black and white – no gray allowed. The result of not abiding in the world is that the world hates us. Jesus said, "If the world hates you, you know that it has hated Me before you" (John 15:18). The word "know" could be a command instead of a statement.[2] Facing the hatred of the world, Jesus commands us to know they hated Him first, either first in time or first in importance. Our union with Jesus establishes a fault line with the world leading us to expect persecution from the world. Christ's enemies are the Christian's enemies because we own a different loyalty (15:19). We associate ourselves with Christ, so we owe our allegiance to a higher authority than any earthly authority.

In December 1995, Hussein (Robert) Qambar Ali who was 44 years old and a Christian for only two years, announced publicly in Kuwait that he had converted to Christianity. On May 29, 1996, a Kuwaiti Islamic court convicted him of being an apostate from Islam and stripped him of his nationality and civil rights for abandoning Islam. Hussein told a reporter, "Apostasy in the Islamic world is serious. Anyone, even an ordinary person, has the right to kill me without penalty." He was forcibly divorced from his wife and refused any access to his children. Death threats followed and Hussein went into hiding, moving from one home to another to avoid detection. He lost everything. He eventually fled to the United States with the help of Christian Solidarity International and married an American woman. Shortly before his departure from Kuwait he said, "I cannot take it anymore. The pressure is mounting. I am trying to leave this country now."[3]

WHY HATE CHRISTIANS?

The world in this verse is not the physical, material globe we call earth. It is the world system which stands against Jesus Christ. The church and the world are mutually exclusive. This world system wears many "ugly faces."[4] Whether it is totalitarian communism or immoral lifestyles; whether it is Islamic fundamentalism or greedy materialism; the faces of the world have the same origin. Satan himself drives this world system. Friends of Jesus are not of this world system although we live in the world system. We must live in the world, but we are not of the world nor do we live for the world (John 17:14-15). Therefore, it should not surprise us when the world hates us.

Jesus states two reasons why the world hates us. The first reason is that Jesus chose us for Himself.[5] "I chose you out of the world, because of this the world hates you" (John 15:19). Three times Jesus uses the same prepositional clause "out of the world" in this one verse. "If you were out of the world the world would love its own; but because you are not out of the world, but I chose you out of the world, because of this the world hates you." The preposition "out of" can indicate either origin or separation.[6] The first clause expresses origin – often used in the sense of family origin. If our birth family is the world, the world would love us. However, we are not out of the world in terms of our birth family any longer. We originate from Jesus. We have a new birth family as those who abide in Jesus. Our point of origin rests in His choice – electing love. He chose us "out of the world." The final clause indicates separation. The world is the place from which Jesus separates us by His choice to become part of His birth family. The world hates us because Jesus chose us.

The second reason the world hates us is that they do not know God the Father. "But all these things they will do to you for My name's sake, because they do not know the One who sent Me" (John 15:21). Ignorance of God the Father leads to persecution of the Son and His followers. Ignorance of the nature of God leads to failure in recognizing Jesus. When people don't know who God is, they cannot know who Jesus is. Jesus has said that to know God the Father you must know Jesus (John 14:6, 9). Now Jesus reverses the truth – to know Jesus you must know God the Father.

Intimacy with Jesus precludes intimacy with the world. If I am intimate with the world, I cannot be intimate with Jesus. If I am intimate with Jesus, I cannot be intimate with the world. The world will notice the difference and hate me for it. People simply hate those who are different and Christians are different. There is great pressure to conform to this world's ideas and standards. It is when we refuse to conform to this world system that we become marked as different and exposed to hatred and attack. It is for that reason that we tend to want to "fit in" not to be different, and we will do what we can to conform. Sooner or later our Christianity will be challenged, and we will have to take a stand. It is then

181

we find out that the world hates Christians because we are chosen to be different.

Jesus said earlier, "You did not choose me, but I chose you" (John 15:16). So Jesus Christ personally selected people out of this world for Himself. This divine selection of certain people and not others is the root of hatred. God chose us, and we responded to His choice by deciding to shift our loyalty from anything in this world to God. God's choice is a great offense to the people around us who reject Him. "What makes you so special?" the world screams at us. "I am special because God chose me for Himself, to be His friend." This truth makes us special. We are chosen to be different and, for this reason, the world hates us.

PRESSURE TO CONFORM

The world puts pressure on us to be like them because when we conform and stop being different, then it makes those who do not follow Christ feel better about themselves. Our daughter, Katie, when she was in elementary school, came home one day and announced to us that she didn't like her teacher's rules. I asked her what those rules were since we need to learn to obey authority at an early age. She said, "The first rule is 'No kissing boys.'" (I thought that was a particularly good rule myself!) "The second rule is no praying in school and the third rule is no talking about Jesus." The pressure to conform to the world – to not be different – comes early in life. We all want to look good and be accepted by others.

John Lennox, a professor of Mathematics at the University of Oxford, experienced the academic pressure from the world to conform early in his career. He found himself seated next to a Nobel Laureate at a dinner while still a student himself. He attempted to engage him in a conversation about God to no avail. After dinner, the man invited him along with some colleagues to join him in his room for coffee. Lennox was the only student present, and the setting felt intimidating. He turned to John and asked him if he was serious about a career in science to which John said, "Yes." The man then said, "Give up these childish ideas of God. They will only disadvantage you intellectually among your peers." When John tried to continue the dialogue about God, the man dismissed him abruptly. Lennox writes:

The pressure is mounting today. If you are going to look good, from the point of view of many scientists and those who follow them, then you had better be an atheist ... If you are going to look tolerant these days, you will be informed that you cannot afford to confess publicly that Jesus Christ is the way, and the truth, and the life (John 14:6). You must recognize that all religions are equally valid ways of searching for some kind of ultimate reality: God, gods, or whatever ... It is, therefore, increasingly difficult to avoid the marginalization that results from stepping out of the politically correct line. It can be an expensive business.[7]

There is a cost to Christianity. In the early church, one of the major charges against Christians which led to the death penalty was that Christians were unpatriotic. Christians owed their allegiance to a higher authority than the Caesar and this unpatriotic stance was a capital offense. It is still true today in many parts of the world. The truth is that we own a different loyalty. Here is the first reason for the hatred, but the real crux of the hatred stems from our association with Jesus Christ. We are hated because we serve a different master. "A slave is not greater than his master. If they persecuted Me, they will also persecute you" (John 15:20).

Jesus used this same expression earlier than night (13:16) when he was talking about washing one another's feet. If the master could wash feet, then we should be capable of serving one another with the same humble spirit. Now He teaches us that this principle also applies to persecution. If the master endured rejection and persecution, then we must expect the same treatment for our Christian faith. If Jesus was ostracized, ridiculed, illegally convicted, and crucified, then we cannot expect much different treatment. We act surprised when people criticize Christianity. We ought to be more surprised by the freedom we have had for so many years to practice our faith. We should expect the negative and be surprised by the positive and not whimper and whine because someone criticized our faith. We should expect rejection for the sake of Christ.

Oswaldo (Wally) Magdangal was the forty-two-year-old Filipino pastor of a growing house church in Saudi Arabia in 1992. The Islamic secret police or *muttawa'in* were led to the church by a regular attendee who betrayed his fellow worshippers to the authorities. Magdangal was arrested and repeatedly beaten on his back and the bottoms of his feet throughout his three-and-a-half hours of interrogation. They demanded that he write down the names of other Christians on a pad of paper. He refused. Eventually, he was so weakened that he cried out to Jesus, "Lord, you've got to help me here." He began to write down names like Billy Graham and Charles Spurgeon. After a few days, the authorities came back very angry because they could not locate these people anywhere in Saudi Arabia. Tried and convicted of blasphemy in an Islamic court, he expected to be executed. Friday is the day of execution in Saudi Arabia, and hardly a Friday passes without at least one execution in the public square in Riyadh following the noon prayers. December 25 fell on a Friday in 1992. Magdangal wrote out his last will and testament to his wife and daughter on December 23 and prepared to die. Unknown to him, family and friends had been filing international protests on his behalf. His situation became known even to Fidel Ramos, the president of the Philippines. The story appeared in newspapers, and organizations like Amnesty International issued bulletins about the coming execution. Shortly before midnight on Christmas Eve, Magdangal was taken out of his cell and put on a plane to Manila. After emigrating to America, he learned that King Fahd himself had ordered him expelled immediately. Saudi officials deny to this day that he ever faced a death sentence.[8]

Our commitment to Christ must count the cost. We often say that Christianity is free, and it is – in one sense. However, Christianity makes demands upon us that are extremely expensive, and we dare not ignore those demands. Rejection for the sake of Christ may be part of the cost. The principle cuts both ways Jesus assures us. We can expect rejection for the sake of Christ, but we can expect acceptance by the saints of Christ. Jesus adds, "If they kept My word, they will keep yours also" (15:20). Jesus is not saying here that those who persecute Christians also keep Christ's word. He is saying that the principle works in both directions. Because we serve a different master, Christ's enemies are the Christian's enemies, but Christ's friends are the Christian's friends. We can expect acceptance by the saints of Christ.

We have many different denominations because we have many different flavors of Christianity. The denominational distinctions are important but not essential. I am a Baptist, but I have brothers in Christ who are Presbyterian. We are all followers of Christ – part of the universal church. I do not mean that we can believe or behave any way we want and still be called Christians because there is a core set of doctrines and moral laws which are essential to the Christian faith. I do mean that we are not all Baptists, and we need to stand with each other even in our differences.

I love the story I heard somewhere about the Presbyterians who were holding a convention in Scotland. After a couple of days of sitting on hard pews, a group decided to stretch their legs and go for a walk. Soon they approached a rickety old bridge over a river, but were so busy talking that they missed the sign which read: "Keep off the Bridge." A villager saw them step onto the dangerous bridge and yelled for them to stop. "That's all right," one of the ministers responded. "We're here from the Presbyterian convention." "I dinna care aboot that," came the reply. "But if ye go much further, ye'll all be Baptists!"

There is a very important practice for all Christians in this world. When we present our faith to the world outside the church, we seek to present a unified front. The world should not see us as Baptists or Presbyterians but as Christians. Yes, we have our differences, and they are important differences, but those differences are to be kept in the family. When I was working as a mechanic for GTE Sylvania many years ago, there was a fellow mechanic who also was a Christian. He went to a different church, and we had some differences of opinion about how things should be done and what we believed in some areas. He seemed intent on making these things an issue at the lunch table and during breaks. He would bring up subjects trying to lure me into an argument before our fellow employees. I finally took him aside and said, "You and I have some important differences, but this is not the time or the place to discuss our differences. So far as I know, we may be the only Christians here, and we need to accept one another before them so that they can see Christ in us. Before them, we must be one whatever we may disagree about in private." The persecution principle works both ways.

HATED WITHOUT CAUSE

The annual *Status of Global Mission* report published by the *International Bulletin of Missionary Research* in 2011 reported 270 Christians were martyred every 24 hours from 2000-2010 – a total of approximately 1 million martyrs in one decade.[9] A friend from India reported to me through email that attacks on Christians occurred almost daily in 2015 throughout India. The country saw 200 major incidents of persecution

185

against Christians. Seven pastors were killed, nuns raped and hundreds arrested as India's anti-conversion laws were being strongly enforced. Hindu fundamentalists are seeking to criminalize the presence of Christians and any Christian social work as a conspiracy by Western political powers thus justifying violence against Christians.[10]

We live in a brutal world where people seek to accomplish their agendas by force. Much of that violence is perpetrated in the name of religion. Nina Shea, director of Freedom House's Puebla Program on Religious Freedom, says, "Christians are in fact the most persecuted religious group in the world today, with the greatest number of victims."[11] Jesus predicted in John 15:21: "All these things they will do to you for My Name's sake." The world hates Christians for the sake of Christ. People hate the name of Christ, and if we associate ourselves with that name, we can expect to receive some of that hatred.

One reason for that hatred is ignorance! The world's malicious hatred proves their ignorance of God. Jesus tells us that men will hate Christians "because they do not know the one who sent me." He adds, "He who hates me, hates my Father also" (John 15:21,23). The basis for this hatred is ignorance of the Father. Sometimes ignorance can be a reasonable excuse. I cannot be blamed if I do not know nuclear physics – unless I am in charge of a nuclear power plant. I cannot be blamed if I do not know how to pilot a ferry – unless I am Captain of a ferry in Casco Bay! One day a Gorham police officer stopped me. He was very professional and very kind, but my inspection sticker had run out. "Oh," I said, "I had not even noticed it." I was ignorant. I still had to pay a fine because I was supposed to know, I was expected to have that knowledge. All human beings are expected to know God enough to be culpable for their ignorance.

> For the wrath of God is revealed from heaven against all ungodliness and unrighteousness of men who suppress the truth in unrighteousness, because that which is known about God is evident within them; for God made it evident to them. For since the creation of the world His invisible attributes, His eternal power and divine nature, have been clearly seen, being understood through what has been made, so that they are without excuse. (Romans 1:18-20)

PRESUMPTUOUS SIN

Presumptuous sin is scary! Presumptuous sin incurs a greater guilt – a deeper culpability – than ordinary sin. A person sins presumptuously when he knowingly and constantly rejects truth to confidently and willfully commit sin. Jesus said, "If I had not come and spoken to them, they would not have sin, but now they have no excuse for their sin" (John 15:22). He is not saying that a person would have been sinless if Jesus had not come. All of us are sinners. Jesus is speaking about the specific sin of conscious unbelief. Jesus came. Jesus spoke the truth. People saw Him. People heard the truth, and people rejected Him and His message. Those people "have sin." The verb means to hold it, grip it or own it! It is conscious sin. They own it without excuse.

Jesus goes on to say, "If I had not done among them the works which no one else did, they would not have sin; but now they have both seen and hated Me and My Father as well" (John 15:24). People not only willfully rejected Jesus' message, but they confidently rejected Jesus' works. They rejected Jesus' words and works in the past but, knowing better in the present, they continue to reject them.[12] Presumptuous sinners not only own the sin but carry the rejection forward without remorse leading to the judgment of God.

The Old Testament Law distinguished between ordinary sin and defiant sin (Numbers 15:30), defining defiant sin as blasphemy! Presumptuous sin is a special category of sin leading to greater culpability. Jesus told the Pharisees that he came to help those who were blind to see and cause those who see to become blind. The Pharisees claimed they were not blind so Jesus retorted, "If you were blind you would have no sin (you wouldn't own it); but since you say, 'we see,' your sin remains" (John 9:41). When we present the message and the works of Jesus to people, they become culpable for their choice. We become, as Paul says, "the smell of death" or "the smell of life" to them (2 Cor. 2:16). A person who knows all about Jesus and still rejects Jesus has greater guilt than one who never hears or knows.

Many people think that they know God. They are very religious. But when people hate Christ it proves that they do not know God no matter how religious they are because Jesus Christ is the revelation of God to man. John wrote in John 1:18, "No man has seen God at any time; the only-begotten God, who is in the bosom of the Father, He has explained Him." Jesus said in John 10:30, "I and the Father are one." Paul wrote in Colossians 2:9 that in Christ, "All the fullness of the deity dwells in bodily form." Therefore, what you do with Christ reveals what you actually feel about God!

The Trinity – the triunity of God – is an essential doctrine of the Christian faith. We may not understand it fully but to deny it is to deny God. Most groups which persecute Christians are made up of people who deny the triunity of God. Many are atheists, but many more believe in other gods or supreme beings. Still more are monotheistic but deny the deity of Jesus Christ. He is the sticking point for most people who reject Christianity. They do not believe that Jesus Christ is God so they are ignorant of the one true God no matter how religious they might be.

THE COST OF FRIENDSHIP WITH JESUS

The world's powerful hatred exposes their personal guilt (15:22, 24). The reason why the world hates Christians is that it hates Christ. Why? Here was a man who never wronged anyone. Never sinned. Never exploited anyone. Why do they hate Christ? There are two reasons in these verses. First, people hated Christ for His words (vs. 22). They "have sin" because Jesus spoke to them. Jesus is not saying that people never sinned until He spoke to them. The second phrase explains the first. They did not know what their sin was before He came and exposed their guilt. They have no excuse for their sin because He spoke to them.

Jesus was never selfish or hypocritical. Jesus was never mean or arrogant so why would they hate his words? Therein lies the reason. He was so pure that dirty people had to get clean or hate His purity. He was so perfect that men could no longer feel comfortable with relative goodness. We can tolerate a little selfishness, jealousy, meanness in ourselves because we can always compare ourselves to someone who is much meaner, more selfish and nastier than we are. When Jesus talks, we suddenly are exposed to such brilliant light that our light looks dark. We hate that kind of exposure so much that we hate the exposer.

Dr. Harry Ironside, the long-time pastor of Moody Church in Chicago during the first half of the 1900s, told a story about a missionary to Africa back when the continent was first being opened to the west. The wife of an African chief happened to visit a mission station. The missionary had hung a small mirror on a tree outside his home, and the woman happened to look at it. She had come straight from her village, and her face was all painted with grotesque symbols, so when she saw her own face in the mirror, she was shocked at its ugliness. Some of us are too, at times! It is so easy to tolerate the ugliness of others, but we hate the exposure of ourselves. She asked who that horrible looking person was inside the tree. The missionary tried to explain that it was her own face but couldn't make her understand until she held it in her own hand. Then she wanted to buy it and was so insistent that he didn't dare refuse. A price was set, and she took the glass. In great anger, she threw the glass to the ground and broke it into pieces as she said, "I will never have it making faces at me again."[13]

There is a second reason that people hated Christ. People hated Christ for His works (vs. 24). The works of Christ are, in fact, the works of the Father (John 14:10-11). His works are so perfect that they make our works look worthless! His works expose the real value of our works. Don't you just hate it when someone is so good at what they do that it makes you look like a chump by comparison!? Christ's works are so perfect that they make our works look shabby. Next to each other we can feel pretty good about ourselves, but next to Christ, who can feel good? Such exposure leads to hatred.

On a lesser scale, we who name the name of Christ also expose sin by our words and our works. The fruit of life in Christ evokes the criticism of the world. At one time Benjamin Franklin was the butt of stinging criticism in various newspapers. His family and friends even received bitter and threatening letters. Franklin's sister, deeply hurt by all the criticism, poured out her heart in a letter to her brother. Benjamin Franklin replied by telling her what his good friend George Whitefield, the English evangelist, had told him. Whitefield said that he had read the attacks on Franklin and was in no position to determine their truth or falsehood. However, he knew by the attacks that Franklin was doing a good job. He wrote, "When I am on the road, and see boys in a field at a distance, pelting a tree, though I am too far off to know what tree it is, I conclude it has fruit on it."[14]

We are by no means perfect, but when we choose to make a stand and confront wrong because of our Christian faith, then we can expect some measure of hatred in return. To the extent that our words and our works reflect Christ, we will suffer the hatred reserved for Christ. Laws are being enacted which are increasingly designed to discriminate against Christians in America. Judge Fred Biery handed down his ruling in June 2011 prohibiting public prayer at the graduation ceremony of Medina Valley High School. He explained his ruling in a lengthy order which ended with the words that the order would be "enforced by incarceration or other sanctions for contempt of Court if not obeyed." Judge Samuel Kent from the U.S. District Court in Galveston County, Texas ruled in 1995 that any student who mentioned the name of Jesus in a graduation prayer would go to jail for up to six months! These are high school students who were threatened with incarceration for naming Jesus in public. He wrote in his order that anyone violating his rule "is going to wish that he or she had died as a child when this court gets through with it." The language used clearly expresses hatred not merely a judicial decision.[15] Following Jesus can be expensive.

Identifying with Jesus can be costly especially if we seek to live out the truth of His words and practice the example of His works. A Christian accountant who refuses to sign falsified documents may lose that client. A shipping clerk who knows that merchandise arrived in good condition but was damaged by an accident in the plant may find his faith tested because he refuses to sign a slip for defective merchandise so as to collect from the shipper. I worked in a drug store in Newark when I was a college student and one day my boss answered the telephone. He put his hands over the mouthpiece and motioned me over. "Dave," he said, "tell this guy that I'm not here and you'll take a message." It may have been what many call "a small lie," but as a Christian, I couldn't do it. I said no. The same hours I once had were suddenly not as available, and the responsibilities of my job were less desirable. It was cost on a micro scale, but it was still a cost for following Jesus. A Christian may not get that promotion. You may not get that pay raise. Another may lose a client or worse; someone may even lose his job in the next layoff. These things happen when we name the name of Christ and live it!

The world's irrational hatred demonstrates the sovereignty of God. Jesus said, "They have done this to fulfill the word that is written in their Law, 'They have hated me without cause'." Every event in our lives has a dual purpose. Satan means it to destroy us. God means it to edify us. How we respond to our circumstances makes all the difference in the world. Even the world's irrational, unreasonable hatred for Christ was part of God's sovereign plan to redeem the world from its sinful hatred! There is no rational basis for hatred of Jesus Christ or anything that he does or says. We may reasonably hate what Adolph Hitler did, but hatred of Christ's actions is hatred without a cause. It is irrational. It is unreasonable. Yet even this irrational, unreasonable hatred served God's purpose. It fulfilled Scripture and was part of the sovereignly superintended process which led up to the cross. Christ came to redeem those who hated him, and their hatred was the very means of getting to the cross by which He could redeem the hater.

All of this was part of God's plan to redeem those who did not know Him and hated Him. Jesus apparently quotes from Psalm 35:19.[16] The author of Psalm 35 had treated his enemies with kindness and grace. He had treated the enemies as brothers, yet they had turned His kindness into hatred in return. So Jesus had done. He had come to give people goodness, but they turned His good into evil. They hated Him without cause. He turned their very hatred into His means of redemption.

God's plan is a great encouragement for all of us who name the name of Christ. The opposition we may endure because of our association with Christ is not out of control. In fact, it is part of His sovereign plan for our lives. We may not see the result of all that God is doing here and now, but we can trust that it is all within the scope of what God allows to accomplish His purposes.

Silas was a pastor of a house church in North Vietnam in 2005. The authorities often jailed Christians for meeting without a permit and Silas did not have a permit. An official warned him to watch out because he was meeting illegally. Silas responded, "I don't have to watch out or be careful; God will care for us." He continued by telling the official, "Your persecution has made us stronger." Pastor Silas went on to witness to the official. He said, "You can shut down our churches, jail us, torture us. It doesn't matter because we'll still love you. We'll love you because God loves you and wants to see you come to know Christ's salvation." The official angrily stalked off into the night.

Time passed. Late in the night, Silas heard a knock on the door, and it was the same communist official. He thought he would be arrested for sure, but the man just wanted to talk, so Silas invited him into his home. Tearfully, the man confessed that he was afraid he might lose his job if he did not hurt Christians. He felt mistreated and overlooked at the office. The government was filled with corruption as men advanced by bribery. Silas shared the message of Jesus with this

191

man. That night he put his faith in Christ. Amazing events soon took place. The new Christian was promoted up the chain of command without bribery. He advanced to a high enough position that he knew when and where the raids were scheduled to take place. He would notify the pastor on Saturday the police were coming on Sunday morning so that when the police arrived they never found any Christians at worship because they would meet in the afternoon or night that week.[17]

God knows what He's about!

15
A COMMON CAUSE

John 15:26 - 16:4

What does God do with a world which hates Jesus? God testifies to that world about Jesus anyway. He leaves Himself a witness so that the world has no excuse in the final judgment court of God Almighty. Jesus leaves behind two witnesses to testify to the world about Him. There is the witness of the Holy Spirit and the witness of the disciples, but both witnesses testify to one Savior. The Holy Spirit is the primary witness, and we are the secondary witnesses. The world hates our witness because it hates the witness of the Holy Spirit first.

"The Blasphemy Challenge" was a $25,000 "YouTube" campaign launched by "The Rational Response Squad to entice young people to deny any faith in the God of the Bible. Participants were invited to post a short video blaspheming the Holy Spirit. Once they uploaded their video, they would receive a DVD of the hit documentary, "The God Who Wasn't There." "You may damn yourself to Hell however you would like, but somewhere in your video, you must say this phrase: 'I deny the Holy Spirit,'" wrote the producers of the challenge. Why? Jesus said that blaspheming the Holy Spirit was the unpardonable sin (Mark 3:29). Publicizing the challenge on all the popular sites with teens, they attracted significant attention and rapid response. The distributor of the DVD donated 1001 DVDs to the campaign. All 1001 DVDs were soon awarded to participants in "The Blasphemy Challenge."[1]

OUR SPECIAL FRIEND

Jesus promised us a special friend who is called alongside us to help in our time of need. The word "Helper" (Paraclete) is hard to translate accurately but is best understood as a legal friend, not a spiritual comforter. The word does not mean comforter in the sense of someone who consoles us although it could refer to someone who encourages us. The most normal meaning of this term in the Greek culture was in the context of their legal system. A Paraclete was not so much a professional legal advisor like a lawyer but rather a representative or advocate who speaks on behalf of someone in a court of law. A paraclete was someone who offered legal assistance in the form of testimony on behalf of someone – in other words, a witness![2]

The Holy Spirit is commissioned by the Son to be our personal friend not merely an impersonal force.[3] Jesus sends Him to us from the Father. The Holy Spirit's commission, to borrow a military term, comes from the Son yet the Holy Spirit actually proceeds from the Father. The Holy Spirit is sent on a mission by command of the Son, yet the Holy Spirit comes from the Father as did the Son in the first place. This language guards the tri-unity of God since both the Son and the Spirit proceed from the Father yet are independent of each other.[4] Jesus had said earlier that He would ask the Father to give us a special friend (John 14:16). Who the Father gives, the Son sends. Who the Son sends is by the authority of the Father. Our friend is the answer to Jesus' prayers for us; the gift of our heavenly Father; and the commissioned representative of the Son. He is the Spirit who speaks the truth.[5]

We need a legal friend to speak the truth at all times even when the truth might be unpleasant or inconvenient for us. He points people to Jesus. Jesus says that "He will testify about Me." The verb means to bear witness to, to speak well of, someone.[6] The most important role our special friend has in our lives is to point us constantly to Jesus. The Spirit of God is the shy member of the Trinity. He does not call attention to Himself but prefers to work backstage – behind the scenes – to magnify Jesus (John 16:14). Any work on earth that is truly Spirit directed, Spirit energized and Spirit stimulated will emphasize Jesus

194

Christ over the Holy Spirit. His job is to witness on behalf of Jesus to a world that hates Jesus.

We often end up speaking about the Holy Spirit as if He is merely a power source. We even use illustrations, I have used them myself, that convey a certain level of truth about the Holy Spirit – like a car engine or electrical power which must be activated to be usable – but also contribute to a misunderstanding of the Holy Spirit. In this way of thinking, the Holy Spirit is sort of a reservoir of potential energy or power for us to use as we try to live the Christian life. Such thinking, while not entirely wrong, is misleading because it teaches us to think of the Holy Spirit as our servant instead of the God we worship. The truth is that He uses us. We do not use Him. He is fully God after all, and God is bearing witness to God. To make the Holy Spirit merely the power source available by our choice – flip a switch and He is there – is to misunderstand the Holy Spirit. He changes us. He doesn't simply wait for us to turn on His power switch. Such thinking reduces the Holy Spirit to someone less than God.

There is a functional subordination within the triune Godhead. There is structure and order. The three persons of the Godhead do not do whatever they please. The Father, Son, and Holy Spirit are all equally, co-equally, God, yet there is a chain of command among them which is theologically significant. The Father is always in charge. The Son is second in command, and the Spirit is always third, so we speak of the persons of the Godhead as first, second and third.

This theological point makes a great deal of difference. Each has a job to do. The Father sent the Son to die. Neither the Father nor the Spirit is our Savior. Only Jesus is the savior. While He came to die, the Spirit came to witness to His Saviorhood. Furthermore, the Son is always incarnate, meaning that He took up residence in human form. He is localized. The Spirit is not incarnate. The Son returns to heaven, but the Spirit is commissioned for a ministry on earth. There is always an important differentiation of the persons of the Godhead, yet all are equally God, and there is only one God. This theology is orthodox Christianity.

WITNESSES FOR JESUS

How, then, does the Holy Spirit testify on behalf of the Son? One way is through us. The Holy Spirit witnesses by witnessing through us. He is the primary witness, but we are the secondary witnesses (15:27). Jesus

195

said, "but you also must testify" indicating that we witness in addition to, or as a secondary witness to, the Spirit's witness. There is a "must" to this statement. It is not said that the Holy Spirit "must testify" for there is no question but He will, but it is said that we must testify. We have an obligation to bear witness to Christ as well. I take great comfort in the order of these verses. I have a responsibility to witness, but my neighbor's salvation does not depend upon my witness. Witnesses don't manufacture information or persuade the jury. Witnesses are persuasive to the extent that they accurately express the truth. That is our obligation.

Early in ministry, I was out on visitation for our church in New Jersey, and I talked to this one young man in his kitchen for three or four hours. It was one of the most frustrating experiences in evangelism that I have ever had. I knew that I did not have the gift of evangelism after that! The man was very interested. He wanted to know more. He asked lots of questions. He acknowledged his sin, but he just couldn't come to the point of making a decision. I felt obligated to persuade him and tried every argument I could muster, but it was all without fruit. Why? I was trying to pick a green apple. It was not the Holy Spirit's time. I have no idea what happened to that man, but I would be willing to bet that two years later he is talking to a friend for five minutes who says, "you know you need Jesus" and "wham!" He believes. Someone is going to walk away saying, "Wow! Who said evangelism is hard? This guy just believed in five minutes, and I didn't do a thing." That's right. Why? It is the work of the Holy Spirit to open blind eyes and set the captives free. We can't do it. All too often we are trying to drag people by the scruff of the neck, kicking and screaming, into the Kingdom, but God is always patient because He knows the heart better than we do. We do so much damage when we try to pick green apples instead of waiting until they ripen in the hands of the Holy Spirit.

Bill (Mac) MacDougall had been coming to our church for a year or two with his wife, Margie. His son was an active member in our fellowship and told me that, while his mother was a believer, his father was not. Still he came. He asked me if I would ride with him to see his brother who was dying of cancer in a town an hour away because he was concerned that he talk with a pastor. I joined Mac and Margie for the drive. We arrived, and I soon discovered that he had recently come to Christ through a local pastor. Mac's brother shared openly about his new faith, and I could see that His unexpected witness moved Mac. We headed home with Mac driving. Margie and I were conversing when Mac suddenly broke in to share that he didn't know where he would go if he were to die. I began talking to him about faith in Christ. He became quite emotional. The car began to weave on the country road as he tried to focus on my words while driving. I suggested that perhaps we should wait until we got home to finish our talk. I was ready to meet God but perhaps not that night! He agreed. Soon we sat together in his kitchen, and he put his faith in Jesus as his Savior and Lord. He was later baptized and has continued as a faithful member of our church even after his wife, Margie, went to be with the Lord. I asked Mac why he kept coming to church for so long before he was a Christian. He told me that he came because I explained the Bible to him. He was tired of people always trying to "get him saved," but I just explained what the Bible said. The Holy Spirit was at work over time to draw Mac to Jesus.[7]

There are three major commands of the Lord in John 15. *Abide in Me* (15:4). To abide is my vertical responsibility. I am to keep a close walk and open fellowship with the Lord unhindered by sin. *Love each other* (15:12). To love is my obligation to other members of the family of God whether they are part of my local church or not. *Witness to the world* (15:27). To witness is my responsibility to those around me who do not know Jesus Christ.

Friends join in a common cause. The cause binds the friendship together. The intimacy of friendship develops as we stand shoulder to shoulder on a mission. C.S. Lewis wrote, "Lovers are always talking to one another about their love; Friends hardly ever about their Friendship. Lovers are normally face to face, absorbed in each other; Friends, side by side, absorbed in some common interests."[8] Jesus calls us to carry out a mission to reach this world with His message. His mission is our mission. The intimacy of our friendship with Him grows as we band together with each other to carry out His mission. We diminish our friendship with Him when we become absorbed with each other instead of being absorbed together in His mission. I do not mean to suggest that we cease to care about each other as we pursue our common cause. The opposite is true. The cause enhances our friendship. Jesus calls the church to be a community of His friends who share a common cause, and His Spirit, our special friend, binds us together in friendship as He empowers us to carry out His mission.

A healthy church, Jesus' community of friends, is outreach oriented. If we are not constantly reaching out to our community in tangible ways, then we are a dying church. Ingrown churches who focus on their personal wants will die. It is a recipe for decline. We tend to sit inside our little cocoons and point fingers at the world around us from the safety of our haven, but let one of those people come into our church, and we don't like it. They don't use the right language. They don't wear the right clothes. Jesus reached out in love toward the demoniac who was running around without any clothes on at all. Jesus loved him as he was making even nakedness an acceptable dress code for sinners to whom we witness, as one writer observed tongue in cheek.

I was in Panama teaching a group of pastors in a conference when the subject of reaching the Guyami Indians came up. The men were notorious for an immoral lifestyle. There was no formal marriage in their culture. If a man walked by and nodded at a woman she followed him into his home and became his "wife." Later he might leave her and nod at another woman. Since the Guyami had no formal marriage or divorce, the courts did not recognize their marriages as legal which left the church in a dilemma. How should we deal with such people in the church? Our conclusion was that we can't ask people to give up their sin before they come to church, but Christ would bring the changes necessary in their lives. I said that a Guyami man will need to learn to stop nodding at women once he becomes Christian! When Christ cleans us up, we are not the same again. When we start asking people to clean themselves up before they come to church, and before we will love them, how can we expect to reach people for Christ? When we get serious about reaching people for Christ, our comfort zones will be stretched out of our conservative, suburban, middle class, comfortable Christianity.

WHO IS THE SOUL WINNER?

I sat under the teaching of a brilliant and godly professor named John Whitcomb in seminary. He told us that he used to travel the country debating skeptics on university campuses regarding creation and the God who created our universe. He stopped. He told us that he found it counter-productive. He pointed out that the debate was often "no contest!" He could argue the skeptic "under the table." He could win the argument but lose the person. Which was more important, winning the battle or winning the war? We have not converted a person just because we can shut them up!

The reality is that most people come to Christ not because of an expert pastor or teacher but because of the witness of a spouse, close friend, co-worker or neighbor. The greatest testimony to your sphere of relationships is you! We must start with our theology. The primary witness is the Holy Spirit. We are only the secondary witnesses. He uses us. We don't use Him. God chooses to use the average and the normal among us to do His extraordinary work. God chooses to use our friendships to draw people to the friend of sinners, Jesus Christ. He works through us and sometimes in spite of us! That takes the burden off from our shoulders. It is not the brilliance of our arguments, but the persuasiveness of the Spirit that wins souls to Christ. It is not our skill at evangelism which wins souls for heaven. It is the Spirit of God working through our feeble efforts to transform lives. We need to be ourselves and reach out to others with the message of Jesus. We should not try to be clever and brilliant in our arguments. We should be "real." Phonies are easily spotted by people.

I worked for four years in a factory after I graduated from Bible College. The education I received working the graveyard and evening shifts in that factory proved to be as important to my growth as any class I took in college. I learned to understand people. One man I worked with was a skeptic. He often ridiculed Christianity. He was clever and cynical. He thought Christians were nothing more than hypocrites even though I'm not sure he had ever had a friendship with a real Christian. I chose not to try and answer all his arguments but rather to become his friend. He was a smart, funny and compassionate man despite his antagonism to Christianity. We developed a friendship and, in time, he softened his attacks on Christianity when he found out he couldn't offend me. He began to listen more when I shared Jesus with him and didn't immediately make fun of what I believed. In time, he invited me to come to his home to talk about Christianity "off duty." We had many conversations over coffee that delved into faith more deeply. Slowly he moved from his cynical skepticism to an openness to faith in Jesus. I moved away to go to seminary before we could solidify his embryonic faith, but God, the Holy Spirit, was clearly at work in his heart, and I expect to see him in heaven one day. God, not me, will finish the work He began in that man's heart.

AVOIDING THE BAIT STICK

According to legend, a young girl was trudging along a mountain path to her grandmother's house. It was bitterly cold. When she was within sight of her grandmother's house, she heard a rustle at her feet and looked down. She saw a snake trying to stay warm. The snake said to her, "I am about to die. It is too cold for me up here in the mountains, and I am starving. Please put me under your coat, and take me with you." "NO!" replied the girl. "I know your kind. You are a rattlesnake. If I pick you up, you will bite me, and your bite is poisonous." The snake objected, "No, No. If you help me, I will treat you differently." The little girl sat down on a rock to rest and think. She looked at the snake and had to admit it was the most beautiful snake she had ever seen. Suddenly, she said, "I believe you. I will save you." The little girl reached over, put the snake gently under her coat and proceeded toward her grandmother's house. Within a moment, she felt a sharp pain in her side. The snake had bitten her. "How could you do this to me?" she cried. "You promised that you would not bite me, and I trusted you!" "You knew what I was when you picked me up," hissed the snake as he slithered away. Jesus said in John 16:1, "All these things I have spoken to you, that you may be kept from stumbling." Yet, so often, we still pick up the snake and play with it never realizing the danger in which we place ourselves. We mean well but the results are devastating.

Why did Jesus warn us about suffering and persecution in this world? He wanted us to expect hardship so that we might not stumble under the pressure. The Greek word for stumble is the word from which we get our English word "scandal" or "scandalize." Jesus warns us so that we will not be scandalized by the sufferings we experience in life. It is a fascinating word which was used of a bait stick holding up a rock or a deadfall trap for small animals.[9] The trap was a crooked stick which, when pulled, brought the trap down on the unsuspecting victim. The word was also used for a snare or a net. The word could be used to describe a military strategy to entrap soldiers and even something like a wolf pit which men would fall into when they were not careful. The word later came to mean a stone or other obstacle over which a person tripped and fell. All of this leads to the general meaning, *cause to ruin or destroy* a person's life.[10]

The verb meant "cause to sin" (to fall) and in the passive meant being led into sin through unbelief or apostasy.[11] A professing Christian is scandalized when pressure entices him to fall away from the truth he once clung to by faith. In the parable of the soils, the seed that fell on the rocky soil sprouted quickly (Mt. 13:20-21). The person received the gospel with joy "yet he has no root in himself, but is temporary, and, when affliction or persecution arises because of the word, immediately he falls away." Pressure causes the person to strike the bait stick in his agitation and be crushed by the enemy's trap. Jesus predicted that there will come times of persecution (pressure) when Christians will be hated. "At that time, many will fall away and will betray one another and hate one another" (Mt. 24:9-10). The lie that God promises us prosperity and popularity is Satan's bait stick leading many to fall away from Christ.

Avoid the bait stick! How? We must remember Jesus' warning that suffering, pressure, and persecution will come to us (John 16:4) so we will be prepared to face the hardships with faith. As the saying goes, "forewarned is forearmed." The best defense against the scandal of suffering is to expect the suffering. If we are not prepared for hardship, we will fall away and cause others to stumble with us. After Jesus told the disciples that He would suffer and be killed, Peter vehemently objected. Peter told Jesus not to think this way (Mt. 16:21-22). Bad things wouldn't happen to Jesus because God wouldn't let them happen according to Peter. I recognize my own false trust in this same bait stick many times. Peter was the epitome of positive thinking. Jesus called him, "Satan," and said that Peter was a bait stick in Satan's trap because he was not setting his "mind on God's interests but on man's" (Mt. 16:23).

John Lennox draws an analogy to a road map.[12] We don't need road maps when the road is broad and well-lit with clear signs marking the turns for us. We need road maps when the way gets confusing, rough and dark. A good map is helpful when confusion sets in or the traffic is so intense that we have little time to choose our turns on the road of life. Then we can use the advance information that Jesus gives us in these verses. We don't have to be surprised by the sudden turns in life or the pressure of traffic that stresses our choices. We are at war, and Satan's strategy is to destroy us, to ruin us. Pressure is the devil's bait stick to destroy us.

Christianity is the hardest life you could lead. If you want an easy life, don't become a Christian. The devil will use every bait stick possible to destroy you. He will even use our best intentions as bait sticks to spring the trap, but the fundamental means for entrapping Christians is pressure! Pressure forces us into poor choices. Pressure drives us to make stupid decisions. An animal which is very hungry is more likely to take the bait, and a Christian under pressure is a prime target for the enemy.

FORMS OF PRESSURE

Jesus identifies two primary forms of pressure and the reason behind that pressure (16:2-3). Jesus said, "they will make you outcasts from the synagogue." This pressure is social persecution. One Greek word translates this phrase, "outcasts from the synagogue." The word meant to excommunicate someone, to place them outside the context of the synagogue. It was not like they could just go to another synagogue and worship. It was far more devastating than that. The synagogue was not just the religious center of Jewish life in each city; it was the cultural, economic and social center of life as well. The person was cut off from friends and family who could not eat or talk with him. He was banned from the Jewish community so that he would lose his job. If he were self-employed, his customers would leave. He would even be refused the right of an honorable burial.

Such excommunication could occur for a variety of offenses. In the Jewish community of Qumran, a man could be excommunicated for thirty days for falling asleep in the worship service! If he interrupted a speaker, he could get ten days, and it was three months for talking foolishly. Such expulsions were temporary, but permanent excommunication was enforced for leaving a congregation and speaking against the synagogue. You could be permanently expelled if you gave food or property to someone who had previously been expelled.[13]

In much the same way, the devil still works today. Employees at the Johnson Space Center had gathered during their lunch hour to pray, sing and study the Bible. The JSC Praise & Worship Club announced the theme of their next meeting in the Space Center's newsletter on May 28, 2015, as "Jesus is our life." Attorneys for NASA called the organizers and told them that they could not use the name "Jesus" in any announcements because it was deemed "sectarian" and would cause NASA to violate the

First Amendment of the Constitution. No more Jesus allowed at NASA![14] Satan often uses social and economic pressure to force us into positions of compromise. When we are cut off from our social support system and our jobs are threatened so that we could suffer financial ruin then we become prime candidates for sinful decisions. We need to know that strategy and be alert to how the Devil will work to destroy us.

The second form of pressure which Jesus mentions is physical persecution. Jesus said "An hour is coming for everyone who kills you to imagine he offers a sacrificial service to God." The word which is translated "service" here is a common word in the OT for the Passover. It was commonly used for sacrificial service, meaning priestly service connected to the sacrifices. The word is only used five times in the NT but three of those times it is directly connected to sacrifices. This is the word used in Romans 12:1 where Paul wrote: "I beseech you, therefore, brethren, by the mercies of God that you present your bodies a living and holy sacrifice acceptable to God which is your reasonable service." The concept of sacrifice clings to the word. Jesus is saying here that people will kill Christians as human sacrifices to God. It sounds barbaric, but church history bears out the truth of this prediction.

Balthasar Hubmaier was a brilliant theologian in the 1500's. He had a Doctor of Theology degree and taught at the University of Ingolstadt. He resigned his positions and became an Anabaptist. The Anabaptists were called that because they believed in baptizing again, which is what the word Anabaptist means. In other words, they did not believe in infant baptism but believed in baptizing only believing adults. The Anabaptist movement produced the Mennonites, Brethren, Baptists and Quakers in the modern world. In 1526, Balthasar Hubmaier was arrested by the town council of Zurich under the direction of Ulrich Zwingli another Protestant reformer but one who believed in infant baptism. Hubmaier was tortured on the rack until he recanted. He moved to Moravia to lead another Anabaptist church but was captured in 1528, this time by the Roman Catholics, and burned at the stake. His wife was dropped into the Danube river with a stone around her neck. All in the name of service to God.[15]

Why? This pressure is spiritual persecution (16:3). "People who do these things have not known the Father or me," Jesus says. Such actions are inconsistent with any real knowledge of God no matter how religious people might be. This was a slap in the face to the Jewish leaders of Jesus' day who prided themselves on knowing God. Throughout this discourse, Jesus has been saying that a person does not really know God until they know Him, Jesus Christ because to know Jesus Christ is to know the Father. Jesus said, "I am the way, the truth, and the life, no man comes to the Father but by me."

No matter what religious banner people use, persecution of Christians demonstrates that a person does not know God. Does this mean that anyone who persecutes Christians is beyond hope? Not at all. Saul was on the way to kill Christians and had been killing Christians when he met Jesus Christ, believed and became Paul the great preacher of the gospel. But such persecution demonstrates that we are engaged in spiritual warfare. People are misguided and ignorant of God when they persecute Christians.

Just because someone is very religious and does much in the name of God does not mean that they are following God's word. We need that warning today. Satan is so skillful at using religion and religious leaders to destroy Christians and bring them to ruin. Jesus tells us all of this so that we will be prepared to face the enemy in this war. Pressure is the devil's bait stick, but preparation is the Savior's solution (16:4). To paraphrase what Jesus says to us: "I am telling you these things now so that you will remember that I prepared you when their hour comes. I didn't tell you this earlier because I was with you and their anger was directed at me. Now the Devil will no longer be able to get at me so you will become his prime targets. Be ready. Be prepared."

Xiao Biguang came to Christ after the Tiananmen Square massacre in 1989. A Chinese intellectual, he quickly attracted attention with his preaching of Christ and was arrested in April of 1994. His trial took place April 10, 1995, and he was not seen for years. Periodically, Chinese officials came to his wife Gou Qinghui and asked for money for her husband whom she had not seen in two years. Gou lost her teaching position at a government sponsored theological seminary, was detained by police four times and remained under close police surveillance for years.[16]

Sergey, a Christian from the Ukraine, experienced the dramatic "Orange Revolution" that brought down the corrupt government in 2004. Christians organized prayer gatherings to teach one another to pray. He writes, "Most of us have only known the long, formal, boring prayers we hear in churches. We are just now discovering the privilege of talking to God as to a friend!" He speaks of the struggles that many have gone through during the Communist years. A friend from Moldova would tell his atheist parents that he needed to use the outhouse but would jump over the fence to pray with a neighbor. Christians chopped through the ice to baptize new believers in frozen lakes. They distributed Christian literature that had been smuggled into the country through their secret network. Many pastors spent time in prison. Yet now that they have the freedom, Sergey is afraid that they are becoming complacent in their faith. He says, "It seems we handle persecution better than prosperity."[17]

We do not face that kind of pressure in our culture yet! It could come. We do face pressure in a variety of other ways designed to attack our faith. We tend to think that a ministry or a movement is God's only when it is numerically successful. The "prosperity gospel" is perniciously popular in America. Such thinking leads us to expect success and not defeat, so when hard times come and the struggles begin in our Christian lives, we can easily fall into the traps of the enemy through despair.

What happens when things don't go well in our business or personal lives? What happens when we are cut off from good sound spiritual advice, or worse, we cut ourselves off and refuse to take the advice? When we struggle to keep all those plates spinning – and some come crashing down – do we despair? When the pressures of physical, material, mental, social or emotional problems threaten to destroy us, will we blame God? Will we turn our backs on Him and fall into the pit which Satan has dug for us?

Persecution is not the only way that the Devil can destroy faith. Pressures of all kinds and shapes are favorite weapons to bring us to the point of making sinful decisions. Our expectations of success can make the fall even more devastating spiritually. We do not always find God's success in the spotlight. It may come in the back alleys and the dark corners of this world where people labor unknown and unseen.

C.T. Studd was born a wealthy man in England. He was gifted athletically and was known for those athletic skills all over the country. Educated at Cambridge University, he turned his back on his wealth and served Christ for decades in China and later in Africa. He wrote:

> Some want to live within the sound
> of church or chapel bell;
> I want to build a rescue shop
> within a yard of hell.

We need that same kind of passion for faithfulness — a passion that looks at the horrible problems and struggles and says, "I remember. I remember that Jesus said it would be this way. I remember that Jesus said that it would be hard. We're on the winning side, and I must be ready for every attack. I must be smart enough to recognize the attack because God's road is not the easy road around the mountain but the tough road right over the top of the mountain!"

We are most ready for battle when we most expect the attack!

FINAL LINKS TO
DEEPER LOVE

16
FOR OUR GOOD!

John 16:5-7

I am like James and John.
Lord, I turn to you
to get the inside track
and obtain special favors,
your direction for my schemes,
your power for my projects,
your sanction for my ambitions,
your blank checks for whatever I want.
I am like James and John.[1]

Jesus has more users than followers today. We use Jesus to sanctify our success and stimulate our worship experiences. Blinded by our self-interests, we often seek a Jesus who serves our needs and promises our prosperity. Our hearts grow restless and bored unless the sermon shows us quickly how Jesus can meet our wants now – today – at this moment! We care more about our earthly Jesus than our heavenly Lord. We are using Jesus more than following Jesus.

Jesus saw these tendencies in His first disciples as well. He wistfully said, "Now I am going to Him who sent Me; and none of you asks Me, 'Where are you going?'" (John 16:5). Peter had just asked Jesus that very question only a few hours earlier (John 13:36). How do we harmonize the two verses? What is the question Jesus longs to hear from us?

Some have suggested that the answer is in the present tense of the verb "ask" as if Jesus was saying that no one was asking Him the question at that precise moment. He was not thinking of what Peter said hours earlier that evening. However, such a solution seems a bit disingenuous, as if Jesus cared more about the timing of the question than the heart of the questioner. It gives me the impression that Jesus is groveling as if trying to evoke sympathy the way we do many times.

Peter had asked the right question with the wrong motives. Jesus knew Peter had asked the question that Peter cared about instead of asking the question Jesus wanted Peter to care about. The words are the same, but the intent is so very different. Peter didn't care about the destination of Jesus only that he felt abandoned by Jesus, and it led to a false bravado in his infamous pledge. The disciples were devastated that Jesus was leaving them (John 16:6). They were not interested in the plans of Jesus only the loss they feared for themselves. They only cared about the problems for them not the purposes of the Lord.[2] They were not concerned with His plan. They were obsessed with their loss. They felt abandoned by someone they loved. They felt the sting of rejection. And that is all they could see.

THE HEART OF THE QUESTIONER

We, too, seek selfish answers for life on earth not serious inquiries to understand the glories of our Lord in heaven. When my daughter, Katie, was a child I could tell her that we will take this Saturday to go to the playground or ride bikes. Saturday comes, and she is excited about the plans. Then the telephone rings. It is an emergency, and I have to go to the hospital or the office. She asks, "Where are you going?" Now she is not concerned with where I am going at all. She cares about her loss, not my destination. She cares about her expectations, not my plans. It is the same with us. We suffer a loss in one form or another. In that loss, Jesus is trying to teach us about Himself, about His plans, about His character and His future for us. All we care about is our loss. In the midst of His teaching we, like the disciples, say: "Yeah, what about me?" Instead we should be saying: "Lord, tell me more about you! What do you want me to learn about your plans, your goals, your purposes for my life?"

Jesus cares more about the heart of the questioner than the form of the question. A follower of Jesus wants to know everything there is to know about Him and His eternal purposes even if the knowledge is not immediately applicable to his earthly situation. A user of Jesus only cares to know what will meet his problems in that specific moment and cares little to know that which is not an immediate life app! What drives our questions shows the shallowness – or depth – of our relationship with Jesus. We experience deeper love for Jesus as we learn to care about His plans, not our losses. As long as we can only see our loss, we will never enjoy a deeper love with Him.

The disciples had built up such great expectations for the future. Jesus is blowing those expectations away. They knew that Jesus had powerful enemies. They knew that there was unrest, criticism and attack but they had faith! They were confident. They believed that Jesus would take care of all of those problems because they were kingdom bound. It would all work out, and everything would be fine. Now Jesus was telling them that it wasn't going to work out. The enemies would win. One of their own would betray Him. He would die! He was leaving them, and they couldn't come where he was going. Their confidence was shattered. Their bravado was gone. Faith turned to doubt and despair.

We are prone to overconfidence. Studies have long demonstrated the Achilles Heel of human thinking. We overestimate our knowledge, our skills, and our expectations.

> 90% of drivers consider themselves above average.
> 94% of college professors think they are above average professors.
> 90% of entrepreneurial business owners believe their business will be successful.
> 98% of students taking SAT tests say they have average or above leadership skills.
> 99% of people in the computer industry overestimated their knowledge before taking a test.[3]

We build up our expectations for success so high that the fall is devastating. We think that if we have enough faith, everything will work

211

out, and it doesn't work out. We fall into the pit of despair. Our emotions fill us with rage and grief to the point where we are blinded by our self-absorption. We cannot see that God has a greater purpose in all of this, and so we run away. We quit.

Elijah is "Exhibit A." He has that mountain top experience with the 400 prophets of Baal. He challenged the false prophets to a duel of the gods in front of thousands of Israelites and King Ahab. God wins. Fire consumes the sacrifice and altar. The people rise up and kill the 400 false prophets. Rain comes after three years of God predicted drought. But the next day finds Elijah running for his life in the Judean wilderness crippled by his emotions, thinking he alone was left of all God's people. We get so melodramatic in our thinking when we let our emotions run wild, don't we?

Many commentators tell us that Elijah ran in fear from the terrible Jezebel. It is possible, but I don't think so. I don't think that the prophet who stood before the king many times and defied the 400 prophets of Baal would so easily turn tail and run even from a powerful woman. I believe he was driven by a much more powerful emotion than just fear. He ran in despair. He ran in discouragement.

After his triumph on the top of Mount Carmel, Elijah tells Ahab to ride his chariot home for the long promised rains are coming. Elijah, on foot, overtakes the chariot pulled by powerful horses. He runs ahead of the chariot into the city of Jezreel (2 Kings 18:46). We picture an athlete of "Olympic" skills outrunning horses, but I think we might be missing the point. The Hebrew could be translated that way but is better understood as "running before Ahab until you are coming to Jezreel."[4] In other words, he ran in front of the chariot, not in a competitive sprint but a triumphal procession. The position of a runner before the chariot was a position of honor in the culture. The honored warrior was leading his king into the city.

Elijah believed that God had won a great victory. He knew Ahab to be a weak, politically correct king who feared Jezebel, his wicked wife, and her powerful minions. He had sold himself on the altar of expediency. Elijah thought, "At last. We have won. The King is going to put Jezebel in her place. He is going to tell her where she can go. He is going to kick her derriere right out of the palace. Elijah goes dancing home that night to celebrate the victory. The next day, Elijah gets a private message from Jezebel (2 Kings 19:2). She is no fool. She is a master politician. It is a private threat because Elijah is in no real public danger right now. The note reads: "You know what happened to those prophets. May the same happen to me if I don't get you first!" The Hebrew says, that Elijah "saw" and ran.[5] He saw the truth. And He ran, not so much in fear. He ran in the prospect of success gone sour! Her threat shattered his overconfidence.

> When is it going to end, Lord? When will that woman be gone? When do we win, Lord? Where are you, God? What has happened to your kingdom?

Elijah ran the way many of us run when emotions cloud our vision. He went AWOL in the middle of battle. So do we. We forget a basic spiritual lesson. Great gain comes from great loss when it serves a greater purpose. We think we are all alone in the fight. We cannot understand, like Elijah in Israel and the disciples at the cross, that Jesus has a greater purpose, and, if we would just stop letting our emotions run wild, we might begin to see His plan instead of our loss.

ABSENT BUT PRESENT

Jesus raises a perplexing question in the minds of the disciples. Why is it better for Jesus to leave them than to stay with them? Up until now, He has walked and talked with them; taught them and showed them how to live; and encouraged and strengthened them with His presence. How could it possibly be better for their friend and teacher to leave them now? Jesus said it. It must be true (John 16:7).

Jesus tells his followers that it is to our "advantage" that he goes away. Jesus says it is profitable, or expedient, for them that He go away.[6] It is the same word which Caiaphas, the Jewish High Priest used in John 11:50.[7] The Jewish Sanhedrin was debating what to do with Jesus. They were worried that the Romans would take away their political power if he continued to excite the people. So Caiaphas stood up and made a speech in which he said, "You leaders are so ignorant that you don't realize it is expedient (profitable) that one man should die for the people so that the whole nation should not perish." Caiaphas thought it was expedient for Jesus to die, and so it was, but not for the reasons he was considering. It is more profitable that Jesus go away because He goes away to die so they might live. God uses the wicked acts of human expediency to accomplish His perfect purposes in this world. Jesus and Caiaphas agree. He must go away. He must die.

The self-absorbed disciples did not grasp the greater purposes behind Jesus' departure. Jesus had come to die. The cross was God's purpose for Him from before time began. He was also leaving them so the Holy Spirit, the Helper, could come. The Spirit's purpose in coming was to glorify Christ, but the Spirit must have a glorified Christ to glorify (John 7:39). The ascension of Jesus, following His cross work, glorified Him. He left to be glorified, and the Holy Spirit continues to magnify Him as the risen Lord. The glorification of Jesus leads to the empowering of the disciples through the Holy Spirit.

The personal presence of Jesus would eventually hinder the personal growth of the disciples and the expansion of His kingdom on earth. As long as Jesus remained in bodily form, His presence was limited to His physical location on earth. Omnipresent indwelling was only possible if Jesus left them and ascended into heaven as the glorified Christ. It was better for Jesus to depart so that He could always be with them as they scattered around the globe (Mt. 28:20) through the presence of His Helper wherever they might be.

Jesus goes on to say that He must go away from this world to a new world because if He does not leave this world the Holy Spirit, the Paraclete, the one called alongside us, cannot come to us. Simply put, the Holy Spirit cannot come to fulfill His new commission until Jesus goes away because Jesus must send Him and the sender cannot send someone somewhere until the sender is no longer there! The Holy Spirit does not merely replace the absence of Jesus on earth. He completes His presence in our lives.[8] We can experience the depths of spiritual intimacy with Jesus in our lives because Jesus departed and the Holy Spirit arrived. The Holy Spirit fills our daily lives with the empowering presence of Jesus in ways that would be impossible if Jesus still walked this earth.

Why must the Lord go away before the Spirit comes? There are three good theological reasons why it is necessary.

1. Christ's physical presence hinders our spiritual growth (Jn. 16:12-13; Acts 1:8; 4:31). The disciples must avoid becoming dependent on His bodily presence because Jesus could only be in one place at one time in bodily form. Jesus had a worldwide vision for what he was going to accomplish. The book of Acts teaches us that the Holy Spirit supplies the

power to reach the world for Christ. Jesus tells us in John 16:12-13 that there are some lessons he cannot teach them now because they are not ready. The Holy Spirit will teach them these lessons.

The best education is on-the-job training. Some lessons cannot be learned in advance. In fact, some spiritual lessons simply could not be learned if the visible presence of Christ was in our midst. If Christ walked and taught in our midst, it would be difficult to learn to walk by faith because we would be walking by sight. We would have him here before us to show us what to do in each situation. Real spiritual maturity comes when we can follow the invisible master as He guides us through each turn in life. We must make our decisions on faith, not sight.

Our daughter, Katie, learned to ski through the Maine Handicapped Ski program. I often watched the instructors as they taught the students to ski. The ones who amazed me were the blind skiers! The blind skier wore a bright pink vest and stayed directly behind the instructor as they went down the mountainside. The instructor called out each turn and told them how to make the turn. The blind skier could not see the instructor, so he had to listen closely to the instructions and stay right behind the instructor. The blind skier had to trust and obey the instructor without hesitation. In John 16, Jesus is telling us that the Holy Spirit will be like the ski instructor calling out the turns of life that lay ahead. We must listen carefully and go by faith.

2. The work of the Spirit depends on the cross work of Christ (Jn. 15:26; 16:8-9; Acts 2:33). The cross is the grand essential of the Christian faith. Salvation only comes by the cross of the Christ who dies in our place. The commission of the Holy Spirit is to apply the blood of Christ to human lives so that we can have eternal life. The Spirit cannot testify to the cross work of Jesus Christ until Jesus has completed His cross work. He must die for the Spirit to testify about His death.

3. The Holy Spirit must have a glorified Christ to glorify (Jn. 7:39; 16:14). The ministry of the Holy Spirit is to bring glory to Christ but, until Jesus has completed His ministry, He has no glory. That is why in John 17:5 He pleads with the Father to have His glory back. Each person of the Trinity has a job to do. Jesus must do His job first before the Holy Spirit can do His job, so one follows the other. The result is to our advantage,

our profit. We are always better off if we will let God accomplish His purposes in our lives. Our gain rests on God's purpose.

We achieve our greatest glory as we live in total dependence on the Spirit. God's Spirit energizes our lives to accomplish His goals. He is Christ's parting gift to us that makes our lives significant and our works meaningful. The Holy Spirit makes His home in us transforming the ugliness of what we are into the beauty of who Jesus is. It is far, far better that Jesus went away so that the Spirit could make our lives His home. Following Jesus by the power of the Spirit is for our good no matter what our circumstances.

Philip Yancey saw the presence of God's Spirit transforming the life of a suffering woman on a trip he and his wife, Janet, made to Nepal. They were touring the Green Pastures Hospital where leprosy patients are rehabilitated. He noticed in the courtyard one of the ugliest humans he had ever seen. Her body had been deformed by the ravages of leprosy with stumps for feet and a face that had been hollowed out by the disease. Bandaged and blind she pulled herself across the courtyard on her elbows, dragging her body behind. He pulled away, repulsed, but Janet never hesitated. She bent low and put her arm around the woman. The woman laid her head on Janet's shoulder and quietly began to sing in Nepali, "Jesus loves me, this I know, for the Bible tells me so." The language was unfamiliar but the tune unmistakable. The physical therapist informed them that her name was Dahnmaya and she came every day to the chapel at the hospital to pray and welcome visitors to the hospital. Philip Yancey took a picture of Dahnmaya and Janet, which he keeps near his desk as a reminder because, not long after they left, they heard that Dahnmaya had died. Yancey writes:

> Whenever I feel polluted by the beauty-obsessed celebrity culture that I live in ... I pull out that photo. I see two beautiful women: my wife, smiling sweetly, wearing a brightly colored Nepali outfit she had bought the day before, holding in her arms an old crone who would flunk any beauty test ever devised except the one that matters most. Out of that deformed, hollow shell of a body, the light of God's presence shines out. The Holy Spirit found a home.[9]

216

17
PROSECUTING ATTORNEY

John 16:8-11

Bramwell Booth, who succeeded his father as General of the Salvation Army, once asked one of his officers about his conversion. "How did you come into the army?" His story was remarkable. The man was in a horrible state one evening as he wandered through Hyde Park in London. He noticed a large crowd that had gathered around a speaker. The man listened to the speaker for a few minutes and then, bored, he started to walk away. At that precise moment, the speaker shouted: "Now, remember what I said," and he quoted a Bible verse which meant nothing to the man. He shouted in a loud voice, "John three and sixteen." The words, "John three and sixteen," shocked the man. He went home, and all he could think about were those words. He could remember nothing else that was said, but he could not get those words out of his head. He couldn't sleep and finally, in desperation, he turned to Christ for salvation. Booth asked him "what was there about the words "John three and sixteen" that convicted you? Well, you see, Chief," the man replied, "my name is John, I have been married three times, and I have sixteen children!"[1]

The Holy Spirit certainly has unique ways of getting the attention of people and convicting them of their needs. We do not always understand how He works, but we see the results of His work in human lives. Jesus predicted that the Holy Spirit "when He comes, will convict the world." Here is the one place in Scripture where the Holy Spirit is said to perform a work *in the world.*[2] The word *convict* is a key word for understanding His role in the world. We have seen that the Holy Spirit is an encourager and defender of believers. We know the Holy Spirit is our defense attorney, but the world cannot know the Holy Spirit in this way. In John 14:17 Jesus said that the He is "the Spirit of truth, whom the world cannot receive, because it does not ... Know Him, but you know Him because He abides with you and shall be in you." The Holy Spirit is our defense attorney, but He is the world's prosecuting attorney.

The word convict means to convince, meaning that the Holy Spirit convinces humans so that they acknowledge their guilt. A common use of the word in a legal setting in the first century meant to convict in the sense of bringing to light the true character of a person and his conduct whether or not he ever acknowledges that character or conduct.[3] The Holy Spirit convicts the whole world. He does not convert the whole world. The verb was used in a legal setting meaning "to cross-examine for the purpose of convincing or refuting an opponent."[4] The Holy Spirit is not the judge or the jury. He is the prosecuting attorney who exposes the truth. The prosecutor's role is to prove sin, righteousness and judgment to the world whether the world changes or not. The prosecutor proves the guilt to the world so the world can see where they stand before God. The guilty verdict has already been pronounced on the world (Jn. 3:18, 36), but the world needs to be convicted of their guilt before they will ever accept a Savior.[5] The following preposition often translated *concerning* is repeated with all three categories of conviction and is better translated "about," indicating that the Spirit convicts the world of the facts about sin, righteousness and judgment. The conviction does not guarantee the conversion. Conviction is the necessary prerequisite to conversion, but conversion requires regeneration to be complete.

How does the Spirit do His convicting work in the world? He does it, at least partly, through us. Twice in these verses, Jesus uses the second person pronoun, not the third person pronoun showing us that He is addressing the disciples, not the world. Jesus sends the Holy Spirit *"to you"* (Jn. 16:7) meaning the disciples. He also addresses the

218

disciples by saying *"and you no longer see Me"* (Jn. 16:10). So Jesus speaks of the work of the Holy Spirit in the world but sends the Holy Spirit to believers transforming believers into the Spirit's conduit to the world.[6] The Holy Spirit uses us to bring conviction to the world, but He alone accomplishes conviction. This truth simultaneously relieves our pressure and endows us with confidence as we witness. We don't have to convince anyone by ourselves, and yet our words are invested with His convicting power!

MAN, CHRIST AND SATAN

The Holy Spirit convicts the world about sin, righteousness and judgment (John 16:8). The first conviction is "manward" in emphasis, the second is "Christward" and the third is "Satanward." The explanatory clauses point toward the emphasis in each case (John 16:9-11). First, Jesus says that the Holy Spirit convicts the world "concerning sin because they do not believe in Me" (John 16:9). Jesus emphasizes human failure. Jesus says "sin" not "sins." The prosecution proves the sin. Sins are symptoms of the disease. Sin is the disease! The disease of sin is unbelief! Unbelief in Jesus is the grounds for the conviction.[7]

Jesus does not say that people are convicted because they break the Ten Commandments. Those are sins but not sin itself. The Holy Spirit does not convict people of breaking the Ten Commandments except as a means to prove the sin of unbelief. Breaking specific laws are sins but not sin itself. Sin, the heart of the disease, leads to lawlessness, the symptoms of the sickness. John wrote: *"Everyone who practices sin also practices lawlessness; and sin is lawlessness"* (1 John 3:4). The Holy Spirit uses the Law to prove sin like a doctor uses an MRI to expose a cancerous tumor. The disease at the root of all our sins is the sin of unbelief. The sin of Adam and Eve in eating of the fruit of the forbidden tree (Gen. 3:6) was an act that demonstrated a faithless heart. Unbelief generates rebellion and leads to lawlessness. Paul wrote, "Whatever is not from faith is sin" (Rom. 14:23). Jesus said that people are convicted because they do not believe in Him.

The ultimate sin is a sin of omission, not commission. The ultimate sin is something we don't do instead of something we do! Not believing in Jesus is the source of all sins. No matter how many good things we do in life, they cannot outweigh this one thing that we do not do. The one sin which encompasses all other sins is the sin of not believing in

219

Jesus Christ. We can do all the most wonderful works in the world. We can do many kind and good deeds for people. We can devote ourselves to helping the poor and needy. We can give our money to the church but sooner or later the unbelief produces sinful actions. Just as a gardener must pull up the weeds by the roots, so the Holy Spirit must convict us of our sins at the root. We can do many good works, but, if we do not believe in Jesus Christ, we stand guilty before God's eternal court. The prosecuting attorney will never rest his case until our guilt is exposed.

A police officer in a small town was out on patrol while town officials were proudly installing the first traffic light in the town. He drove through that intersection on the day the light became operational and saw the city officials, including the mayor and chief of police, admiring the new traffic light. He honked and waved. Later, his chief informed him that he'd earned the humbling distinction of being the first person in the town to run a red light, and he'd done it in a patrol car! Guilty! Exposed! We think we are doing well only to have the prosecutor prove our failure by the law.

The Holy Spirit convicts the world "concerning sin and righteousness and judgment" (John 16:8). He clearly convicts the world of the world's sinfulness (John 16:9), but whose righteousness is in view in the second work of the Holy Spirit? He convicts the world "concerning righteousness because I go to the Father, and you no longer see me" (John 16:10). Is He convicting the world of its own righteousness or Jesus' righteousness? Some argue that the three convictions must be consistent. The Holy Spirit convicts the world of its own sin, its own righteousness, and its own judgment.[8] To maintain the consistency, we must flip the meaning of righteousness to unrighteousness. He convicts the world of its own, sort of, "bad" righteousness – self-righteousness is proven to be unrighteousness. Otherwise, it is argued, we must change the meaning of convict to convince. There is, however, no great semantic distinction between convict and convince.[9] The work of convicting is the work of convincing.

Each convicting work of the Holy Spirit contains its own explanatory clause.[10] The cause for convincing the world about righteousness is the return of Jesus to the Father and the fact that the disciples no longer will see Jesus. So, the explanation for conviction of righteousness is Christological. The risen and ascended Christ is the focus. The Holy Spirit's work is to convince the world of Jesus' righteousness.

220

The resurrection is the proof of His perfection which is why belief in the resurrection is foundational to our salvation.

The world has an inverted view of righteousness. We think we are righteous (Luke 18:9), and Jesus is a sinner (John 9:24). The people in Jesus' world saw it this way,[11] and it is still the way the world views righteousness today. In one form or another, we consider ourselves good and Jesus not so good – or, at least, measured by our goodness. We measure Jesus by our goodness instead of measuring ourselves by His goodness. Therein lies a fundamental problem for mankind, so the Holy Spirit convinces people that Jesus is "Perfect Righteousness" in human flesh! He is the standard by which we are measured and fall short. Here is the starting point for our salvation. We have no hope of righteousness in ourselves when measured by His perfection, and any attempt to bring Jesus down to our level leaves us hopeless in our unrighteousness. Our only hope for righteousness rests in His perfect righteousness imputed to us by God when we believe (2 Cor. 5:21). The Holy Spirit convinces us of Jesus' righteousness, so we will not rest our faith in our perfection but His! The Holy Spirit's job is to expose the truth about Christ's righteousness to a world with a warped sense of right and wrong.

What ammunition would the Holy Spirit have to expose Christ's righteousness to the world? The very events by which He went to the Father, namely His death, resurrection and ascension, prove Christ's righteousness. Communion pictures the perfection of our Savior and illustrates the basis of our salvation. The only hope for a guilty person is in the righteousness of Christ offered to us on the cross. The righteousness of Christ on the cross is our only grounds for forgiveness. Our best righteousness is awful shabby next to His righteousness, so our only hope is to trust His not ours. Verse 9 focuses on man's condition in sin. Verses 10 and 11 tell us the two options which are available to man. We can enjoy Christ's righteousness or join Satan in His judgment. Ultimately, every man is going in one direction or the other. The Holy Spirit's job is to expose the truth about both results.

The Holy Spirit convicts the world concerning judgment, but it is not the judgment of the world that is the focus of the conviction. The Holy Spirit is not bent on convincing the world that they will be judged. He convinces the world that Satan, as the world's ruler, has already been judged. The ruler of this world has been condemned. Jesus said that the Spirit when He comes, will convict the world "concerning judgment, because the ruler of this world has been judged" (John 16:11). If we are to take the explanatory clause seriously, then the judgment pertains to Satan, not the world. The Holy Spirit convicts the world of its sin, Christ's righteousness and Satan's judgment (John 16:8). Each convicting work has a clause explaining the convicting work.

Jesus says that Satan, the ruler of this world, *has been judged.* Jesus treats this act as an already accomplished fact.[12] He is looking ahead to the cross because it is on the cross that the judgment of Satan is pronounced. So certain is Christ of this fact that He treats it as already accomplished. A sentence of condemnation was pronounced on the ruler of the world when Jesus died on the cross.[13] God turned the tables on the malevolent ruler who orchestrated the crucifixion. The one condemned by the world pronounced condemnation on the one condemning Him. The cross was a victory, not a defeat. The Holy Spirit convinces the world that God has sentenced their ruler. Some sinners in this world will respond to the Spirit's message, confess their sin and trust in the righteousness of Christ. Every sinner whom God rescues from the clutches of this world's ruler pounds another nail in the coffin of the condemned ruler.[14]

On the cross, God judged Satan! How is Satan judged on the cross? It would appear that the cross was Satan's victory, not His defeat. It may help to think of this passage in a legal context rather than a military context. The defeat of Satan is not so much a military victory as it is a judicial sentence. Jesus sentenced the devil on the cross. In God's courtroom, Satan has already been tried and sentenced to the Lake of Fire. We live in the period between the sentencing and the carrying out of that sentence. Satan is on death row! It is during this interim period that the Holy Spirit does His convicting work.

The Spirit convicts people, who consider themselves good, of their badness. The Spirit convicts people, who consider Jesus unrighteous, of Jesus' perfection. The Spirit convicts people, who owe allegiance to the ruler of this world, of his condemnation. Sadly, some will choose to ignore the conviction and to side with the condemned ruler rather than trust the righteous Savior because they cannot accept their sinfulness. One day, the one condemned by the world will condemn the world, and all will know what the Spirit taught was true. Until then, the Spirit continues to convict the world of sin, righteousness and judgment.

MANIPULATION OR PERSUASION?

I was in high school when a rock band came to put on a concert in the gymnasium. The band was made up of Christians who toured the country performing rock concerts to attract attention and use the forum to talk about Jesus. They contacted area churches in advance to prepare us for follow up but insisted that no one know that the concert would conclude with a message about Jesus. The band members performed in an assembly to advertise the evening rock concert. The place was full of young people that night drawn by the promise of a free rock concert. They sang all the popular rock songs of the day without any mention of Jesus until the concert drew to a close. Then the lead singer and guitarist came out and gave his testimony and talked about Christ. Cards were passed out and an invitation given. I found out from talking to my friends later that many felt ambushed by the bait and switch technique. They felt used and manipulated by the gospel.

In college, one of the staff set up an evangelistic event. A helicopter would carry a junk car high in the air and drop it into a large empty lot in the city. The event was advertised heavily, and we were enlisted to share the gospel with those that gathered. The idea was that the helicopter drop would gather a crowd, and we would walk around and seek to engage the people in conversation about Jesus. I declined to participate. I considered it a manipulative gimmick, not an ethical persuasion. There is an important distinction we need to maintain between manipulating people with methods and trusting the Holy Spirit to persuade people with His power.

It is true that the Holy Spirit witnesses primarily through us to the world (John 15:26-27). It is true that our witness should include exposure of human sin. We need to hold up Christ's righteousness as the standard of measurement, and we need to confront men with the prospect of joining Satan in his judgment. But all too often we think the Holy Spirit needs our help to get the job done. We place our faith in techniques and methods. We focus on preparation and training. If we have not had the training, then we cannot witness effectively, or so we think. But Jesus placed the emphasis in evangelism on the Holy Spirit, not us. It is far more important to pray for the power of the Holy Spirit than it is to master the finest techniques of evangelism. It is much more valuable to ask God to touch

223

human hearts through His Holy Spirit than it is to put our faith in the latest principles of church growth. Real church growth comes when the Holy Spirit moves in the hearts of men. Real salvation comes when the Holy Spirit exposes the truth to men and women in such powerful ways that they cannot escape the glare of that exposure and trust Christ. It is not our skill that brings salvation. It is His power! It is not our words, but His truth that changes lives. Sometimes we need to get out of His way and let Him work.

This prosecutor never rests his case without a conviction!

Louis Lapides was walking along Sunset Strip in 1969 when he struck up a conversation with some Christians who challenged him spiritually. He was quick to respond with the usual philosophical arguments until one of the Christians asked him about Jesus. Lapides replied that he was Jewish so he couldn't believe in Jesus. A pastor with the group asked him if he had ever read any of the prophecies about Jesus in the Bible. "Prophecies. I've never heard of them," Lapides replied. The pastor began quoting from the Old Testament, which got his attention because he knew they were the Jewish Scriptures. The pastor offered him a Bible. He took it but told the pastor that he would only read the Old Testament and not the New Testament. "Fine," the pastor said, "but ask the God of Abraham, Isaac and Jacob to show you if Jesus is the Messiah." One of the Christians said to him as he was leaving, "You're either on God's side or Satan's side."

Louis set out to prove Christianity wrong. He asked his Jewish stepmother to send him a Jewish Bible so he could check it out himself. He didn't trust the Christian Bible. She did and, to his surprise, he found it was the same as the Christian Bible. He read the Old Testament and found that over and over again there were predictions that pointed to Jesus – dozens of them! He struggled with what he was learning until he finally decided to open the New Testament. He half expected to be struck by lightning as he opened the first page. Matthew's words caught his attention. "A record of the genealogy of Jesus Christ, the son of David, the son of Abraham ..." He kept reading and came to the place where Matthew quoted Isaiah 7:14 about the virgin birth! He thought, "What's going on here? This is about Jewish people!" He couldn't put it down and read through the rest of the Gospels and then the book of Acts.

He was confronted not only with the claims of Jesus but also the growing realization that if he accepted Jesus for who the Bible said He was that he would have to change his life. He couldn't continue with his drugs and sex. He didn't grasp that God would bring about those changes. He thought he had to do it on his own. Lapides and some friends went to the Mojave Desert for some fun. One night he was sitting alone wrestling with his deeper inner spiritual conflict. He said, "God, I've come to the end of this struggle. I have to know beyond a shadow of a doubt that Jesus is the Messiah. I need to know that you, as the God of Israel, want me to believe this." It was as if God spoke to his heart that night, and he chose to follow Jesus. He said, "God ... I don't understand what I'm supposed to do with him, Jesus, but I want him. I've pretty much made a mess of my life; I need you to change me."

God began to make changes in his life. His friends noticed that he was different, but he couldn't explain why to them. Then he met a Jewish girl named Deborah who was a follower of Jesus. She took him to church with her one Sunday, and it turned out that the pastor of the church was the same one who had challenged him on Sunset Strip months earlier. The pastor was shocked – delightfully surprised – to see what God had done in the life of Louis Lapides. Louis went on to marry Deborah, go to seminary and become a pastor and Bible professor. The God of Abraham, Isaac and Jacob had shown him Jesus and changed his life forever![15]

18
MASTER
COMMUNICATOR

John 16:12-15

Meet Marlo Morgan, a middle-aged American woman who spent a few months in Australia working at a pharmacy and fabricated a top selling book about the aborigines. She claimed that she was their "Spiritual Guardian" after living among them learning thirty thousand years of wisdom from them. She told her story in the book *Mutant Message Down Under* which sold over a million copies. She originally sought to publish it as non-fiction but when the publisher couldn't verify her story they forced her to publish it under the fiction label although she continued to maintain for many years that the story was true. Journalist Dick Staub asked her about the truth of her story, and she told him that it didn't matter because "what is true for me is true for me, and what is true for you is true for you!"[1] Truth has become whatever we want truth to be for us. My truth, your truth, it is all truth but really no truth. Francis Schaeffer once said, "Modern man has both feet firmly planted in mid-air."[2]

The devil thrives on lies, half-truths, misinformation, rumor, and innuendo. What better way to deceive people than through misinformation and half-truths which sound good but are lies? The devil is the master of lies, but the Holy Spirit is the master of truth. Three times in the upper room discourse, the Holy Spirit is called *The Spirit of Truth* (14:17; 15:26; 16:13). He is the master communicator of truth and truth is the greatest defense against the fiction of Satan.

Jesus said that when the Spirit of Truth comes "He will guide you into all the truth" (John 16:13). The word for *guide* is a composite of two Greek words which means "to lead in the way." So the job of the Holy Spirit is to lead people in the way of truth.[3] In the Septuagint, the Greek translation of the Old Testament, the word is used for the "pillar of fire by night and the cloud by day, to show you the way in which you should go" (Deut. 1:33). The noun form is used to describe Judas, who became an escort for those who arrested Jesus (Acts 1:16). The Spirit is our guide who escorts us in the way of Jesus by leading us into all truth.[4] The Holy Spirit guides us in the sphere of truth as we walk on the path of Jesus. Truth envelopes the way of Jesus.

Jesus said "I am the way and the truth and the life." Nobody comes to God, the Father, except through Jesus (John 14:6). How can we walk on the way, know the truth and so live an eternal life? Jesus promised that the Holy Spirit would guide us into all truth (John 16:13) so that we can live His life and walk in His way guided by His truth. The job of the Holy Spirit is to instruct Christ's followers in the way, the truth and the life of Christ.

NEED TO KNOW

The Holy Spirit is the ultimate teacher of Christian truth, and He taught that truth to the disciples on a need to know basis. The disciples could not take the whole truth dumped on them all at once. Jesus could not unload all of that on them that night for they could not bear it, and neither can we. The more of God we know, the more responsible we are before God for our knowing. The deeper we penetrate into God's truth, the greater is the weight we carry for God's truth. The closer our friendship with Jesus, the greater our burden of intimate knowledge becomes, so the instruction of the Holy Spirit is a progressive instruction. (v.12)

Jesus said, "I have many more things to say to you, but you cannot bear them now" (John 16:12). God's revelation is given piecemeal and progressively down through history. Here, Jesus refutes the false notion that only the gospel accounts were inspired. Jesus pre-authenticates the rest of the New Testament Scriptures with these words. More revelation was coming as God progressively revealed Himself in the collection of writings called the New Testament. Jesus is thinking of more than chronological progression with these words. Jesus allows for our spiritual progression. He accommodates Himself to our level of spiritual growth. He gives the disciples and, by extension, us the knowledge we can bear at any given time. The word *bear* was used of carrying a heavy burden. Truth can be burdensome.[5] The truth is simply too heavy to carry sometimes. We are not ready for it, and the Lord knows that. He understands our limitations and never pushes us beyond our capacity.

Jesus says that the Holy Spirit guides us into the whole truth along the path we are walking. It is a figure of speech for a guide leading travelers through an unknown country. The Spirit guided the disciples into the body of truth we call the New Testament and guided those disciples step by step throughout their lives. The guiding was progressive. At any one time, they did not have all the answers. They did not know what was ahead.

We, unlike the disciples, have the full canon of Scripture to examine, but we, like the disciples, may not be able to carry the full burden which comes with that knowledge. The Holy Spirit is our guide leading us in the way of Christ. The way is not a sudden revelation but a steady illumination. He lights the path. Now He does not usually shine that light far ahead. It is a step by step process. We may not know what the next step looks like until we take the step He is directing us to make. We are never going to have all the answers ahead of time. We have to follow His lead by faith. We are responsible for taking the next step before we find out what follows. He helps us understand His truth progressively – one bite at a time. He feeds us daily at His dinner table so we can assimilate His truth into our lives. He illuminates His truth on a "need to know" basis. He teaches us what we need to know when we need to know it and not before we can bear it.

Walking on the way is not accomplished without the cooperation of the one led. Our responsiveness to His leading is vital to the process. He leads. We respond. If we do not respond, then He waits for us to learn that lesson before He can take us to the next lesson. Sometimes the Lord deliberately places us in situations and circumstances where we feel as if we have been sidetracked or derailed. We don't really understand why we are where we are. Sometimes the Lord crushes us outwardly to grow us

229

inwardly. We may feel as if we have no value at that point. We must remember that the Lord wants to teach us some lessons in those circumstances, and, until we learn those lessons, the master teacher cannot move on with us. The path to deeper intimacy is sometimes slow and meandering because of our lack of responsiveness to the Spirit's instruction.

GREATER INTIMACY WITH JESUS

The Holy Spirit performs three functions for the believer (John 16:13-15) parallel to the three functions He performs for the world (16:8-11). With respect to believers, the Holy Spirit will guide us, teach us and glorify Jesus to us (vv.14-15). The teaching work of the Spirit is mentioned three times (vv.14-15). The verb means to report, disclose, announce or proclaim.[6] The primary preaching work of the Holy Spirit is not revelatory, as in disclosing new information, but a proclamation, as in announcing truth to us.

The Spirit receives from Jesus what He teaches us.[7] Jesus is the source of the Spirit's information because the Father is the source of His information (v.15).[8] Jesus is not separate from the Father for they hold all knowledge in common (John 17:10). The Spirit communicates knowledge in perfect unity with God the Father and God the Son. What the Holy Spirit communicates to the disciples is exactly what God wants to be communicated. He takes the revelation and announces *what is to come*. When we realize that this expression is given to the disciples prior to the cross, then we realize that Jesus is not so much talking about prophecy here as He is talking about the whole body of truth which we call the NT. James, the half-brother of Jesus, who still did not believe at this point, would write by the inspiration of the Spirit. A Gentile doctor named Luke would write a quarter of the New Testament, and a Jew named Paul would write volumes under the direction of the Spirit. What each wrote would be exactly what God wanted to be written. There is no communication problem between God the Father, God the Son and God the Holy Spirit.

The measure of truth is God's nature. The Spirit's job is to announce that truth to us. He holds up the yardstick by which we measure our lives. Ugandan Archbishop Janani Luwum was challenged about his relationship with the evil dictator, Idi Amin. He said, "The best way to show a stick is crooked is not to argue about it or spend time denouncing it, but to lay a straight stick alongside it." He was arrested and executed shortly after making that statement.[9] The Spirit holds up Jesus to show the crookedness in our lives and, in this way, He announces truth to us.

Once again, the symmetry of the Godhead is perfect. The Spirit communicates what He receives from Jesus, who shared the knowledge of the Father. In this way, the Spirit glorifies the Son, who glorifies the Father for they are one (John 17:4-5). The goal of the Spirit is to glorify Jesus.[10] The glorification test is an important measuring tool for our ministries. Any ministry claiming to be led by the Holy Spirit will not be characterized by an emphasis on the Spirit but by an emphasis on Jesus. The Spirit guides and teaches in a manner that honors Jesus. If the chief work of the Holy Spirit is to glorify or exalt Christ not to call attention to Himself, then any movement claiming to be led by the Spirit will not be characterized by glorifying the work of the Spirit but by glorifying Christ. Beware of church movements which so emphasize the work of the Spirit that they have lost sight of the work of the Son.

The Holy Spirit is an invisible promoter of Christ. He calls attention not to Himself but to Christ so Christ must be central to a biblical ministry. The Holy Spirit is an unseen pointer to Jesus. It is Jesus who is the way, the truth and the life not the Holy Spirit. It is Jesus who is our friend, and the Spirit nurtures our friendship with Jesus. We will never cultivate a deeper love for Jesus without relying on the Spirit to nurture that love in us. He teaches us and guides us into greater intimacy with Jesus, but the goal is always to cultivate our love for Jesus not market the ministry of the Spirit.

KNOWING JESUS

There are two major implications of this concept for our lives today.

First, we are called to live for a person, not a vocation. Paul David Tripp has correctly warned us of the danger that develops when our calling becomes our identity – when our ministry supplants our relationship with Jesus. Jesus calls us first to be His friends because then, and only then, can we serve Him well. The order is critical. If my ministry comes to define my identity, I am headed for disaster. If my biblical and theological knowledge is the measure of my maturity in Christ, I will end in despair. If I confuse ministry success with God's approval of my life, I will be filled with pride. I have been there. I know the danger firsthand. The results were ugly in my personal life but, more importantly, in my relationship with Jesus. I lived what Paul Tripp warns us about.

> Ministry had become my identity. No, I didn't think of myself as a child of God, in daily need of grace, in the middle of my own sanctification, still in the battle with sin, still in need of the body of Christ, and called to pastoral ministry. No, I thought of myself as a pastor. That's it, bottom line. … It was me in a way that proved to be more dangerous than I would have thought. … My role as pastor was the way I understood myself. It shaped the way I related to God. It formed my relationships with the people in my life. My calling had become my identity, and I was in trouble, and I had no idea. … Biblical maturity is never just about what you know; it's always about how grace has employed what you have come to know to transform the way you live.[11]

It is not just pastors who struggle with these issues. All Christians can allow what they do and what they know to replace their communion with Jesus as friend and confidant. What we do in life is not nearly as important as who we belong to in life. What we know about Jesus pales in importance to how we cultivate intimacy with Him. We are called to live for a person, not a vocation, and the Holy Spirit's job is to guide us deeper into our friendship with Jesus.

Second, the real Jesus is the same Jesus as the Jesus of the early church. There is simply no other Jesus to know than the Jesus revealed to us in the pages of the New Testament. We are constantly deluged with self-appointed experts rewriting the story of Jesus to fit their favorite fictional caricature. Jesus is often pictured as a champion of the economically deprived – a social revolutionary. A week before Christmas, an article appeared in our local paper about a new book which had been written by a lawyer from Hollis, Maine entitled *Jesus Didn't Go to Church*. Charlton Smith had undertaken to study the life of Christ and uncover the real "undiluted" Jesus behind all the church traditions. He writes: "Jesus was a religious, political, social and economic revolutionary. His positions on almost every issue of importance are largely unacceptable in practice to the vast majority of people who call themselves Christians."[12]

The book is nothing new at all. People have been writing books for hundreds of years which purport to uncover the real Jesus behind the Jesus of the Bible. This "quest for the historical Jesus" spawned the infamous "Jesus Seminar" which is often quoted by the media as well as numerous other revisionist writers in recent years. Truth has become whatever we want it to be, and the story of Jesus becomes a figment of our creative imaginations. Ravi Zacharias, addressing this phenomenon in his book, *Jesus Among Other Gods*, illustrates this attitude toward truth with a story about a leading Indian philosopher named Shankara. The philosopher explained to the king that material reality is merely a delusion of the mind, so the King released an elephant rampaging through the garden. Shankara climbed a tree to escape the elephant. The king asked Shankara why he climbed the tree if the elephant wasn't real. Shankara replied, "What the King actually saw was a nonreal me climbing up a nonreal tree!" Zacharias incisively comments, "That is a nonreal answer."[13]

The basic assumption behind all of these attempts to find the real Jesus is that the New Testament church has deliberately obscured the truth about Jesus so that we have to peel back the layers of the accounts to find the real Jesus. Jesus clearly says in these verses that the Holy Spirit will take from Him and disclose that information to the disciples so that the information which the disciples recorded is, in fact, exactly what Jesus communicated. There is no discrepancy between the real historical Jesus and the writings of the New Testament writers according to Jesus Himself. It is only the arrogance of modern scholarship which sets our rational powers above the revelation of Scripture to think that we, after 2,000 years, can somehow disassemble the writings of the early Christians and rewrite them to make them right.

What the Father has, He gives to Christ. What Christ has, He communicates to the Holy Spirit and what the Holy Spirit has, He reveals to the church. The doctrine of the Trinity is the foundation of Christianity. The three persons of the Trinity are a perfect team (v.15). There is a functional subordination within the Godhead. The Holy Spirit is the perfect team player because His job is to point to Christ. I heard a story once about the conductor of a great symphony orchestra who was asked what was the most difficult instrument to play. He responded by saying, "the second violin. I can get plenty of first violinists, but to find someone who can play the second violin with enthusiasm – that is a problem. And if we have no second violin, we have no harmony." The Holy Spirit is the perfect "second fiddle" to Jesus Christ.

The role of the Holy Spirit is to teach us and guide us into all truth while glorifying the Son. He discloses the mind of Jesus to us to nurture our intimacy with Christ. The work of the Holy Spirit does not only apply to revelation but illumination as well. The Holy Spirit draws us deeper in love with Jesus so that we show His love to the world. He illuminates Jesus to us so that we can illuminate Jesus to others.

Author and Bible teacher, Joe Stowell, boarded the last flight out from O'Hare Airport in Chicago bound for Toronto late one Saturday night. He had noticed a young woman during pre-boarding who was clearly nervous about the flight. To his dismay, he discovered that he was seated next to her. He had a briefcase full of work and considered asking to change seats when he saw how agitated she was, but He sensed the Holy Spirit's silent rebuke about his selfishness and took his seat next to her. He knew that Jesus would most certainly have wanted to sit next to her to help calm her fears. She looked up at him with tears streaming down her cheeks and said, "I miss my daddy! I miss my daddy so much!" She was probably in her twenties and obviously cognitively impaired. She spoke loudly about her fears, and one man asked to be moved immediately. As the flight got under way, Stowell was busy helping her change the time on her watch to Toronto time and listening to her talk out loud to her imaginary friend Michelle. He tried to keep her calm and help her through the flight.

Joe Stowell learned that her name was Krista, so he asked her, "Krista, where are you from?" "Wisconsin," Krista replied. "Where in Wisconsin?" Union Grove." Joe Stowell knew that this was the location of Shepherd's Home, a Christian ministry for mentally disabled adults, so he asked her, "Krista, are you from Shepherd's Home?" She replied excitedly, "Yes. I'm from Shepherd's, and tomorrow night when I get home to Toronto my daddy will take me to People's Church" (a leading evangelical church in the city)! Stowell confessed that his attitude changed completely. Jesus had put him next to this young, frightened Christian girl to serve her needs. What had seemed like a chore before was transformed into a wonderful privilege. It was as if God said to him, "Stowell, your assignment is to sit there and help us get Krista safely home from Chicago to Toronto."

Later, as Joe Stowell stood in the baggage claim area, the man who had asked to be relocated away from Krista stood next to him. He said, "Excuse me. Could I ask you a question? Did you know the lady you were sitting next to?" When Joe told him no, he said, "You're kidding. Are you a therapist?" "No." "Are you a psychologist?" "No." "Well, what do you do?" Joe Stowell replied, "I am a minister." The man looked at him and said, "I knew you had to have something different in your life to do what you did on that plane." Then he got his bags and left.[14]

The Spirit of Jesus transforms our lives as we learn His love and live His grace.

19
GRIEF'S RESERVOIR

John 16:16-22

It is dark and quiet in the streets of old Jerusalem now. Most people have gone to bed in preparation for the great feast. The disciples follow Jesus through the winding streets, stopping periodically for him to teach then breaking into clumps of two or three to talk as they walked. They had rounded the corner of the great eastern wall of the temple and walked alongside the massive eastern gate. Soon they would cross the Kidron and enter the garden on the lower slopes of the Mount of Olives. They knew where they were going, yet they sensed in their souls that they didn't! It wasn't easy to understand what Jesus was telling them, and they questioned it among themselves. They were confused and upset. They were entering what St. John of the Cross called "the dark night of the soul."

Just like the disciples, we are often confused and upset. We do not understand what the Lord is sometimes doing. And just like the disciples, our confusion leads to tears of frustration and fear. We enter our dark nights of the soul, a necessary step on the path to intimacy with Jesus. A foreboding sense of looming loss engulfs us. Confusion! Fear! The disciples' response is typical. They don't ask Jesus their questions but instead whisper and wonder with one another. We do the same. We seek solace with a friend, sympathy from a spiritual leader or lapse into brooding despair. Dark nights can seem so endless.

SEEING JESUS

Jesus anticipates what they are thinking and predicts that their current confusion will lead to tears. Twice in these verses, he tells them the riddle which keeps them wondering. "A little while, and you will no longer behold Me; and again a little while, and you will see Me." It has been a puzzle for theologians for 2,000 years now. What exactly did He mean by that statement? The first half is clear enough. Jesus is talking about the cross. He has been talking about the cross before. The cross is the source of their sorrow but what is the source of their joy? What does Jesus mean by the second half of the expression?

Jesus could be talking about the second coming. He could be referring to His return in glory to claim the world for Himself. The problem with this view is that it would then make the time of sorrow or grief this entire age. Jesus would be saying that the time of tears is the entire period of church history until He comes again. It would appear from this context that Jesus implies that the time of sorrow is a short while, not an entire age. He uses the imagery of a woman in labor which implies a short time span, not an entire age.[1]

Some think that Jesus must be talking about the coming of the Spirit. He has been saying much about the Holy Spirit in these verses, so it fits with the context. However, there are two problems with this view. First, it requires two different kinds of seeing. They soon will not see Him as they do now with their physical eyes but will see Him with spiritual eyes. The interpretation is possible but awkward. The second problem is that the disciples are filled with joy long before the Holy Spirit comes upon them in power (John 20:20).

Jesus likely has His resurrection in mind here. The seeing is a reference to the resurrection appearances of Jesus Christ. It is the resurrection that changes their sorrow into joy. It is the resurrection that transforms their tears into hope. It was only during the days when Christ was in the tomb that the disciples were overcome with grief. As soon as they saw Him alive, it changed everything. Then they understood what He was saying – yet not fully! The sight lacked insight. The resurrection filled them with joy, but the joy was short-lived. They needed a joy that would carry them through life without Jesus physically present. The Spirit of God is the source of that kind of joy, so there is a sense that Jesus saw farther than His post-resurrection appearances here. He saw what we need today.

Seeing Jesus involves more than merely seeing Jesus! Helen Keller, blind from birth, once said, "The saddest thing in the world is people who can see, but have no vision."[2] Seeing Jesus through the eyes of faith involves spiritual insight, that is to say, insight produced by the Spirit of God. Two different verbs are connected to two time sequences ("a little while"). The first "little while" is the interval of time until His death on the cross. After the cross "you no longer see Me."[3] The seeing, in this case, is sensual in nature. It means to "be a spectator, look at or observe."[4] After the cross, the disciples ceased to see Jesus with their physical eyes for a little while. Jesus goes on to say that you will see Me. The second verb used here refers to spiritual insight.[5] Jesus combines Easter with Pentecost. The resurrection appearances certainly involved physical sight, but, when the Holy Spirit arrived on Pentecost, the understanding was transformed into spiritual insight. The second "seeing" carries this double sense. The Holy Spirit turns physical sight into spiritual insight.[6]

However, we must be careful not to over spiritualize this insight as if it is only a spiritual vision without any reference to actual physical sight as some do.[7] The post-resurrection appearances of Jesus were bodily appearances verifiable by physical eyes, not mere visionary spiritual experiences. One clue that the physical sight and the spiritual insight are both true is found in the parallel expression where Jesus says, "After a little while the world will no longer see Me, but you will see Me" (John 14:19). The same verb is used in both sightings – the pre-death and the post-resurrection sightings[8] – making a distinction between sight and insight irrelevant in this statement.

Seeing Jesus involves more than merely seeing Jesus but not less than seeing Jesus. The post-resurrection sightings of Jesus were actual physical sightings not merely visionary experiences of faith. The bodily sightings of Jesus were understood by the spiritual insight of the Holy Spirit even as He was actually visible to those who saw Him. Seeing by the eyes of the body and seeing by the eyes of faith converge to form a single seeing, protecting our faith from both mysticism and rationalism.

BIRTH PANGS OF JOY

There are times when life is confusing and painful. We feel like we have wasted our time and our energy. We feel like God has abandoned our dreams and ambitions. Our world has crashed and burned around us leaving us nothing but the blackness of the storm clouds. Because we are confused – we cry! We give up. We quit. In 1916, Oswald Chambers gave a talk to a group of soldiers in the YMCA hut at Zeitoun Camp in Egypt as World War I raged around them. He died a year later at the age of forty three while serving as Chaplain with the British troops in Egypt. Chambers told them, "Watch out for the shallow optimism that proclaims every cloud has a silver lining. There are some clouds that are black all through."[9] There are times in life when even the most mature believers are confused. That confusion leads to tears as we cry out to God that we do not understand what He is doing. We can see no silver lining, but we can cling to a golden promise! Jesus tells us that eventually our tears are turned to joy (16:20-21).

Paul Brand, the renowned leprosy surgeon, writes: "I have come to see that pain and pleasure come to us not as opposites but as Siamese twins, strangely joined and intertwined."[10] I came across this proverb somewhere. "The soul would have no rainbow had the eyes no tears." Ed and Betty Hinds had become good friends since I worked with Betty at the college. We kept in touch after she left the job and we prayed together over Ed's declining health. One day I visited Ed in the hospital. It was the highlight of my week. Ed had a severe stroke a month earlier and had been unable to speak or move much since. That day he was up in a wheelchair. His mind was sharp, and he could say some words. He could move in the wheelchair. Ed, Betty and I cried with joy together. I left with tears of thanks in my eyes for the grace of God. I say this gently but truthfully; there is a greater joy in seeing Ed now than the joy I had in seeing Ed before although Ed may never be the same again. The greater joy comes through deeper pain.

Ravi Zacharias tells the story of meeting two missionaries who had served in Iran for fourteen years. He joined Mark and Gladys Bliss with a group of Iranian Christians for fellowship one night. The Iranian host told him their story. Mark and Gladys were driving with their children and some friends to visit a church some distance from Teheran when they met with a tragic accident. All three of their children were killed. The other couple also lost a child in the accident. Ravi looked across the room at Mark and Gladys as his new friend told him the story. He marveled at the peace they exuded despite burying three children while faithfully serving the Lord in Iran. How does a person carry on under such weight? "Their testimony became a shining light in our community," his Iranian host continued. "Only their faith in God carried them through."[11]

The process of spiritual growth Jesus is modeling in this passage develops our faith by not always answering our questions. We have questions just like the disciples. We want answers just like they did, but Jesus does not always give us answers to our questions. The words which Jesus uses in verse 20 for weep and mourn are funeral words. They depict the weeping and wailing of those who mourn at a funeral. Jesus is not answering their questions at all. Instead, He prepares them to suffer, grieve and ultimately rejoice. He doesn't tell them what they want to know. He tells them what they need to hear. Our needs are the focus of Christ, not our questions.

The first word for weeping was used for expressing the intense emotion of deep sorrow at the death of a loved one. In the Old Testament, it indicated the act of wailing as a form of dependence on God instead of an expression of total despair. The second word for weeping was used for a funeral dirge. The bewailing of death was often characterized in public by striking the chest and singing dirges in a loud voice.[12] The first two words refer to outward expressions of grief, but the third word speaks of inner suffering.[13] The only other time the word is used in John described Peter's feelings when Jesus asked him after the resurrection if he loved Jesus. Peter was grieved (John 21:17). The contrast between all who grieve and the world that rejoices intentionally intensifies the pain of grief for the believer. The joy of the world makes their tears more painful, but, of course, the story does not end with their tears and the world's joy.[14]

Their tears will not merely be replaced with joy.[15] The very event – the cross – that causes their tears will become the event that brings them joy. So today, the symbol of the cross – the source of sorrow – has become the symbol of faith – the source of hope. The very same event can change pain to joy. Jesus uses the example of childbirth to illustrate the point (v. 21). Birth pangs had long been associated with the coming of the messianic figure in the Old Testament (Isaiah 26:17-18; 66:7-8; Hosea 13:13). Jesus is predicting the birth pangs of the Messianic Age. Pain is often the precursor to joy in our lives. Suffering on earth leads to the joy of heaven. Our tears at death are the birth pangs of our joy in life with Jesus forever.

PAIN: THE SETTING FOR HIS JEWEL

Many times in our lives today Jesus chooses to meet our needs not answer our questions. Our need is for a friend, not an answer man. We need someone who walks with us through life, not a computer that can predict the future. We need to grow spiritually and sometimes the only way we can grow spiritually is to endure the struggles of life. Many of our greatest griefs, our greatest struggles provide the means to grow the greatest in our faith. The cross is the only grounds for grace, and we will only enjoy the grace when we accept the cross. The difference between Peter and Judas was three days! Peter denied the Lord and Judas betrayed the Lord. Both sinned. But Peter hung around for three days and Judas hung himself. Suicide has a way of making decisions permanent. Both sinned horribly, but surely the forgiveness of Christ would have been equally offered to Judas as it was to Peter. Judas was not there to receive the forgiveness because he made his final decision. The difference was three days of waiting on the Lord. One enjoyed the joy of God's grace, and one felt the sting of Christ's judgment. The waiting was the difference!

An ancient Hindu parable speaks of a master who was teaching his young apprentice about pain. The apprentice was complaining about his lot in life, so the master placed a handful of salt in a glass and told him to drink it. He took a gulp and immediately spit it out. The brine was bitter. The master then took him to a lake and threw a handful of salt in the lake. He told the apprentice to drink from the lake. He did and was refreshed. The pain in life is the salt; the master taught him. How much bitterness you taste depends not on the salt but on the container that holds the salt. Pour the glass of pain – the bitter brine you taste – into the lake of God's grace. Our pain is absorbed in His grace turning our grief into joy.[16] Christ may never answer our greatest questions in this life, but he will meet our deepest needs.

Our tears are the seeds of joy not merely the forerunner to joy. Jesus says, "Your grief will become joy." He is not saying that grief is merely the precursor to joy. He is not saying that joy will eventually replace the grief. Joy is not the substitute for tears. Tears are not the promise that joy will come eventually. What Jesus is saying is that the same event which caused the tears is the event which brings the joy. *Your grief will be turned into joy!* Every mother knows this principle which is why Jesus uses the analogy of childbirth. I had the privilege of being in the room for the birth of both my girls. I marveled at my wife. We had waited eleven long years to have children. She had endured multiple surgeries and months in the hospital to give birth to a child. The process had been long and hard. The birth itself was filled with suffering for her. During the pain of labor, there were great tears, and those tears did not stop with the birth. They were the same tears, but now the tears had been turned to joy. The same event brought both grief and joy.

Elisabeth Elliot wrote, "God's ultimate purpose in all suffering is joy."[17] Jesus does not take away the tears to give us joy. He does not replace our tears with joy. Instead, the tears of pain become the tears of joy. There is a pain which is purposeful. The cross of Christ brings first great pain, but the same event is the means of great joy. In our lives today, the event which brings the greatest suffering and loss is also the very event by which Christ gives us the greatest joy in life.

> God, who whatever frenzy of our fretting
> Vexes sad life to spoil and destroy,
> Lendeth an hour for peace and for forgetting,
> Setteth in pain the jewel of His joy.[18]

OWN THE PAIN

In January of 1956, five missionaries landed their plane on a little sandbar on the Curaray River in Ecuador. Nate Saint, Jim Elliot, Roger Youderian, Ed McCully and Peter Fleming were trying to reach a tribe of Indians known as the Aucas with the gospel of Jesus Christ. All five were murdered by the Aucas leaving behind nine children in shock. Steve Saint was one of those children. In 1996, Steve wrote an article entitled, *Did They Have to Die?* He told the untold story behind the murders.

Rachel Saint, the sister of Nate, and Elisabeth Elliot, the wife of Jim, surprised the world by returning to the Aucas to live among them. Eventually, most of the tribe accepted Jesus Christ as their Savior. Steve Saint spent many a summer vacation living among the men who had killed his father. No one ever really knew what had happened or why because the Aucas never talked about it. The families had pieced together much of the story from diaries and pictures. Even though Steve had made friends with the very men who killed his father, he never asked them what had happened because it was his right to avenge his father's death as the oldest son, and he didn't want them to think he sought details out of a spirit of revenge.

Then in 1995 Steve heard the whole story from four of the men who killed the missionaries. One man in the village had wanted to marry a young girl, but the family did not approve of the marriage much to the frustration of the young man. One day the man followed the young woman into the woods. An older woman went with them as a chaperone. They ended up with the missionaries, and the man was taken for a plane ride. All was going well until the young girl and the man slipped off into the jungle while the older woman stayed behind. They met a group of Aucas including the girl's brother. The brother accused him of compromising his sister. The man knew that he would be killed, so he told them that the missionaries had attacked them. A lie told to save a man's life became the basis for the murderous attack the next day. The Aucas murdered the missionaries because of a lie. Steve Saint asks the question: *Did they have to die?* And he answers it with a yes. The death of the missionaries was something these Auca people never could understand. They had guns but did not defend themselves when attacked. It was this event, filled with so much pain for all involved, which melted the hearts of these people and eventually resulted in so much joy for all eternity.[19]

Our tears are turned to joy, and our joy is a forever joy (16:22). No one can take that joy away. Here we have the cycle of Christian joy which is played out for the disciples in those three days of agony. It is played out in our lives as well. There is the pain of the cross which is followed by the hope of the resurrection. Then we see the power of hope to change the disciples from disillusioned and defeated to bold and victorious. Finally, there is the assurance of joy which comes by faith. It is the joy no one can take away from us. The joy comes by faith. We must trust God that whatever he takes us through there is a purpose to the pain, and, even if we don't understand the purpose, the pain can be used to bring great joy – a forever joy – which no one can ever touch. This transforming joy is the power of the resurrected Christ in our lives.

Purposeful pain produces permanent joy we embrace by faith. Martin Luther was prone to depression. He would sometimes isolate himself for days on end from everyone. His family would remove any dangerous item in the house for fear that he might hurt himself. One time, his wife, Katherine, dressed for a funeral and entered his room during one of these times of blackness. Luther asked her who had died. She replied, "No one." But then she added that from the way he was acting, she thought God had died![20]

Jerry Sitser lost his wife, Lynda, his four-year-old daughter and his mother in a tragic car accident in 1991. Killed by a drunk driver, he had to pick up the pieces of life as he cared for his other three children all under the age of eight. His loss was horrific, and he plunged deeply into the darkness of despair. He had a recurring dream that the sun was setting, and he was running as hard as he could after the sun only to see it set plunging him into darkness. Terror would grip his soul. He thought he would live in darkness forever. The dream dominated his thinking until his sister, Diane, told him that the quickest way for someone to find the sun was not to run west chasing it into the darkness but to run east embracing the darkness until the sunrise![21]

Joni Eareckson Tada, who has taught us so much about suffering over the years since her tragic diving accident that left her a quadriplegic, spoke at a conference I attended. She challenged us that we have to own our weakness for God to begin His work in our lives. She told how she struggled with despair for two years until she learned His lesson. She and a group of friends had enjoyed a night out and ended up in Penn Station at 10:30 at night. They were feeling happy and having fun, so they started singing. The acoustics made the singing sound great. An officer, thinking they had partied too much, came over and told them to leave. It was a public area. He turned to Joni in her wheelchair and said, "Missy, put that wheelchair back where you got it." She was shocked and replied, "But it's my wheelchair!" They all laughed that night, but her friend said to her that the moment was powerful because for the first time in two years she had called it "my wheelchair!" It was the beginning of her healing. Joni had to own her pain to experience God's joy. She often says that she wouldn't trade the wheelchair for anything because through that wheelchair God has given her the gift of His joy.

When we are going through our days of darkness, we must remember the cycle. The same events that bring us so much pain now will be used of God to teach us a forever joy in Him. It is the pain of the cross which brings the greatest joy. Never get far from the cross.

20

HAVE YOU ASKED?

John 16:23-24

He preached his first sermon at the age of thirteen and later pastored the famous Westminster Chapel in London, but he was rejected by the first church he applied to pastor. G. Campbell Morgan was twenty-five when he showed up at the Litchfield Road Church in Birmingham, England to candidate for the Methodist ministry. The auditorium was large and the congregation few. Morgan preached poorly that Sunday and was rejected by the church. He sent a note to his father who also was a minister. The note contained one word: "Rejected." Morgan wrote in his diary entry for that day, "Very dark everything seems. Still, He knoweth best." Morgan's father wired back to him, "Rejected on earth. Accepted in heaven." Years later Morgan said of that experience, "God said to me, in the weeks of loneliness and darkness that followed, "I want you to cease making plans for yourself, and let Me plan your life." So He surrendered to God's leading, eventually entered the ministry and became one of the greatest preachers of his day. He authored over sixty books, becoming a leading figure in evangelical Christianity.[1]

Rejected on earth. Accepted in heaven. Those words form the backdrop to Jesus' lesson on prayer. The lesson is set in the context of rejection. Jesus has just said they will weep and wail while the world rejoices in verse 20. In verse 22 He predicts that the pain of the cross will be transformed into the joy of the resurrection. They will be rejected but rejoicing. Just like the disciples, we synchronize our souls with His purpose so we can rejoice in His will. As E. Stanley Jones says: "Prayer is surrender – surrender to the will of God and cooperation with that will. If I throw a boat hook from the boat and catch hold of the shore and pull, do I pull the shore to me, or do I pull myself to the shore? Prayer is not pulling God to my will, but the aligning of my will to the will of God."[2] Prayer refreshes the soul with the pleasure of God.

GETTING IN SYNC

The prerequisite for prayer is to be aligned with God. Jesus said, "In that day you will ask Me nothing." There are two kinds of asking in our relationship with God. We can ask a question or we can ask for a favor. We can seek information from God, or we can make a request for God to do something for us. Both kinds of asking are seen in John 16:23. The first asking means to ask a question. It is a different word than the second word translated *ask*. The first verb does not refer to prayer. It refers to the asking of questions.[3] The same word is used back in verse 5 where Jesus said, "None of you asks Me, 'Where are you going?'" This word is used again in verse 19 where Jesus knew that the disciples "wished to question Him."

The presence of Christ was a hindrance to their prayer life because He was the ultimate answer man! He was always there providing the answers to their questions. Now He was going away. Jesus literally says, "In that day *Me* you will ask nothing." The *Me* is placed out of order for emphasis. The reference is to His resurrection and ascension to the Father. In that day, they will no longer be able to ask Him all their questions.

Prayer changes things. No. Prayer changes me! As my thinking moves in sync with God's thinking, I learn to share God's burdens and stop asking my questions. I figure out what God wants and pray accordingly. The burdens I feel in prayer are the burdens God has placed in my heart, so my confidence in His power grows as I align myself with His will. George Muller had been praying for two men to come to Christ for fifty years. Someone asked him if he believed that God would save these two men. He replied, "Do you think God would have kept me praying all these years if He did not intend to save them?" One man came to Christ shortly before Muller died and the other man shortly after Muller's death![4]

Jesus may never answer all our questions, but He does promise to meet our deepest needs. There comes a time when, like the disciples, we must let go of our obsession for answers and be at rest with God's will. Prayer is not our hotline to heaven which gives us the information we want when we want it so that we can make the decisions we want to make. In fact, prayer is not about getting information from God at all. Like the disciples, we must come to the point where we have no more obsessive questions for the son because the soul is at rest with the Father's will. Proverbs 3:5-6 says: "Trust in the Lord with all your heart and lean not on your own understanding. In all your ways acknowledge Him and He will direct your paths."

William Sangster, an English preacher, once visited a young girl in the hospital who was going blind. "God is going to take my sight away," she told the pastor. After he had thought for a long moment, Sangster replied, "Don't let Him, Jessie. Give it to Him. Try to pray this prayer: 'Father, if for any reason I must lose my sight, help me to give it to you.'" There is the key. Rest in the Father's will. The prerequisite to prayer is to be aligned with God not to line God up with ourselves. Jessie did lose her sight but not her faith. She attended church with a guide dog who would wake up and howl after sleeping through the first twenty minutes of the sermon. After its howling didn't stop the sermon, the dog would go back to sleep.[5]

Jesus said that in that day "you will ask *ME* nothing" but you will ask the Father in my name. The second asking means to make a request. This is the language of prayer. It is the new medium of communication for the disciples. Jesus is saying that they will no longer be constantly asking for information from Him . Instead they will learn to ask the Father for His favor. Prayer is the language of a suppliant making a request of a superior.[6]

Herein lies the subtle danger of prayer. We come to treat prayer in mechanistic ways losing our relational connection with the Father. Philip Yancey tells about visiting Nepal and buying a Buddhist prayer wheel that spins a prayer repeatedly to God. Buddhists with computer skills download prayers to their spinning hard drives to replicate the giant versions of prayer wheels turned by the priests outside the temples. Taoist temples in Taiwan sell "ghost money," something like Monopoly money but paid to the gods. The money is burned in large incinerators in the temples seeking protection from the ghosts in this world. Yancey points out that we are not so very different in our ideas about prayer. We "say a prayer" before a meal as if it is a ritual that earns favor from God. We treat prayer as a "transaction" with God. It becomes a duty. We give God our prayers, and He gives us what we want. Our relationship with God becomes more like our relationship with a bank manager. We deposit our prayers in our heavenly bank account keeping up a proper business relationship with God so that when we have to ask for a favor God is inclined to treat us well.[7]

I confess that I have often treated prayer like a spinning prayer wheel as if God will be impressed with the quantity of my words spun heavenward. I slip into prayer wheel mode when I put my faith in the volume of my prayers instead of the relationship I have with the Father. I think that God will listen to me more if I get more people repeating my prayer to God so I enlist lots of people to pray in the hopes that God will give me what I want. More often, I treat God like my bank manager. Prayer becomes transactional, not relational. I do my part, and God will do His part. He owes me pay back for what I have paid into my account. I forget that He owes me nothing! It is I who owe Him everything. He invites me to refresh my soul with His pleasure through prayer.

ACCEPTED FOR INTIMACY

Sometimes we talk about the power of prayer as if prayer is the Christian equivalent of a nuclear missile. We give the coordinates to God by prayer, and He obliterates the enemy. Jesus teaches us that the real power of prayer is not found in manipulating God but in being accepted by the Father in the person of the Son. We have a new relationship with God on the basis of the cross. We now have direct access to the Father. The Old Testament believer did not have this experience. It is new because of the mediatorial work of Jesus. The veil between God and us has been torn down. For the disciples before the death of Christ, prayer to the Father had been hindered by the presence of the Son. Now they went directly to the Father because the Son's mission was to connect them (and us) with the Father. We are accepted by the Father no matter what our past. We can ask anything of the Father and, wonder of wonders, He listens. Why? Not because of our merit but Christ's! Jesus has been accepted so we are accepted in Him. The intimacy of prayer characterizes our relationship with the Father through Jesus.

Here is the power of prayer, to be accepted in Christ! Prayer is relational language. It is the language of intimacy. I will never enjoy the intimacy of prayer as long as I hide my real struggles from God. I can hide behind the façade of religious formality. I go to church, pray nice prayers, sing great songs but underneath I am bitter, unforgiving and guilt-ridden. God seems distant – formal – far away. I can only experience true intimacy with God through honest prayer. I must level with God. He knows it all anyway so who am I kidding? He accepted me in Jesus warts and all. His acceptance opens up the possibility of intimacy but only in honesty. C.S. Lewis said, "We must lay before Him what is in us, not what ought to be in us."[8]

The very essence of a request is that I cannot presume that God will grant my request on my merits. I cannot presume that the Father will hear me apart from Christ. Yet in Christ, I can be confident that God hears me. Twice Jesus uses the expression *in My Name*. The expression means that the Father hears me on the merits of the Son. I file my claim on His credit. If I go to the bank and sign my check for a million dollars, I will go away empty handed! If I have a billionaire friend, who has co-signed my check for a million dollars, that makes all the difference in the world. Jesus has co-signed my heavenly check. I ask the Father in the name of the Son. His co-signature is the power of prayer. I file my claim on His credit, so I receive my gift in accord with His character.

How we view God has a lot to do with how we pray to God. If we think of God mostly as a mean-spirited, capricious and judgmental God, who rewards us according to our actions, then we will pray like that. Such a view of God is the sad result of legalism. We must use certain terminology. We must attend certain meetings. We must perform certain functions. We must act certain ways. We do these things to gain a hearing with God. Do you see the warped nature of such prayers? The emphasis is on our actions. We feel that God will hear our prayers and reward us with answers based on whether or not we have earned His favor. It is all backward. Prayer is not like that at all.

Scholars debate whether the expression *in my name* in verse 23 goes with the request or the gift. I believe that the condition goes with the asking, not the giving.[9] We are to direct our requests to the Father in the name of Jesus. This is the normal order of prayer for us. The expression *in the name of* refers to the merits or credit of the person, but it also refers to the character of that person. In the ancient world, people's names were important because they were named to represent their character. The name "Jesus" means "Jehovah saves"! His character is a gracious saving character for all who repent and trust in Him. What the Father gives to us in answer to our request is always on the merits of Christ and in accord with the gracious character of our Lord – the same Lord who calls us friends (John 15:14)!

How we view God has much to do with how we talk to God. Christ revolutionized that relationship. We do not ask the Father based upon our own merits, and we do not receive from the Father anything because of our righteousness. The performance trap depends on our merits for our answers. It will leave us striving to please God so that he will listen to us. Prayer is not a hocus pocus formula for getting God to listen to us. Jesus says, "I have already earned that hearing for you. You are my friends. Ask the Father anything you want. What He gives you is always in accord with my gracious character." The wonderful power of prayer is simply to be accepted by the Father in Christ. We don't have to earn His favor. We can enjoy it.

THE PLEASURE OF HIS SMILE

The purpose of prayer is that joy will fill our lives (16:24). The purpose of prayer is to fill us with abundant joy not burden us with another obligation. Joyless Christians are prayerless Christians. The disciples had surely prayed much in their lives. They were devout Hebrews who had been taught all the prayers of their faith. There were daily prayers and festival prayers. They knew all about prayer. They knew about asking God in prayer. What was new was asking in Jesus' name. Here the name is clearly connected to the asking. Jesus says, "Ask and you will receive." He stresses the continuous nature of asking – keep on asking and you will receive. There is a persistence in prayer that is critical not because God likes lots of words but because we are in contact with the Father. We are enjoying a relationship by prayer. To ask in His name is to ask in accord with His desires. To ask according to His desires is to tap into His power. He promises to give what we ask when we ask in accord with His name.

Philip Yancey says, "Prayer is a designated instrument of God's power, as real and as 'natural' as any other power God may use."[10] We tap into God's power by prayer, but the prayer that taps into God's power is the prayer that is fixated on God's purposes. John Piper points out that prayer is focused on two purposes of God. First, we pray to produce fruit in our lives – God's fruit (John 15:7-8). Second we pray because we are on His mission in this world.[11] Too often we pray for our selfish desires instead of praying to accomplish victory in His battles. We pray like we are on a cruise ship instead of praying like we are on a battleship. Piper writes: "Could it be that many of our problems with prayer and much of our weakness in prayer come from the fact that we are not all on active duty, and yet we still try to use the transmitter? We have taken a wartime walkie-talkie and tried to turn it into a civilian intercom to call the servants for another cushion in the den."[12] Prayerlessness produces joylessness because we are focused on selfishness and fruitlessness. The power of prayer comes from the power of God to accomplish the purposes of God.

Prayer is not a magic formula whereby God is moved to do what we want. Prayer is simply a conversation with God whereby we ask Him to teach us His desires. When we ask in accord with Christ's desires, then God always does what we ask. The key is to learn His desires. Prayer is the language of love not the language of duty. So when we ask in accord with His desires, we enjoy the pleasure of His smile. Prayer is relational language, not religious language. Jesus knew something about relationships. It is not the getting of our way that brings the joy. That is a childish and self-centered relationship. In fact, sometimes Jesus will give us what we want just to show us that there is no joy in it. It is shallow and superficial. The joy comes from the relationship. The asking and receiving are relational. The purpose of it all is joy. When we understand that principle, then we begin to understand prayer.

It was late 1964 in Zaire, Africa. The communist Simba rebels had taken the town of Bunia. They were arresting and executing any who were "enemies of the revolution." Pastor Zebedayo Idu was arrested in the purge. The following day a great festival was planned in front of the statue of Patrice Lumumba, the leader of the revolution. The prisoners were to be executed by firing squad in front of the monument. The next day the prisoners were herded into a truck to be taken for execution. But the truck would not start. So they were all unloaded and ordered to push-start the truck, but when the truck stalled again right in front of the police commissioner's office, they ordered the prisoners out. They counted off by twos and then all the number twos marched to the monument. The rest, including Pastor Idu, were taken back to prison where they heard the gunfire in the distance. Pastor Idu seized that moment to share the gospel with the other prisoners and eight accepted Christ as their Savior. He had hardly finished praying when a messenger came and announced that he had been arrested by mistake and was free to go. The pastor left the prison and went back to his house where he found the congregation gathered in prayer. Obviously, there was great rejoicing at God's answer to prayer.[13]

"Ask and you will receive that your joy may be made full." The Greek text emphasizes that our joy may be filled up and continue on with great and overflowing results. Jesus doesn't want us just to enjoy Him for a moment. He wants us to enjoy Him forever. Do we enjoy the pleasure of His smile today? Prayer is the language of friendship. Simon Chan writes: "Petition makes perfectly good sense when it is understood in the context of friendship, not in the context of physical cause and effect. ... Real asking, giving and receiving are deep interchanges between friends."[14]

If you have lost your joy, then prayer is the way you will find it! But be warned! Some of the most miserable saints I have ever known, pray the most! They pray long, interminable, boring prayers of obligation and duty. They know nothing of the joy of talking with God. Their prayers are filled with themselves, not God. I am not talking about such prayer. Simply spend time alone with God. Talk to him in simple everyday language. Cultivate a relationship of prayer where you do not need a special place or special language. Just tell him your heart and let him fill you with His joy! When you come to the Father in that spirit, your soul will be refreshed with the pleasure of God. You will feel His smile again in all you do. The danger for all of us is to lose the joy of His smile in the duties of religion.

Let me suggest several things you can do to enjoy Him more through prayer.

1. Keep your language simple and ordinary. Don't try to be eloquent or flowery. Be real! When I first wake up in the morning, I lie in bed and talk to God about whatever is on my mind.

2. Talk to the Father about what is bothering you or about what is important to you. As a father, there is nothing I enjoy more than to hear my daughter tell me about her day even if the things she is excited about are rather silly. So it is with our Father in heaven.

3. Keep your prayers short. Nothing kills a prayer life faster than long, wordy prayers just like nothing kills a friendship faster than long, wordy friends!

4. Pray frequently and in all sorts of places. He is with you always. Cultivate prayer in your everyday life. I like to use my car as a prayer closet. I turn off the radio and talk to Jesus.

George MacDonald was asked, "Why, if God loves us so much and knows everything before we ask, do we need to ask?" He said: "What if He knows prayer to be the thing we need first and most? What if the main object in God's idea of prayer be the supplying of our great, our endless need – the need of himself? What if the good of all our smaller and lower needs lies in this, that they help drive us to God?"[15]

21
TO BE LOVED BY GOD

John 16:25-28

Vaneetha Rendall contracted polio as a child long after it was supposed to have been eradicated in America because the doctor misdiagnosed her symptoms leading to partial paralysis. Thirty years later a substitute doctor in the hospital took her baby off a life-saving drug saying he didn't need it. Two days later her baby died. Why God? Why? The question haunted her for years. She writes:

> Not knowing why, having to trust God in a senseless situation – when the world feels like it has exploded and we are left picking up the splintered fragments of our life – seems impossible. God is asking the unthinkable. To trust him in the dark. To accept his will when we don't understand. To submit to his sovereignty in the midst of uncertainty. To believe he has a purpose when nothing makes sense. Unthinkable as it is, God keeps asking me to trust him.[1]

Sometimes we cry out to God for answers, and He gives us riddles. Jesus knows that He has spoken to the disciples in figurative or mysterious language (16:25). The word means "dark sayings," words and sentences that are hard to understand.[2] Jesus has been talking about leaving them; His coming sacrifice for them; the hatred of the world, and His going to the Father. He has talked about suffering grief and loss using the example of a woman experiencing childbirth. Surely these are dark sayings for the disciples to hear! They are dark sayings not because Jesus was intentionally concealing information from them or because they were intellectually incomprehensible words. They were dark sayings because the teachings were emotionally unacceptable. The disciples were not ready to embrace His teachings. The darkness was in them not in Jesus.[3]

When will they understand? Jesus promises clearer language later. This sense of confusion will not last forever. Jesus will speak *plainly* or openly about the Father in due time. The disciples certainly think that time has come now! They assume that He has started to speak plainly to them at last (vs.29) but little do they understand it all yet. The time of speaking plainly has not yet come. The time for plain speech comes after the resurrection which is why Jesus goes on to say (vs.26) that they will ask the Father *in that day*. That day is after the resurrection when Jesus can explain openly to them the events and the Scriptures concerning Himself. Luke records the fact that in Christ's post-resurrection appearances to the disciples He explained to them "what was said in all the Scriptures concerning Himself" (24:27), and "He opened their minds so they could understand the Scriptures" (24:45).

We, too, experience the dark sayings of Jesus when we struggle emotionally to understand and accept our loss, our grief, and our suffering in this life. The deep waters threaten to overwhelm us even though we have the rest of Scripture to bolster our faith. We still need the Holy Spirit as our "Special Friend" to disclose Jesus' dark sayings to us because of the darkness that sometimes shrouds our minds. The Spirit helps us understand the dark sayings of Jesus as we experience the sufferings of life. Jesus knows that we grow in His love by learning His lessons in life. We come to understand the dark sayings of His word as we experience the dark nights of our souls.

DIGGING DEEPER

Growing through our struggles is the constant pattern of our lives. We never stop learning from the Lord. As the saying goes: "the person who graduates today and stops learning tomorrow is uneducated the day after." We never graduate from the school of Christ until we get to heaven. So we must be ever living with an attitude of learning, and we learn from this Word. The Bible is our source book for spiritual education. We cannot learn of Christ apart from His Word. There is much talk today about spirituality, but spirituality apart from the Bible is impossible. The Holy Spirit used the Bible to guide and govern our spiritual growth. When we get out of touch with what the Bible says, we will get out of touch with God. A relationship with the Lord cannot be sustained unless we stay in His word.

The classic passage in the NT on this subject is James 1:19-22. James gives us two practical lessons to help us learn from God's word. He tells us that we must learn to listen. James is speaking about our response to the Bible when he says: "Let everyone be quick to hear, slow to speak and slow to anger." We need to cultivate our hearing so that we listen to what the Lord is teaching us in His word. The Rabbis had a saying, "Men have two ears but one tongue, that they should hear more than they speak. The ears are always open, ever ready to receive instruction, but the tongue is surrounded with a double row of teeth to hedge it in, and keep it within proper bounds."[4] How quick are we to hear God's word? There is so much that can get in the way of our listening to Him. If I am so busy trying to tell Him my feelings and my concerns, I hinder my listening ability. If I fill up with candy and cookies, I will not eat many vegetables at supper. In the same way, if I fill my soul with the world's "all you can eat buffet" of goodies, I will not dine much at the banquet of Christ. We must also learn to practice. "Prove yourselves doers of the word and not merely hearers who delude themselves" James writes. I delude myself when I think that I can listen to a sermon on Sunday and fill my life with garbage the rest of the week and still learn the lessons the Lord is teaching me. The garbage I fill my life with will warp my ability to listen and to practice God's word.

We grow in His love by learning from His Word but learning from Him takes discipline and commitment. A cartoon appeared in a magazine depicting a church with a large sign out front. The sign read: "The lite church" – 24% fewer commitments, home of the 7.5% tithe, 15-minute sermons, 45-minute worship services. We have only eight commandments – your choice. We use just three spiritual laws. Everything you've wanted in a church ... and less!!"[5] Jesus said in John 14:23: "If anyone loves me, he will keep my word; and my Father will love him, and we will come to him, and make our abode with him." Obedience is the key to growing in the love of God. We cannot expect to enjoy His love while disobeying His word. It will never happen. Commitment is foundational to growth.

By learning from Him, we grow in His love and by praying to Him, we enjoy His love (16:26-27). Jesus teaches us that prayer is talking to the Father in the name of the Son (v. 24). So in prayer we claim Christ's credit, ask in accord with His character and the wonder is that the Father listens when we pray. One of Jesus' purposes for prayer is to fill us with joy which means if we have lost our joy then we must check our prayer life. Now Jesus expands on that thought. There is a danger in asking in His name. We may think of that expression as a formula for success. We may use that name as a superstitious means of gaming the system! If so, Jesus says, we totally misunderstand prayer. Prayer in his name is not a way of gaining His support for our pet projects. Prayer is not a matter of political connections. We do not go to the Son and ask Him to talk to the Father on our behalf because He has more pull with the Father. As D.A. Carson says, our answers are not "wheedled out of the Father" by prayer through the Son.[6]

FRIENDSHIP LOVE AND PRAYER

My Father loves me. He is happy to hear me when I pray. Here is the key to joy. The Father listens to our prayers because He loves us.[7] He loves us because we love Jesus! Jesus certainly intercedes for us. We are told that elsewhere in Scripture (Rom. 8:34; Heb. 7:25; 1 Jn. 2:1). The joy of prayer comes in realizing that we are welcome to talk directly to the Father not just because we know the Son but because the Father loves us! Prayer is relational language, not religious language. Prayer is the language of love which leads to joy. It is not performance but relationship which counts. The Father does not listen to me based on my past successes or failures. He listens to me because He, Himself, loves me.

A lady in our church was very ill in the hospital when her husband, Chet, died of a heart attack. Frances Heath was having a very difficult time dealing with her grief while struggling with sickness. Several weeks later, I was reading a bedtime story to my nine-year-old daughter, Katie. She is our special needs child with cognitive disabilities, and I am never sure how much she understands about things that are happening outside her personal world. I noticed a scribbled note on her nightstand as I prepared to leave. It read, "Dear God, please help Mrs. Heath." She knew and understood the joy of talking to God herself. Because God loved her, she knew He heard her.

V. Raymond Edman was a missionary in Ecuador and later became president of Wheaton College. He came so close to death during his days in Ecuador that his wife dyed her wedding dress black so she would have something to wear for his funeral. Dr. Joseph Evans back in Boston, Massachusetts, not knowing anything about the situation in Ecuador, was prompted by the Spirit of God to pray for Edman. He led his prayer group in a time of intense prayer burdened for the missionary and his wife for reasons they could not explain. They continued in prayer until Dr. Evans concluded by saying, "Praise the Lord! The victory is won!" V. Raymond Edman recovered and went on to serve the Lord for more than forty years.[8] Our Father hears us because our Father loves us.

Jesus said that the Father Himself loves you because you yourselves have loved Jesus. God, the Father, loves you right now because you loved Jesus in the past and you continue to do so. The word for love which is used here means affection. The normal word for God's love is "agape." This love is a love of the will. It is a choosing to love even the unlovely. However, the word which is used here to describe both our love for Jesus and the Father's love for us is "phileo," a word used for friendship love, emotional affection. The Father does not just love us with rational love which is somewhat cold and unfeeling. He loves us with all His emotions as well.[9] For this reason, the Scriptures can speak of His jealousy which is a byproduct of His love. He is jealous for our affections because He loves us with a friendship love, and we love Him back with a friendship love. Friendship love is the basis of our prayer life and results in our joy as we pray.

THE FOUNDATION FOR THE FATHER'S LOVE

Jesus gives us two reasons for the Father's love.[10] First, the Father loves us because we love His son. This love is different than His love for the world (John 3:16). The affection He feels for those who love His son is an affection He does not feel for those who do not love His son. He loves us in a different way than He loves the world. Like the father who loves a young man because the young man loves his daughter, our heavenly Father loves us because we love Jesus. Our love for Jesus "seals the deal" on His love for us.

> My Father loves me.
> This I know.
> For my Savior
> Tells me so!

Jesus says that the Father loves us because we have loved the Son. He does not mean, of course, that the Father only loves us if we love the Son first. In fact, the Scriptures teach us that the Father loved us before we ever loved the Son (John 3:16, Romans 5:8). The Father chose to love us in our unlovely state but when we respond to that love and love the Son then the love which the Father has for us reaches new heights of intimacy. Augustine wrote, "He would not have wrought in us something he could love, were it not that He loved us before He wrought it."[11] The relationship we enter into in Christ deepens His love even as our love for Jesus deepens. Relational language is the language of prayer. As we pray, we experience this deepening relationship which promotes an ever-deepening joy. The better we know Jesus, the better we pray to the Father. The failure of our prayer life is directly connected to our failure to know Jesus.

We must cultivate a life of prayer if we want to enjoy His love. Thomas Kelly taught us how to develop "an amazing inner sanctuary of the soul" at all times and in all places. He writes: "There is a way of ordering our mental life on more than one level at once. On one level we can be thinking, discussing, seeing, calculating, meeting all the demands of external affairs. But deep within, behind the scenes, at a profounder level, we may also be in prayer and adoration, song and worship, and a gentle receptiveness to divine breathings."[12] The secret to intimacy with Jesus is found in this inner sanctuary of the soul – a holy place where we can commune with God despite the noise of our surroundings.

We can live on two planes – actually multiple levels – at once? I tell listeners they are doing it as I preach! They are listening to me speak, but their minds are also functioning on another level. They may be thinking about the Lord or one of the hymns we sang. They may be thinking about some application which my words have triggered. Or maybe they are just thinking about the ballgame this afternoon or the roast in the oven! We understand that we can live on more than one level at once because we do it all the time. So it is with prayer. We can be mowing the lawn, working at the computer even sitting in a business meeting – and pray! By cultivating this kind of relationship with the Lord, we enjoy His love.

Prayer becomes a cold and lifeless thing when it does not spring out of worship and appreciation for the Lord's grace. E.M. Bounds wrote, "When the angel of devotion has gone, the angel of prayer has lost its wings, and it becomes a deformed and loveless thing."[13] The second reason for the Father's love is because we have believed. Ours is not a nebulous faith. We believe that Jesus *"came forth from the Father."* It is not enough to believe that Jesus was born into this world. We must believe that Jesus was sent from the side of the Father.[14] John 16:28 is a one-verse summary of the grand foundation of the Christian faith. Here is a mountain top view of Christ's work of grace on our behalf. It is a panoramic view – a snapshot with a wide angle lens. Jesus makes four assertions about His life and work which are summarized by theologians in four theological words.

Preexistence: He is God. Jesus said "I came out from the Father." Earlier, Jesus had said, "Before Abraham was, I am." (8:58) Later He would ask the Father to glorify Him together with the Father, with the glory which He had with the Father before the world was (17:5). He existed with the Father long before the world was ever created. This assertion emphasizes His deity. Faith in the pre-existence of Jesus is essential to enjoy the personal love of the Father.

Incarnation: He is man. Jesus said "I have entered into the world." At His birth to the Virgin Mary, He became a man. He took on human form. We call this the incarnation. God became man. The verb form here is different than the first word. The first word merely says that He came from the Father. This verb means that He entered in the past but continues to live in the form of man. In fact, Jesus is, from His birth onward, always and forever incarnate – God living in human form.

Atonement: He is Savior. Jesus said "I leave the world." Whenever Jesus spoke words like these in the latter stages of John's gospel, he was referring to the complex set of events we call the "Passion" – the trial, the

263

cross, the tomb and the resurrection. The Passion was the path of His departure. And He did it all for us. He is our savior.

Ascension: He is Lord. Finally, Jesus said, "I go to the Father." Jesus was not merely redundant. He was referring to his ascension. He ascended to the Father because His priestly work was done, the author of Hebrews teaches us. The point of the ascension is forecast by the angels. "This same Jesus, who has been taken up from you into heaven, will come in just the same way as you have watched Him go into heaven." He is the master. He will return as King.

What a panorama of Christ's life. From the cradle to the return, from the manger to the warrior, this is the foundation of our faith. I like what Joe Bayly wrote in his *Psalm of Anticipation:*

> Lord Christ
>> Your servant
>> Martin Luther
>> said he only had
>> two days
>> on his calendar
>> today
>> and that day
>> and that's
>> what I want too.
>> And I want
>> to live
>> today
>> for
>> that day.[15]

We live our lives in His love!

GOD PROVIDES!

As I wrote this chapter my 25-year-old nephew, Jacob Bartley, was preparing for a kidney transplant to save his life. My sister, Dorcas, told his story in a post on the internet this way!

Scott Gardner is a match!

A few weeks ago, Scott and Sarah flew into Charlotte to complete his testing to give Jacob a kidney. He passed with flying colors! His many years of running, his age and blood type and his desire to serve God in how He saw fit created quite an impact with the Kidney Transplant Team here. ...

We are still in awe of how God provided for Jacob.

This story actually started many years ago when two girls met in 7th grade at First Baptist Church in Portland, ME. Sallie, Scott's mom, and Dorcas, Jake's mom, became fast friends. Teen years passed, marriages were performed (Sallie to Bob, Dorcas to Greg) and families were formed. Gregory was born and the delight of all four of us. When Bob and Sallie found out that they were pregnant, we were ecstatic! Devastating news was given to us before Scott's birth. Gregory was diagnosed with Leukemia and was in the hospital for many weeks receiving chemotherapy. During that time, Scott made his appearance! It was good to have a celebration during such sorrowful times and what made it just a little sweeter? Sallie and baby Scott were just down the hall from where Gregory was staying for his chemo treatments. Late night talks and snuggles with our boys brought us all comfort!

Three more boys, Jacob, Michael, and Adam, and the cutest baby girl from Korea, Min, created busy lives for us all! Friendships continued through the years as they all grew up. Vacations, church outings, school events and then .... weddings! Jacob was in Scott and Sarah's wedding, along with Gregory and friends. He was delighted to be included!

The next summer brought a potential move for us from Asheville to Charlotte, NC. Gregory was working in Charlotte, and we fell in love with the area. We decided to move there unknowing of upcoming events. Dorcas' dad was willing to move with us as his beloved wife had passed away earlier that year. It seemed like such a great option for all of us. Jacob had not felt well for a bit, so doctors' appointments were made. ... We couldn't understand why Jacob's kidneys had failed or how we had missed any possible signs. A kind nephrologist explained that Kidney disease is a silent disease and is commonly found out in later stages. That's where Jacob was – end stage Renal Failure. He needed Kidney dialysis and a kidney transplant.

God already had a provision in place!

While Asheville did not do Kidney Transplant surgeries, Charlotte did! We moved with the help and prayers of many to a quiet cul de sac filled with friends who welcomed us like family! Jacob was also able to be in another family/friend wedding! Michael and Julia's wedding took place just two weeks after Jacob was hospitalized. We were so thankful that Jacob was able to stand with his friends and be a part of such a sweet experience. Many of you know that Julia was diagnosed with Leukemia just seven weeks after being married. We covet your prayers for her as she fights her way through two-and-a-half years of chemotherapy! We well remember those days for Gregory!

Jacob continued with many hard days of dialysis. He has lost thirty pounds, and his body has struggled in many ways to maintain a comfortable lifestyle. We started the process right away for a Kidney match. As you know, Greg was not a match, and we sadly accepted that fact.

God already had a provision in place!

266

Even though Scott and family were so burdened for their Julia, Scott wanted to try.

That's where this story is now!

No human being could have orchestrated this!

God provides.

In different ways, in difficult times, with loving arms.

What's next? We covet your prayers!

Hebrews 12:1 says, "Since we are surrounded by such a great cloud of witnesses [that's y'all praying for us], let us throw off everything that hinders and the sin that so easily entangles. And let us run with perseverance the race set before us!"

Jacob is running a race right now, fighting for his life here on Earth. Scott is not running the Boston Marathon this year, but he is running a race.

We persevere to the surgery which is coming up soon! Please pray for those details to be worked out. Please pray for continued health for all.

God provides. Jehovah-Jireh.[16]

22

BATTERED BUT NOT BROKEN!

John 16:29-33

Have you ever listened to someone talking and had absolutely no idea what they were saying, but you couldn't let on that you didn't know? So you nod your head and say, "uh-huh." This is exactly what the disciples are doing at the end of John 16. The fact is that, often in life, we congratulate ourselves in our confusion. Jesus' disciples all nod their heads and say, "Ah, now we understand what you are telling us. You are speaking openly and not talking in riddles anymore. Now we know that you know everything (especially since we can't understand half of what you are saying). Now we know that we don't have to interrogate you all the time because we know that God sent you."

Their confidence has some basis in faith. They are not lying here. The disciples sincerely think that they have understood. There is a level of faith here which is important, but they have merely arrived at the starting point of real faith. Surely, after three years of intense training, they should have arrived at a deeper level of faith than this. This level of faith is not much different than Nathaniel back when Christ first called him three years earlier (John 1:47-50). The reason that Nathaniel believed was that Jesus told him his thoughts before he spoke them. In John 16:30, the reason that the disciples believe is because they are taken back by his ability to discern their questions before they ask them. Have they progressed so far in three years? The teacher has been pouring Himself into them for three years of Bible school. Now they are on the eve of final exams. They are confident that they know the answers and are prepared for the test, but Jesus knows the fog that shrouds their minds.

We, too, are often confident that we are ready for the test. We've learned the lessons. We can take whatever comes. There is a measure of faith in this, but it is a faith filled with self-satisfaction and founded on confusion. We are just as ignorant in our faith as the disciples were on that night. We're just not going to admit it. We think that we understand, but even our greatest expressions of faith are tinged with ignorance. Our faith quickly wobbles in the face of disappointment, failure, broken promises and unfulfilled expectations.

ABSENT WITHOUT LEAVE

Jesus corrects us as He did the disciples. He knows what He's about, and it's a good thing for us. Verse 31 could be read as an exclamation, "Now you believe" or as a question, "Do you believe? Is this the moment you now believe?" It is probably best understood as a question because of the correction which follows in the context. It is as if Jesus is saying, "Do you really believe? Let me show you how confused and ignorant you really are."

Jesus then predicts what will happen to the disciples in their hour of testing. They will run away. They will go AWOL. They will flunk the test. They will abandon the Lord who came to save them. This failure is recorded in Scripture for all to read about down through history. We are not so very different! The church of Jesus Christ depends on what Christ has done for us not what we do for Him. Success is not found in us but Him. It is not our courage or our cleverness that wins the battle. It is not even our faithfulness for we fail all too often. The battle is won by His grace not our grit.

Jesus says that the hour is fast approaching when they will all be scattered.[1] The time has arrived for the greatest event in human history to take place. The enmity between the seed of Satan and the seed of the woman (Gen. 3:15) will come to its decisive hour. Mark records the fulfillment of this prediction (Mark 14:50). In the Garden of Gethsemane, the disciples watch in bewilderment as Jesus allows the soldiers to arrest

Him. He will not allow them even to fight for Him. Then Mark writes: "And they all left Him and fled."

Jesus must face this battle alone. The hour has come for the disciples to leave Him alone as they are scattered (John 16:32) "each to his own." When we are scattered from the Lord and each other, we individually enter into our own things. The expression is used for John taking Jesus' mother into his own household (John 19:27). It could be translated "each for himself." The adjective refers to our possessions and our relationships. Our human nature drives us to seek our own personal goals – the matters we control – whenever we abandon the Lord. After the cross, we see the disciples wandering in confusion. They each begin to make plans to return and pick up the lives which they left to follow Jesus. Each sets in motion steps which will lead back into their own little worlds once again. It is what they know. We do the same.

We isolate ourselves by our choices. Confused and discouraged we slip away. We go back to what we knew. In their case, it was fishing or business or family or farming. Where do we go? Wherever it is, the result is isolation – brokenness! A mother wrote: "One morning after her dad resigned the pastorate and moved in with another woman, my little girl was crying so hard that I told her to be strong; and she said, 'Mommy, my strong is broke.'"[2] Our strong is broke! We slip away to our own little worlds. We return to our past and isolate ourselves by the choices we make. The worst thing is that we abandon Him in our fears. Jesus predicted that they would leave Him alone. It is one thing to leave a church. That is understandable, maybe even God's will, in certain situations. But it is another to leave the Lord! The disciples left the Lord.

They left Him all alone and yet He was not alone. The Father was with him in this experience. Human abandonment cannot leave him alone, yet he would be alone at one point. He would not be alone because they left him, but He would be alone when the Father left Him. Jesus cried out on that cross, "My God, My God why have you forsaken me." It is the cry of abandonment. At that moment, an eternity of the Father's wrath poured down on the Son's shoulders. At that moment, he experienced absolute, infinite, utter, cosmic aloneness. He did it for us. Some think there is a contradiction here. There is not. Jesus is speaking here of human abandonment, and human abandonment can never render Him alone. In that moment of human rejection, He is surely not alone, but He is not saying that the father would never leave Him alone. In that crisis moment of all salvation for all humanity, He walked that road alone for us. That is salvation.

SCATTERED BUT NOT ABANDONED

They abandoned Him, but He never abandoned them. The easiest thing in the world is to walk away from the Lord when He fails to meet our expectations. "O, I've got bigger fish to fry. I tried this "god thing" and it didn't work for me. He didn't get me out of my jam. He didn't solve my problems. I've wasted enough time on religion. It's time I got on with my life." We abandon Him, but He never abandons us!

Henry and Richard Blackaby were attending a large convention when a pastor shared his story with them. He had served as pastor years before but conflict developed in the church. Some of the church members became very critical of his leadership and attacked his character and his family. He was crushed by the attacks and resigned from the ministry. He vowed never to return to the ministry. A business friend hired him as vice president of a new company. The company was very successful, and the former pastor became wealthy. The church he was attending began studying the Blackabys' course entitled *Experiencing God,* and the Spirit of God touched his heart. He told them with a big smile but tears in his eyes, "God got hold of me! I'm a pastor again!"[3]

The scattering and subsequent abandonment are introduced by an important conjunction indicating purpose.[4] God always has a purpose in our pain. Jesus used the scattering of the sheep as a description of Satan's work (John 10:12) when the hireling shepherd abandons his sheep. Jesus didn't abandon His sheep, but Satan did scatter the sheep in this hour. Satan's scattering work must be seen as within the scope of God's overall purpose. In the garden at His betrayal, Jesus said, "All this has taken place to fulfill the Scriptures of the prophets. Then all the disciples left him and fled" (Mt. 26:56). Zechariah had predicted the scattering when he wrote, "Strike the Shepherd that the sheep may be scattered" (Zech. 12:7). God intended to scatter the sheep leaving Jesus alone to battle Satan on the cross. The apparent victory of Satan was part of God's sovereign plan for the disciples. Satan's work accomplishes God's purpose. We cannot understand, sometimes, why Satan seems to win in this world. We scatter, like the disciples, to pursue our own things in life feeling like Satan has won; forgetting, in our despair, that God has a purpose even in the victories of Satan!

God does beautiful things in brokenness!

J. Oswald Sanders wrote: "God does not waste suffering, nor does He discipline out of caprice. If He plough, it is because He purposes a crop."[5] Elisabeth Elliot wrote: "It is a merciful Father who strips us when we need to be stripped, as the tree needs to be stripped of its blossoms. He is not finished with us yet, whatever the loss we suffer, for as we loose our hold on visible things, the invisible become more precious – where our treasure is, there will our hearts be."[6]

PEACE UNDER PRESSURE

Success is not found in us, but peace is found in Him. "These things I have spoken to you, so that in Me you may have peace. In the world you have tribulation, but take courage; I have overcome the world" (John 16:33). Jesus draws three contrasts between our two spheres of life.

In Me vs. In the world
Peace vs. Pressure
Might have vs. Have

We simultaneously experience two spheres of life. The "in Me" sphere of life should be the dominant reality. The expression is emphatic both in position and form. The "in the world" sphere of life, while seemingly the dominant reality, should be secondary, not primary. The two spheres of life are characterized by two contrasting experiences. In Christ, we have peace while in the world we have pressure. We can experience peace and pressure at the same time because we live in both spheres simultaneously. Peace and pressure co-exist in the life of every Christian. Peace is not the absence of pressure. We can have peace in the middle of our troubles.

Pressure in the world is a given while peace is a possibility.[7] Peace is not guaranteed unless the following command is obeyed. The command is to *"take courage."* Peace under pressure comes from courage

273

under fire. We can have courage because Jesus has established a new reality for us. "I have overcome the world."[8] We might have expected Jesus to say, "Take courage. You have overcome the world." He doesn't say that, of course, because the victory is not in us but Him. Jesus says that He has already won the victory even before the cross, so certain is He of the outcome of the looming battle.[9] Jesus faced the cross with the assurance of total victory. He goes to the cross with confidence that He will conquer the enemy despite the horror He faces in battle. We must take courage in His victory. We have victory because He has victory. We are conquerors because He is conqueror (Romans 8:37). We can have peace under pressure because we take courage that He is the conqueror.

Regina Kuruppu huddled under a desk with her co-workers, holding hands and praying. "Heavenly Father: Watch over my family," she said. "Watch over us." When the fire alarm had sounded, she thought it was just a drill until she made her way downstairs and saw the bodies on the floor. She ran back upstairs and several of them barricaded themselves in an office with the door locked and a bookcase shoved up against it. Regina prepared to die. She thought about her son and texted her sister. "I'm going to leave this world," she thought to herself. The mass shooting in San Bernardino, California by the husband and wife team of terrorists, Syed Farook, and Tashfin Malik, killed fourteen and wounded twenty-one that day in Building 3 at the Inland Regional Center. Regina had started her day putting final plans in place for her vacation. After the horror of that day ended, she tried to pick up the pieces of life and make sense of it all. A day later she told a reporter, "Fear is not what God wants us to feel. He wants us to feel peace."[10]

Peace is not the absence of conflict. It is not the satisfaction of all our wants and desires. It is not the fulfillment of our dreams and ambitions. Peace is the bird huddled in the crevice of the rock sleeping in the midst of the storm. Peace is inner contentment while trouble rages around us. Peace is the spirit that picks up the pieces of our shattered dreams and adapts life to the new direction God has for us. We find that peace in Christ. When we isolate ourselves by our choices and abandon Him in our fears, we will never find peace. The path to peace is to remain in Christ. This is the lesson of John 15. "Abide in Me and I in you," Jesus said (15:4). Abiding is the way to find lasting peace.

Jesus goes on to emphasize a powerful contrast between the peace of Christ and the pressures of this world. "In the world you have trouble –

tribulation," Jesus said. The word "tribulation" means pressure. It could be translated affliction or distress. The same word is used back in John 16:21 when the woman after childbirth "remembers the anguish [trouble] no more." No one ever has the perfect job, the perfect marriage, the perfect home, and all dreams and ambitions fulfilled. Life is a struggle. It is filled with pressure, distress, unfulfilled dreams, unsatisfying jobs, conflict, turmoil, hurts, and pains. Why? Because we live in a fallen world populated by sinners.

OVERCOMERS!

Jesus says, *"Take courage."* The word meant to be cheerful under fire – courageous in the face of pressure – strong in the presence of suffering. It was used in the Septuagint (the Greek translation of the Old Testament) by an angel speaking to Rachel as she was dying in childbirth (Gen. 35:17). "Take courage, Rachel!" It was used by God encouraging those who were grieving the death of loved ones in Zephaniah 3:16-17. Take courage! When Paul was locked in prison by the Romans after the mob of Jews almost killed him, the Lord stood by his side in the dark of that night and said, "Take courage!" (Acts 23:11) Take courage when everything is going bad. Take courage even in death. Such an encouragement would be almost sadistic if it were not for what Jesus says next. *"I have overcome the world."* Jesus said that before he died and rose again. He said it before the affliction yet to come. The expression indicates that the victory has been won, and the results of that victory continue today. We live in the glow of His victory over death. "Really? It doesn't look like it Lord, not from where I stand right now."

Walt and Marty Russell were overwhelmed with grief at the death of their son, Christopher, who died suddenly at eighteen months old. The Russells had been on vacation with a friend when they got the call. At the graveside service, Walt said it was the most painful experience of his life, and he felt like he was in a deep pit of despair and faithlessness at that moment. He sensed the Spirit touch his soul. Walt said, "I began to experience profound, soulish comfort in the deepest recesses of my being as God used His Word to renew hope and courage in me."[11]

Take courage; I have overcome the world! The word "overcome" is an athletic or military term. It was often used of winning the games or races of the Greco-Roman world. It was also very common as a description of

275

the emperor after he won a great military battle. What Jesus is saying here is that all who stand opposed to God have already been defeated. They just don't know it yet. We have already won in Christ; we just can't see it yet!

John continues this theme of the overcomer throughout his writings in 1 John and later in the book of Revelation. We are overcomers in Christ.

> For whatever is born of God overcomes the world; and
> this is the victory that has overcome the world – our faith.
> And who is the one who overcomes the world, but he who
> believes that Jesus is the Son of God? (1 John 5:4-5)

The word for "victory" used here is a form of our word for overcome. It also occurs in a letter from Emperor Claudius on a diploma of membership in the *Worshipful Gymnastic Society of Nomads*. He thanks the gymnastic club for the golden crown which they sent to him when he defeated Britain in a military campaign in A.D. 43.[12] All true believers are overcomers. True believers persevere to the end. Persevering faith is what it means to be born again. We overcome by faith in Jesus who has overcome the forces of sin in this world. Victory is guaranteed because victory does not depend on us but Christ. We overcome the pressures of this world by faith in Christ.

Mark Wellman is a paraplegic who gained national attention in the summer of 1989 when he climbed the sheer granite face of El Capitan in Yosemite National Park. It took him six days. He and his partner, Mike Corbett, slept in hammocks attached to the rock wall as they climbed. At the summit, Wellman addressed the crowd of about fifty waiting to see him. "No one in my situation has ever done anything like this, and that I'm proud of. I felt like the whole world was watching," he said. He wore the same hiking boots he had been wearing at the time of his fall seven years earlier when he fractured his vertebrae and was left paralyzed from the waist down. His partner, Mike Corbett, actually scaled the 3,000-foot mountain twice so that he could help Mark Wellman up once. The scariest part of the climb was the last leg when Mike had to carry Mark on his back because the spikes Mark needed to pull himself up the slope would not hold in the loose gravel. One slip and they both would have slid off the face of the cliff.[13]

Christ already went to the top for us! He already climbed the mountain. He is with us today as our shepherd helping us to scale the rock He has already climbed for us. He brings us the nourishment we need. He stays with us when the storms come up. He shows us the best handholds and footholds we need to climb the cliff. He encourages us when we are down. He knows the way, and we find our way by following Him. We win because He won!

Jerry Sittser, whose mother, Grace, wife, Lynda, and youngest daughter, Diana Jane, were all killed in a drunken-driving accident, tells about a conversation he had with his eight-year-old son, David, sometime after the tragedy. They were riding in the car and David was quietly reflective. He broke the silence with a question: "Do you think Mom sees us right now?" Jerry thought a moment and then said, "I don't know, David. I think maybe she does see us. Why do you ask?" "I don't see how she could, Dad," David replied. "I thought Heaven was full of happiness. How could she bear to see us so sad?" For a few moments, they rode in silence as Jerry struggled to answer his son's question. "I think she does see us," he finally replied. "But she sees the whole story, including how it all turns out, which is beautiful to her. It's going to be a good story, David."[14]

Peace is knowing the end of the story is good.

EPILOGUE

Dear Dave,

How is your soul doing? You have been so busy lately. I know it is all good stuff. It's not like you are avoiding me. The merry-go-round of responsibilities consumes your days. Church, ministry, and family concerns fill up your time with little left over for me. You are busy helping others with their spiritual needs, but I miss our talks together. I watch you work, and I think that ministry has become your identity. You define yourself more and more by the success of your work. What you do for me is more important to you than what you do with me. You have become so caught up in the rush of service that you have lost a sense of my presence in your ministry.

Stop the whirlwind of activity and settle your soul in silence with me for a while. A little solitude will do wonders for your soul. Spend some time with me. Even better, let me into your daily life. Pause in the rush of your work to open your heart to me as you serve me. Let me experience with you what is happening as it happens. I'm not looking just for prayer appointments that you set aside on your calendar for me. I want to be in your life as you live it. I want to share your experiences with you and have you enjoy my presence in each moment of your life.

Talk to me. Share your thoughts and feelings, good and bad. Tell me your joys and frustrations. I care about your ups and downs because I love you. Don't be afraid to open up to me about your struggles. Talk to me about the criticism someone blindsided you with the other day. Share with me how that hurt your feelings, but you couldn't say anything about it. Bring it to me. I'm here for you. Tell me about your worries for your children. Let me carry the weight of worry for you. You pray a lot. Intercession for others including your children is good, but what about you? I want to hear how you feel. I would love it if you shared your dreams and ambitions with me more often. It is good to dream big, but I'd like to be part of those dreams.

Talk to me not just about the big things but the little things too. You could have shared that beautiful sunset with me last night if you hadn't been so intent on getting to your meeting on time. How about the songbirds I sent to serenade you when you woke up three mornings ago? I was saying "good morning" to you, but the clock told you that you overslept and would be late for work so you couldn't enjoy the moment with me. Then there was the irritation you felt last week as you drove home from an appointment but the radio was blaring incessantly so you didn't bother to share it with me. I could have helped.

Walk with me. You do well to follow my directions for the most part. It is not like you are disobeying my word in any public way, but it is easy to get distracted by things that don't matter eternally. You can lose your focus in the spam that fills your daily life. The picture you saw at the news counter or the commercial on television can fill your mind with impure images. That television show you were watching the other night stimulated thoughts that were dishonorable to me. Guard your thought life. Think on excellence because it is easy for bad thoughts to crowd out the good thoughts until you are no longer walking in my ways.

The path gets a little steep at times, rocky too, but as long as you are walking with me, you will find that it's worth it. I ask you to face some tough situations. It is part of the path I ask you to walk with me. The loss of a loved one, the sickness you experience, the financial setback, are all part of the path. You may not be liked or respected in this world. Others may be more successful. Don't look at anyone else. Your path is not their path. Your path is the path I have chosen for you. Walk with me on that path I have for you. You may like the looks of another path but don't wander away. I'm on this path – the path I have for you. If you wander to another path, I'm not there with you on that path. I'm here for you on your path so walk with me through it all.

Hear my heart. Take your Bible and read it by yourself and for yourself. Don't just read it for sermons or Bible study preparation. Find time to read it looking for my heart for you in the words you read. I left my word to share my heart. Listen to my Spirit as you seek my heart. He will show you what I care about and what is important to me. He will disclose my heart to you. Ask Him to help you see the world through my eyes. Ask Him to help you hear my words with your inner ears. Open your spiritual eyes to see – really see – me in your life. I am always with you, but you often don't see me. Ask the Spirit to tune your mind to my mind. I want you to be so in sync with me that you think my thoughts and feel my feelings. Then you will hear my heart for you and this world. My heart will be open to you as you open your heart to me.

Your friend,
Jesus

ENDNOTES

PROLOGUE

[1] C.S. Lewis, *The Four loves: An Exploration of the Nature of Love*, Mariner Books, Houghton Mifflin Harcourt, 2012, p. 59.
[2] Lewis, pp. 70-71.

CHAPTER ONE: WASHING UP FOR SUPPER

[1] Matthew Kelly, *The Seven Levels of Intimacy: The Art of Loving and the Joy of Being Loved*, A Fireside Book Published by Simon & Schuster, 2007, p.8.
[2] James Montgomery Boice, *The Gospel of John: An Expositional Commentary, Vol. 4, John 13:1-17:26*, Zondervan Publishing House, 1978, p.13.
[3] Kelly, *The Seven Levels of Intimacy*, p. 113.
[4] D.A. Carson, *The Difficult Doctrine of the Love of God*, Crossway Books, 2000, pp. 16-21.
[5] Boice, *John*, Vol. 4, p. 17.
[6] James Hope Moulton, *A Grammar of New Testament Greek*, Vol. 1, Prolegomena, T & T Clark, 1978, p.90.
[7] J.I. Packer, *Knowing God*, InterVarsity Press, 1973, p. 115.
[8] Leon Morris, *The Gospel According to John: The English Text with Introduction, Exposition and Notes*, Wm. B. Eerdmans Publishing Co., 1971, p. 616, fn. 19.
[9] Alfred Edersheim, *The Life and Times of Jesus the Messiah*, Wm. B. Eerdmans Publishing Co., 1971, One Volume Edition, Book III, p. 493-494.
[10] Leon Morris, *The Gospel According to John*, p.617.
[11] Klaus Issler, *Wasting Time with God: A Christian Spirituality of Friendship with God*, InterVarsity Press, 2001, p.43.
[12] Matthew Kelly, *The Seven Levels of Intimacy*, p. 9. Em Griffin, *Making Friends (& Making Them Count)*, InterVarsity Press, 1987, p. 167.
[13] Ray Stedman, *Expository Studies in John 13-17: The Secrets of the Spirit*, Word Books, 1975, p.14.
[14] Em Griffin, *Making Friends*, p. 167.
[15] Em Griffin, *Making Friends*, p. 174.

CHAPTER TWO: WASH WHOSE FEET?

[1] For her autobiography see Bernice Foss, *Great is Thy Faithfulness: The story of God's faithfulness in one missionary's journey to Africa and back*. Doorlight Publications, 2007.
[2] Deborah Smith Douglas, *The Other Side*, May-June 1991, cited by *Christianity Today*, September 16, 1991.

[3] Mother Teresa, *In the Heart of the World: Thoughts, Stories & Prayers*, edited by Becky Benenate, New World Library, 1997, pp. 70-71.

[4] Boice, *The Gospel of John*, vol. 4, p.33.

[5] Moulton and Milligan, *The Vocabulary of the Greek New Testament*, p. 386.

[6] John Piper, *Desiring God: Meditations of a Christian Hedonist*, Multnomah Press, 1986, p. 73.

[7] Cited by Piper, *Desiring God*, p. 204.

[8] Mother Teresa, *In the Heart of the World*, pp. 28-29.

[9] Robertson McQuilken, *Muriel's Blessing*, in *Christianity Today*, February 5. 1996, pp. 32-34.

CHAPTER THREE: THE DARKNESS WITHIN

[1] 2 Samuel 15

[2] 2 Samuel 17:23

[3] Matthew 26:22; Mark 14:19.

[4] Edersheim, *The Life and Times of Jesus the Messiah*, Book III, p. 494.

[5] Matthew 26:25.

CHAPTER FOUR: LOYAL LOVE AND THE CROWING COCK

[1] Elisabeth Elliot, *A Chance to Die: The Life and Legacy of Amy Carmichael*, Revell, 1987, pp. 241-242.

[2] Richard Trench, *Synonyms of the New Testament*, Wm. B. Eerdmans Publishing Company, 1880 reprinted 1975, p. 220.

[3] George Barna, *Revolution: Worn-Out on Church? Finding Vibrant Faith Beyond the Walls of the Sanctuary*, Tyndale, 2005, p. 49.

[4] Warren W. Wiersbe and Lloyd M. Perry, *The Wycliffe Handbook of Preaching and Preachers*, Moody Press, 1984, p. 257.

CHAPTER FIVE: A FOREVER FAITH

[1] https://ahcuah.wordpress.com/2014/02/11/barefoot-man/ There are several adaptations from John Greenleaf Whittier's "The Barefoot Boy." This one was written in 1948 and called "The Barefoot Man."

[2] H. A. W. Meyer, *A Critical and Exegetical Handbook to the Gospel of John,* Hendrickson Publishers, Inc. Reprint of the Sixth Edition, Funk & Wagnalls, 1884, pp. 406-407

[3] Helen Barrett Montgomery, *The New Testament in Modern English*, Centenary Translation, The Judson Press, 1968.

[4] John of the Cross, *Excerpts from The Dark Night of The Soul*, in *Devotional Classics: Selected Readings for Individuals and Groups*, edited by Richard Foster and James Bryan Smith, a Renovare Resource for Spiritual Renewal, HarperCollins Publishers, 1993, pp. 33-36.

[5] Klaus Issler, *Wasting Time with God: A Christian Spirituality of Friendship with God*, InterVarsity Press, 2001, p. 146.

6 J.H. Bernard, *A Critical and Exegetical Commentary on the Gospel According to St. John*, T. & T. Clark, 1976, II:532

7 Walter Bauer, William F. Arndt and F. Wilbur Gingrich, *A Greek-English Lexicon of the New Testament and Other Early Christian Literature*, second edition by Frederick W. Danker from Walter Bauer's fifth edition, 1958, p. 527

8 Colin Brown, General Editor, *The New International Dictionary of New Testament Theology*, Zondervan, 1981, 3:229

9 Bernard, *St. John*, II:532

10 BAGD, *A Greek-English Lexicon*, p. 822.

11 Moulton & Milligan, *Vocabulary*, p.258

12 Used by permission.

13 The KJV follows a different textual reading at this point and reads: *And whither I go ye know and the way ye know*. In that case, Jesus would be saying that they know both the destination and the route which He will travel. This makes sense since He has just stated His destination is Heaven but the better manuscript evidence points to the shorter reading here.

CHAPTER SIX: SLOW LEARNERS!

1 J.I. Packer, *Knowing God*, InterVarsity Press, 1973, p.20.

2 The protasis (condition) is essentially the same in both cases (minor textual differences), but the apodosis (result) has a major textual problem. The form of the apodosis determines the nature of the protasis. (1) *"You would have known my father."* There are two variant readings in the manuscript evidence. The condition becomes a contrary to fact condition rebuking them for not knowing him as they should have known him. (2) *"You will know my father."* In this case, the condition is assumed to be true resulting in a promise that they will know the father based on what Jesus said in verse 6. The manuscript evidence is strong for both forms of the text.

3 Gary Thomas, *Sacred Pathways: Discover Your Soul's Path to God*, Zondervan, revised edition, 2010, p.23.

4 Thomas, pp. 23-30.

5 Thomas, p. 52.

6 Jacob Neusner, *A Rabbi Talks with Jesus*, Doubleday, 1993, pp. 24, 29. 31, 53 cited by Philip Yancey, *The Jesus I Never Knew*, Zondervan Publishing House, 1995, p. 96.

7 The perfect tense indicative verb emphasizes past action that stands accomplished in the present. Ernest De Witt Burton, *Syntax of the Moods and Tenses in New Testament Greek*, Kregel Publications, 1978, Reprint of Third Edition published by The University of Chicago Press, 1900, p.40.

8 BAGD, *A Greek-English Lexicon*, p. 578.

9 K. Dahn, "See, Vision, Eye" in *The New International Dictionary of New Testament Theology*, Colin Brown, General Editor, Zondervan Publishing House, 1971, 3:515-517.

10 Millard Erickson, *Christian Theology*, Third Edition, Baker Academic, 2013, p. 309. For a full treatment of this doctrine see pp. 291-313.

11 Cited by Erickson, p. 313.

12 Wayne Grudem, *Systematic Theology*, Zondervan, 1994, p.247.

[13] Charles Swindoll, *Intimacy with the Almighty: Encountering Christ in the Secret Places of your Life*, J. Countryman, a division of Thomas Nelson, Inc., 1999.

[14] Klaus Issler, *Wasting Time with God*, pp. 40-41.

[15] J.I. Packer, *Concise Theology: A Guide to Historic Christian Beliefs*, Tyndale House Publishers, 1993, p. 42.

[16] Wayne Grudem, *Systematic Theology*, pp. 249-252.

[17] The word "living" (μενων) is a nominative participle modifying Father. It means enduring, continuing or remaining. The Father is continuously living in Jesus. Jesus says, "The living in me Father" performs (ποιει) – on an ongoing basis – His works, thereby verifying the words of Jesus.

[18] What are we to believe? Jesus defines the content of our faith not the cause of our faith in the expression *"I am in the Father and the Father is in Me."* The particle (οτι) should be translated "that" not "because" (Meyer, *John*, p 412). We are to believe Jesus when He says *"that I am in the Father and the Father is in Me."* This is an essential doctrine of Christianity.

[19] John Piper, *Desiring God*, p.33.

[20] I am indebted to D.A. Carson for his extended discussion of this doctrine in his book, *The Difficult Doctrine of the Love of God*, Crossway Books, p. 34.

[21] D.A. Carson, *The Difficult Doctrine of the Love of God*, pp. 34-35.

[22] Arthur Bennett, editor, *The Valley of Vision: A Collection of Puritan Prayers & Devotions*, The Banner of Truth Trust, 1975, p. 330-331.

CHAPTER SEVEN: THE MYSTERY OF PRAYER IN THE PRESENCE OF POWER

[1] Philip Yancey, *Prayer: Does it Make Any Difference?* Zondervan Publishing House, 2006, pp.75-77.

[2] Leon Morris, *John*, p. 646.

[3] Warren W. Wiersbe and Lloyd M. Perry, *The Wycliffe Handbook of Preaching and Preachers*, Moody Press, 1984, p. 239.

[4] Ibid., p. 218.

[5] Philip Yancey, *Prayer: Does It Make Any Difference?* Zondervan, 2006, p. 59.

[6] R. A. Torrey, *The Power of Prayer and the Prayer of Power*, p. 126, cited by James Montgomery Boice, *John*, 4:146.

[7] Eugene Peterson, *Working the Angles: The Shape of Pastoral Integrity*, p. 43-44 in *Eugene Peterson's Pastoral Library: Four Books in One Volume*, William B. Eerdmans Publishing Company, 1992.

[8] Jesus promised, *"Whatever you ask in My name, that I will do, so that the Father may be glorified in the Son. If you ask Me anything in My name, I will do it"* (John 14:13-14). The expression is awkward. We don't usually request something from someone in his/her own name. In fact, some manuscripts leave out the "me" (με) and insert "the Father" (τον πατερα) in its place. There is, however, strong external manuscript evidence for "me" being the original text and the internal evidence is compelling as well. It seems more likely that a scribe copying the text by hand would make the mistake of omitting

"me" and supplying "the Father" to avoid the awkwardness of the sentence. So the best reading is με not τον πατερα. We can ask Jesus in Jesus' name to answer our requests. Further support for praying directly to Jesus comes from the pronouns in both verses. Jesus says in verse 13, *"Whatever you ask ... I (εγω) will do."* He makes the "I" emphatic in verse 14. *"If you ask Me ... I will do it"* (εγω ποιησω). The εγω reinforces the με and Jesus will do (ποιησω) what we ask Him to do.

[9] Obedience is the natural, but not obligatory, consequence of love. Love does not demand obedience, but obedience expresses love. It is a third class condition sometimes called a "more probable future condition" (H.E. Dana and Julius R. Mantey, *A Manual Grammar of the Greek New Testament*, The MacMillan Company, 1955, p.290). The construction suggests an element of uncertainty expressed in the future tense of the apodosis – *"you will keep my commands."* The majority text uses an imperative (τηρησατε), but the better attested reading is a future indicative (τηρησετε) which also fits better with the third class condition and the future tense of "ask" (ερωτησω) in verse 16. The stress of the apodosis is on **"my"** commands. The pronoun is emphatic (τας εμας). There is absolute authority bound up in this pronoun. Moses told the Israelites, *"These are the things the Lord has commanded you"* (Exodus 35:1). Now Jesus talks about *"my commandments"* recalling the Lord's commands in the Law of God. Yet, instead of making obedience a response to authority, Jesus teaches an obedience that flows from love. Here is no legalistic duty to obey but a free desire to obey with an element of uncertainty in the obedience because Jesus seeks the heart more than the act of obedience.

[10] Yancy, *Prayer*, pp. 121-123.

[11] James Boice, *John*, p. 149.

[12] Boice, *John*, 4:151.

[13] Klauss Issler, *Wasting Time with God*, p. 217.

[14] The verb translated *"will ask"* (ερωτησω) suggests an open dialogue between two people face to face. It meant to ask a question in a conversation. Another common word for "ask" (αιτεω) is used of making a request from an inferior to a superior. When the disciples ask God for anything in prayer, αιτεω is used, but αιτεω is never used of Jesus' own requests to God. The word for Jesus' requests to the Father is either ερωταω or δεομαι. The word ερωταω indicates an intimate conversational setting (H. Schonweiss, "Prayer" in *The New International Dictionary of New Testament Theology*, Zondervan Publishing House, 1971, 2:856-857).

[15] The verb form of this word (παρακαλεω) means "to call alongside" and can be used for either exhortation or consolation (BAGD, *A Greek-English Dictionary*, p. 617). The noun (παρακλητος) can certainly carry a sense of comfort or consolation, and the early church fathers translated it this way. The word can also be used in a technical sense of attorney or advocate. We can see this sense of the word used for Jesus and His role in God's courtroom when we sin. *"If anyone sins, we have an Advocate (παρακλητον) with the Father, Jesus Christ, the righteous"* (1 John 2:1). Jesus is our defense attorney whenever we are charged with sin before a Holy God. The Holy Spirit, in John 14:16, is "another" παρακλητον like Jesus so many opt for "advocate" in keeping with the image of a defense attorney in 1 John 2:1. However, by the time of the New Testament the technical legal meaning of the word had diminished in usage (Arndt and Gingrich, *A*

Greek-English Dictionary, p617) and the word had taken on a more general meaning of a helper – one who comes to the aid of another. This is a common way to understand the word. The context of John 14 supports a meaning that is less technical and more supportive given the emphasis on teaching and peace (John 14:26-27). Helper moves us in this direction, but I think it loses some of the richness of the meaning we find for paraclete.

[16] Moulton and Milligan, *Vocabulary*, p.485.

[17] Morris, *John*, p.649.

[18] Donald Grey Barnhouse, *The Love Life*, p. 187 cited by James Boice in *John*, 4:173.

[19] The external textual support is strong for either a present tense or a future tense, but the context requires a future tense. There would be no reason for Jesus to request another "friend" if the friend was already there in the same way as He will be there later. The future tense of "will give" (δωσει) in verse 16, and the undisputed future tenses in verse 26 require us to understand the coming of the Spirit as future to that day.

[20] In verse 16, Jesus says that the friend "may be with you forever" (μετα). In verse 17, the Spirit "is abiding with" them (παρα). A change is coming and the Spirit "will be in" them (εν). We cannot make ironclad distinctions between prepositions, but, when used in a context like this, we can draw out some nuances of meaning in the contrasting phrases. The base meaning of the preposition μετα is "in the midst of" or with someone in the sense of a union or association (A.T. Robertson, *A Grammar of the Greek New Testament in the Light of Historical Research*, Broadman Press, 1934, p.609). The fellowship of the Spirit is with us in our Christian lives (2 Cor. 13:14). The simplest meaning of the second preposition παρα means beside or alongside of someone. It emphasizes His personal presence with us. Jesus has already been with them in this sense along with the Holy Spirit (14:25), and Jesus promises to continue to be with them in the future (14:23). The idea is that both are with us in the sense of at our homes (Robertson, p.614). The third preposition εν introduces the new role of the Spirit. The emphasis of εν in this context is that our friend will not just be near us but inside of us. This is the basic meaning (Robertson, p. 586), and Jesus implies this very distinction here regarding the changing role of the Spirit.

[21] Joni Eareckson Tada, *A Lifetime of Wisdom: Embracing the Way God Heals You*, Zondervan Publishing House, 2009, pp.108-109.

CHAPTER EIGHT: ORPHANS NO LONGER

[1] www.brainyquote.com/quotes/quotes/j/josephaddi143015.html. Joseph Addison, Retrieved October 28, 2015.

[2] Jesus said, *"In that day you will know that I am in the Father, and you in ME, and I in you"* (John 14:20). The triple repetition of the preposition "in" (εν) indicates "the space within which something is found" (BAGD, *A Greek-English Dictionary*, p. 258).

[3] Erickson, *Christian Theology*, p.312.

[4] Klauss Issler, *Wasting Time with God*, pp. 50-51.

[5] BAGD, *A Greek-English Dictionary*, p. 257; Bernard, *John*, p. 550.

[6] Emory Griffin, *Getting Together: A Guide to Good Groups*, InterVarsity Press, 1982, p. 116.

[7] Ibid., p. 132.

[8] Kelly, *The Seven Levels of Intimacy*, p. 31.

[9] J. Oswald Sanders, *Enjoing Intimacy with God*, Discovery House Publishers, 2000, original edition published by Moody Bible Institute, 1980, p.9.

[10] Kelly, *The Seven Levels of Intimacy*, pp. 56-57.

[11] J. Oswald Sanders, *Enjoying Intimacy with God*, p. 17.

CHAPTER NINE: THE PARACLETE'S PEACE

[1] www.cnn.com/US/valujet.592/, www.cnn.com/US/9611/15/valujet/index.html.

[2] Jill Higgins, "Wednesday Night's 12 Fires Have Biddeford Scared," *Portland Press Herald*, May 17, 1996, p. 1A.

[3] David Seamands, *Healing for Damaged Emotions*, Victor, 2002, p. 129.

[4] Elisabeth Elliott, *A Path Through Suffering: Discovering the Relationship Between God's Mercy and Our Pain*, Servant Publications, 1990, p. 160-161.

[5] Walt Russell, *Playing with Fire: How the Bible Ignites Change in Your Soul*, NavPress, 2000, pp. 63-64 cited by Klaus Issler, *Wasting Time with God*, pp. 166-167.

[6] Jesus leaves (αφιημι) peace to us. The word is often translated "forgive" or "pardon" and can even mean "divorce" in the sense of sending someone away. Here, however, Jesus uses the word in its most common sense of leaving behind something in the manner of a bequest to a loved one. The same word was used in John 14:18 where Jesus said, *"I will not leave you as orphans."* The bequest of Jesus is peace not abandonment. Jesus leaves behind a sense of inner wholeness and order despite outer chaos and conflict.

[7] Jesus gives (διδωμι) us His peace. Peace is a gift or a bestowal in the midst of our personal experiences. Jesus leaves us with a sense of order in life because He is in control, but He also gives us a sense of well-being that we can experience in the middle of our circumstances. We will be alright in the end because He controls the end! Three times He uses the verb to give (διδωμι). Jesus tells us *"I, myself (εγω), give you My (εμην) peace."*

[8] Arthur Somers Roche cited by George Sweeting in *Great Quotes and Illustrations*, Word Publishing, 1985, p. 268.

[9] The disciples were saddened by their coming loss. Their myopic self-interest interfered with Christ's eternal interests making their sadness selfish. The conditional sentence is a second class condition where the condition is assumed to be unfulfilled or contrary to fact (Robertson, *Grammar*, p. 1012). The protasis is "if you loved Me" (ει ηγαπατε με). The imperfect tense indicates they were not loving Him on an ongoing basis. Jesus does not doubt that they have loved Him, but their sadness at His going proves they were not continuing to love Him. If they had kept on loving Him, they would have experienced joy even in His departure (Robertson, *Grammar*, p. 1015).

[10] Only one man in the history of the world had no foothold that Satan could use to rule him – Jesus! Jesus said, *"he has nothing in Me"* (John 14:30). The *"in Me"* (εν εμοι) is placed first in the clause for emphasis. The double negative added further intensity to

Jesus' affirmation (ουκ εχει ουδεν). Literally Jesus says, *"in Me not he has nothing."* The clause is translated idiomatically in several ways. The ruler of this world could find nothing in Jesus that he could use to rule Jesus in any way.

[11] Satan rules this world by finding flaws he can use to dominate people. We are all flawed by sin and Satan uses these sinful flaws to rule us. There were no spiritual weaknesses or sinful flaws in Jesus. Pontius Pilate used a similar expression to announce that he could find no guilt (ουδεμιαν αιτιαν) in Him (εν αυτω) (John 18:38). Jesus was sinless, but His sinlessness was more than merely a lack of sinful actions or behaviors. Jesus claims here that His sinlessness is a "necessary causal condition" (Meyer, *John*, p. 424) for His freedom from the power of the ruler of this world. The sinless perfection of Jesus was intrinsic to His nature giving Satan no foothold in His life.

[12] S. Lewis Johnson, private notes from a course entitled "The Upper Room Discourse" at Grace Theological Seminary, 1983.

[13] Nien Cheng, *Life and Death in Shanghai*, Grove Press, 1986, pp. 142-143.

CHAPTER TEN: THE GARDEN OF HIS DELIGHT

[1] The verb translated "takes away" (αιρει) has three possible meanings (BAGD, p. 24). The first meaning is to lift up or pick up. The verb is used of picking up stones to stone Jesus (John 8:59). The second lexical meaning is to lift up and carry. The man Jesus healed by the pool of Bethesda lifted up and carried his pallet (John 5:8,10,11,12). The third meaning is to take away or remove with the sense of killing someone. The crowds screamed about Jesus to Pilate, *"Away with this man"* (Luke 23:18). So which interpretation would be correct in John 15:2?

[2] The participle "bearing" (φερον) is a present active participle. The branch is not actively producing fruit, and the branch is not currently producing fruit. The time of the participle is connected to the time of the main verb. The main verb in this case is also a present tense verb (αιρει). Therefore, the time of the participle is present time. The Christian in view is not presently bearing fruit. Jesus is not considering a person who has never borne fruit. A professing – not genuine – Christian would never have borne any fruit. Jesus is not talking about such a person here. He is talking about a believer who is not currently producing fruit not an unbeliever who pretended to produce fruit.

[3] H.G. Link and J. Schattenmann, "Pure," in *The New International Dictionary of New Testament Theology*, edited by Colin Brown, Zondervan Publishing House, 1971, 3:102.

[4] James Boice, *John*, 4:229.

[5] Elisabeth Elliot, *A Path Through Suffering*, p. 106.

[6] BAGD, *A Greek-English Lexicon*, p. 503

[7] It is an aorist active command (μεινατε) indicating action that is undefined in terms of duration. However, the two following uses of abide in this verse are in the present tense indicating that the abiding is to be an ongoing abiding as opposed to an event. We must continue to remain in Christ in order to produce fruit because the power that produces the fruit flows from the vine, Jesus Christ.

[8] There are three ways to understand the clause (Morris, *John*, p. 670). 1) Jesus is commanding Himself to remain in them, but this makes little sense. 2) The second command is a continuation of the first one. "Remain in Me and make sure I remain in you." 3) The second condition is actually a promise predicated on the first condition. "Remain in Me and I promise to remain in you." This makes the best sense of the verse (Meyer, *John*, p. 430).

[9] Paul Brand with Philip Yancey, "And God Created Pain: A World Famous Surgeon's Appreciation for the Gift Nobody Wants," *Christianity Today*, January 10, 1994, p. 22.

CHAPTER ELEVEN: ARE YOU ABIDING?

[1] Sadhu Sundar Singh, *With and Without God*, cited in *Devotional Classics: Selected Readings for Individuals and Groups*, edited by Richard J. Foster and James Bryan Smith, HarperCollins Publishers, 1993, p. 310.

[2] Patrick Morley, *The Man in the Mirror: Solving the 24 Problems Men Face*, Thomas Nelson Publishers, 1992, p. 94.

[3] BAGD, *A Greek-English Lexicon*, p. 548

[4] The next three verbs all have plural subjects. *"They gather them and they cast them into the fire and they are burned."* The first two verbs are present active indicatives and the third is a passive, yet all three can be translated as idiomatically passive. All the discussions explaining the identity of "they" in this verse are 'fruitless' discussions! The construction is a Semitic idiom for an impersonal subject (Moulton, *Grammar*, 2:447-448). A third person plural subject was used with an active voice as a substitute for an impersonal passive in the Hebrew style of writing so the identity of the subject is simply impersonal.

[5] Erwin W. Lutzer, *Hitler's Cross: The Revealing Story of How the Cross of Christ Was Used as a Symbol of the Nazi Agenda*, Moody Press, 1995, p. 104.

[6] Ibid., p. 153.

[7] Priscilla Wong, *Anne Steele and Her Spiritual Vision: Seeing God in the Peaks, Valleys, and Plateaus of Life*, Reformation Heritage Books, 2012, p 80.

[8] Ibid. pp. 79-80.

[9] R. Kent Hughes, *Liberating Ministry from the Success Syndrome*, Tyndale House Publishers, 1987, p. 72.

[10] Philip Yancey, *Prayer: Does it Make any Difference?* pp. 292-293.

CHAPTER TWELVE: FRUIT FOR THE GARDENER

[1] Annie Druyan, in an interview for National Public Radio, Feb. 12, 2010 cited by Christopher West, *Fill These Hearts: God, Sex, and the Universal Longing*, Image, an imprint of the Crown Publishing Group, a division of Random House, Inc,. 2012, pp. 3-4.

[2] The words "by this" (εν τουτω) are in the emphatic position at the start of the verse. Jesus is referring forward not backward to the upcoming purpose clause.

[3] There is also a textual problem with the verb. Is the verb "become" a subjunctive (γενησθε) mood or a future (γενησεσθε) tense? The manuscript evidence is evenly

divided, but it is probably better to take the verb as a future because of the grammatical structure of the passage. Often a purpose clause introduced by "that" (ινα) would take the subjunctive. However, this construction has two verbs connected by "and" (και). As such, it is a special case where the first verb is in the subjunctive mood and the second is a future tense. The future tense indicates a further consequence or future result that stands independently of the first one (Blass/Debrunner, *Grammar*, p.186).

[4] The verb (γινομαι) is a fairly loose term with multiple meanings. It can mean to come about or take place – to become. It can also mean to "be" as a substitute for the verb "is" (ειμι). I suggest that the verb used in this context simply acts as the equivalent of "is" or "are" (BAGD, *Lexicon*, p. 160). We can translate the verse this way. *"By this, My Father is glorified that you bear much fruit and you will continue to be My disciples."*

[5] BAGD, *Lexicon*, p. 485.

[6] Jean Vanier, *From Brokenness to Community*, Paulist Press, 1992, pp. 15-16, 47-48.

[7] J. Oswald Sanders, *Enjoying Intimacy with God*, Discovery House Publishers, 2000, p.10.

[8] David Brooks, *The Social Animal: The Hidden Sources of Love, Character, and Achievement*, Random House Publishing Group, 2012, p. 19.

[9] Charles Colson, *Loving God*, Zondervan, 1987, p.138).

[10] "My joy" (η χαρα η εμη) is Jesus' own joy not the joy produced by Jesus (Meyer, John, p. 434). Jesus' joy stood on the twin pillars of eternally abiding in the Father's love and always obeying the Father's commands (Jn. 15:10). The obedience of a slave produces duty, but the obedience of love produces joy so Jesus' joy is the product of His loving obedience. The happiness Jesus enjoyed with the Father is the happiness He wants us to enjoy with Him. We will experience the same joy He experiences with the Father by abiding in His love through obedience to His commands.

[11] Joni Eareckson Tada, *A Lifetime of Wisdom: Embracing the Way God Heals You*, Zondervan, 2009, p. 86.

CHAPTER THIRTEEN: BEST FRIENDS FOREVER

[1] Em Griffin, *Making Friends (& Making Them Count)*, InterVarsity Press, 1987, p. 142.

[2] Griffin, p. 158.

[3] D. A. Carson, *The Farewell Discourse and Final Prayer of Jesus: An Exposition of John 14-17*, Baker Book House, 1988, p. 103.

[4] Charles Colson, *Loving God*, Zondervan Publishing House, 1997, p. 126.

[5] "Rick Bragg, "Oseola McCarty, A Washerwoman Who Gave All She Had to Help Others, Dies at 91," *New York Times*, September 28, 1999. See also, www.philanthropyroundtable.org/almanac/hall_of_fame/oseola_mccarty.

[6] The condition (εαν ποιητε) expresses a degree of "reduced probability" (Louw Nida, 89.62). It is not certain that we will obey so it is not certain that we will experience friendship with Jesus. Jesus invites us to be His friends, but the friendship is conditioned on doing what He commands.

[7] D.A. Carson, *The Difficult Doctrine of the Love of God*, Crossway Books, 2000, p.42.

[8] Griffin, *Making Friends*, p. 211.

[9] Issler, *Wasting Time with God*, p. 141.

10 The author of the words of the hymn entitled "I Sought the Lord" included in many hymnals is listed as anonymous. It was apparently written in 1878 and published in *Holy Songs, Carols, and Sacred* Ballads compiled by the Roberts brothers in Boston in 1880.

11 Jesus says, *"You did not choose* (εξελεξασθε) *Me but I chose* (εξελεξαμην) *you"* (John 15:16). The verbs are both in the middle voice indicating that the choice is a matter of personal interest. We did not choose Him for ourselves, but He chose us for Himself. Jesus chooses us to be His friends. Jesus chooses to disclose Himself to us as His friends. He risks possible rejection to call us His friends. He invites us into his friendship if we will choose to obey Him out of love.

12 Griffin, *Making Friends*, p. 174.

13 George Sweeting, *Great Quotes & Illustrations*, Word Publishing, 1985, p. 177.

14 *The Lord of the Rings: The Return of the King*, directed by Peter Jackson, produced by New Line Cinema, 2003 and based on *The Lord of the Rings* by J. R. R. Tolkien.

CHAPTER FOURTEEN: A FAULT LINE WITH THE WORLD

1 Sarah Pulliam, "YWAM Director Describes Shooting, Forgiveness," *Christianity Today*, www.christianitytoday.com, 12-19-07.

2 Bernard, *John*, 2:491.

3 Kim Lawton, "The Suffering Church," *Christianity Today*, July 15, 1996; *Amnesty International*, "Kuwait Hussein Qambar 'Ali: Death Threats," August 1996, AI index: MDE 17/05/96, DISTR: SC/GR/CO.

4 Carson, *Farewell Discourse*, p. 117.

5 εξελεξαμην - middle voice

6 BAGD, *Lexicon*, p. 234.

7 John Lennox, *Against the Flow: The Inspiration of Daniel in an Age of Relativism*, Monarch Books, 2015, pp. 80-81.

8 Jeff M. Sellers, "How to Confront a Theocracy: The most effective way to address the human rights disaster in Saudi Arabia may be to let Muhammad do the talking," *Christianity Today*, Vol. 46, No. 8, July 8, 2002, p. 34.

9 Cited by John Lennox, *Against the Flow*, p. 138.

10 Private email correspondence

11 Lawton, "The Suffering Church," *CT*, July 15, 1996, p. 56.

12 They "have seen" (εωρακασιν) and "hated" (μεμισηκασιν). The verbs are perfect tense verbs indicating a "seeing" and "hating" that are ongoing into the present moment.

13 Boice, *John*, 4:268.

14 Arnold Dallimore, *George Whitefield: The Life and Times of the Great Evangelist of the Eighteenth-Century Revival*, Crossway Books, 1979, 2:451.

15 Cited by Lennox, *Against the Flow*, pp. 210-212.

16 He could also have been citing Psalm 69:4. We can't be certain of the origin of the quote.

17 Jeff Sellers, "Cure for IDOP Holiday Blues," *Christianity Today*, November 16, 2005.

CHAPTER FIFTEEN: A COMMON CAUSE

[1] John Lennox, *Against the Flow*, p. 192; www.blasphemychallenge.com

[2] TDNT, 5:801-803; Morris, *John*, pp. 662-666.

[3] The word "spirit" (πνευμα) is neuter in gender leading some to imply that the Spirit of God is an influence or force. However, the pronoun used (εκεινος) is masculine and the closest antecedent is πνευμα not παρακλητος. The pronoun indicates personality. Jesus consistently uses a personal masculine personal pronoun when speaking about the Holy Spirit (John 14:26; 16:8,13,14) proving that He is a person not merely a force.

[4] Our friend proceeds from the Father. Twice Jesus uses the prepositional phrase "from the Father" (παρα του πατρος) in this verse. The preposition is used often for Jesus coming from God (John 7:29; 16:27) so the Spirit and the Son both come from the Father. The verb "proceed" (εκπορευεται) should not be understood in terms of eternal procession in this verse but rather in the sense of proceeding from the Father for a specific work. The use of the preposition παρα instead of εκ supports this understanding. The Spirit, as our friend, continues the work of Jesus, as our friend, and both come to us from the Father. All three persons of the trinity are intimately involved with our lives.

[5] Jesus calls Him "the Spirit of Truth" (το πνευμα της αληθειας). The genitive – "of the truth" – is best understood as an objective genitive. He is the Spirit who communicates the truth.

[6] BAGD, *Lexicon*, p. 493

[7] Used by permission.

[8] C. S. Lewis, *The Four Loves*, p. 61.

[9] Colin Brown, Dictionary, 2:707

[10] TDNT, 7:339ff.

[11] BAGD, p. 752, The connection to apostasy is particularly important in the passive voice as in this case. The verb meant to fall away from what was once believed or to be misled from the truth (Colin Brown, Dictionary, 2:708).

[12] Lennox, *Against the Flow*, p. 21.

[13] Emil Schurer, *The History of the Jewish People in the Age of Jesus Christ*. A New English Version Revised and Edited by Geza Vermes, Fergus Miller and Matthew Black, T&T Clark LTD, 1979, 2:432-33.

[14] Todd Starnes, "NASA bans the word Jesus," February. 8, 2016. The ban was later rescinded. www.foxnews.com/opinion/2016/02/08.

[15] Earle E. Cairns, *Christianity Through the Centuries: A History of the Christian Church*, Revised and Enlarged Edition, Zondervan Publishing House, 1981, p.306.

[16] Kim A. Lawton, "The Suffering Church," *Christianity Today*, July 15, 1996, p.57.

[17] Yancey, *Prayer*, p. 119.

CHAPTER SIXTEEN: FOR OUR GOOD

[1] Robert Raines quoted by R. Kent and Barbara Hughes, *Liberating Ministry from the Success Syndrome*, Tyndale House Publishers, 1988, p. 49.

2 Morris, *John*, pp. 695-696.

3 Brooks, *Social Animal*, pp. 218-219.

4 See footnote for 2 Kings 18:46 in the *New American Standard Bible*.

5 See the footnote for 2 Kings 19:3 in the *New American Standard Bible*.

6 The clause "that I go away" (ινα εγω απελθω) is the subject of the verb "it is to your advantage" (συμφερει). The verb carries commercial overtones of profitability (Moulton and Milligan, *Vocabulary*, p. 598).

7 John only uses the term two other times in his gospel (John 11:50; 18:14), and both times it comes from the lips of Caiaphas, the High Priest.

8 Bernard, *John*, 2:504.

9 Philip Yancey, *Prayer: Does it Make any Difference*, p. 274.

CHAPTER SEVENTEEN: PROSECUTING ATTORNEY

1 Warren Wiersbe and Lloyd M. Perry, *The Wycliffe Handbook of Preaching and Preachers*, Moody Press, 1984, pp. 185-186.

2 Morris, *John*, p.697.

3 Hendriksen, *John*, p.325. The verb translated *"will convict"* (ελεγξει) has four possible meanings: 1) to expose; 2) to convict; 3) to reprove; 4) to punish (BAGD, *Lexicon*, p. 249). The same meaning should be applied to all three targets – sin, righteousness and judgment – which eliminates #1 and #4. To merely reprove the world seems rather weak so the best understanding is to convict or convince the world.

4 Bernard, *John*, 2:506.

5 Carson, *The Farewell Discourse*, p. 139.

6 Carson, *The Farewell Discourse*, p. 143.

7 The word translated "because" (οτι) could be translated "that" indicating the content of the conviction, but it is better understood as the cause or grounds for the sin. The Holy Spirit convicts the world individually not collectively. The "world" (κοσμον) is singular. The verb "they do not believe" (πιστευουσιν) is plural. The Holy Spirit proves sin to the world by proving sin to each individual in the world. The sin of unbelief is individual not corporate, and the guilt is personal not collective.

8 Carson, *Farewell Discourse*, p. 141.

9 The verb (ελεγξει) has four possible meanings, but convict and convince are considered to be in the same semantic category – "to convict or convince someone of something" (BAGD, *Lexicon*, p. 249).

10 A causal οτι is used in each case.

11 Morris, *John*, p. 698, fn. 20.

12 The verb translated "judged" (κεκριται) is a perfect tense and passive voice verb. The perfect tense is written from the perspective of a future time. Jesus predicts that, by the time the Holy Spirit comes after Jesus' death and resurrection, the ruler of this world "has been judged!" The passive voice tells us that the judgment is done by someone else.

13 The verb (κρινω) means to be condemned. It is a legal term indicating a judicial verdict has been reached, usually in an unfavorable sense (BAGD, *Lexicon*, p. 450).

---

[14] Frederic Louis Godet, *Commentary on John's Gospel*, Kregel Publications, 1978, p. 871.

[15] Lee Strobel, *The Case for Christ: A Journalist's Personal Investigation of the Evidence for Jesus*, Zondervan, 1998, pp. 191-196.

CHAPTER EIGHTEEN: MASTER COMMUNICATOR

[1] Dick Staub, *Too Christian Too Pagan: How to Love the World Without Falling for It*, Zondervan Publishing House, 2000, p. 40.

[2] Cited by Charles Colson in *The Body: Being Light in Darkness*, Thomas Nelson, 1992, p. 141.

[3] The Holy Spirit is responsible to guide (οδηγησει) us (16:13). The verb means to lead or conduct us along the way (BAGD, p. 553). The etymology of the word helps us grasp its significance. It comes from two Greek words – "lead" (αγω) and "way" (οδος) – and means to "lead on the way" or "to show the way" (TDNT, V:97).

[4] There is a textual problem here. He guides us "into" (εις) all truth or He guides us "in" (εν) all truth. The translation "into all truth" suggests that He leads us toward the goal of all truth – a goal we will never reach in this life. The translation "in all truth" suggests that the Spirit leads us in the sphere of all truth. The manuscript evidence favors "in (εν) all truth" so it is best to understand it this way.

[5] The verb "to bear" (βασταζειν) means 1) to carry or 2) to endure (BAGD, *Lexicon*, p. 137). The word can refer to carrying a literal burden such as a jar of water (Mark 14:13) or the cross (John 19:17). It can also be used figuratively for carrying the cross (Luke 14:27) or the burden of keeping the law (Acts 15:10). We also bear a burden in the sense of enduring the heat of the day ((Matthew 20:12) or enduring the weaknesses of weaker Christians (Romans 15:1).

[6] BAGD, *Lexicon*, p. 51. It is used of Paul's preaching ministry (Acts 20:20,27) in a way synonymous with teaching (διδαξαι).

[7] The verb is future in verse 14 (λημψεται) and present in verse 15 (λαμβανει). It can mean either to take or to receive (BAGD, *Lexicon*, p. 464). The source of information is Jesus. Twice the phrase "of Mine" – literally "out of Me" (εκ του εμου) is used, and, once again, the "Me" (εμου) is in its emphatic form showing us that the Spirit's focus is to point us to Jesus.

[8] Here we see a neuter plural subject, "all things" (παντα) with a singular verb (εστιν) to emphasize that the information being communicated is viewed as a whole mass not specific individual teachings (Dana & Mantey, *Grammar*, p. 165).

[9] *Christianity Today*, October 4, 1999, p. 88.

[10] The clause about the glorifying work of the Holy Spirit is intensive in form stressing His role in the godhead (John 16:14). Literally the text reads, "that one Himself will glorify Me" (εκεινος εμε δοξασει).

[11] Paul David Tripp, *Dangerous Calling: Confronting the Unique Challenges of Pastoral Ministry*, Crossway, 2012, pp. 22-26.

[12] Portland Press Herald, December 17, 1994.

[13] Ravi Zacharias, *Jesus Among Other Gods: The Absolute Claims of the Christian Message*, Thomas Nelson, 2000, p. 81.

[14] Joe Stowell, *Perilous Pursuits: Overcoming Our Obsession with Significance*, Moody Publishers, 1994, pp. 185-188.

CHAPTER NINETEEN: GRIEF'S RESERVOIR

[1] The second "little while" is the interval of time between the cross and the resurrection. The adverb "again" (παλιν) ties the two intervals together negating any identification of this "seeing" with the return of Christ. The two "seeings" are connected closely in time by the adverb.

[2] Quoted by Dann Spader and Gary Mayes in *Growing a Healthy Church*, Moody Publishers, 1993, p. 185.

[3] The verb (θεωρειτε) is in the present, not future, tense which is significant – you see Me no longer. "No longer" (ουκετι) does not mean "never again." The action simply stops (Bernard, *John*, p.513).

[4] BAGD, *Lexicon*, p.360.

[5] A different verb (οψεσθε) is used for resurrection sight, and it is a future tense (from οραω). This verb replaces the former verb because it is always used in John to emphasize spiritual perception (Bernard, John p.513).

[6] TDNT, V:360.

[7] Meyer, *John*, p.451.

[8] Morris, *John*, p.703.

[9] Oswald Chambers, *Baffled to Fight Better*,

[10] Paul Brand and Philip Yancey, "And God Created Pain: A world-famous surgeon's appreciation for the gift nobody wants." *Christianity Today*, January 10, 1994, vol. 38, no. 1, p. 18.

[11] Ravi Zacharias, *Jesus Among Other Gods*, pp. 59-60.

[12] NIDNTT, 2:416-420.

[13] Bernard, *John*, 2:515. The word is λυπηθησεσθε. It is future passive, meaning that something outside the person causes the inner grief.

[14] There is a sharp contrast in the verse which an English translation cannot bring out effectively. The "you" (υμεις) is emphatically placed at the end of the clause immediately adjacent to "the world" (ο κοσμος) beginning the next clause.

[15] The verb is γενησεται which means "to be or become." Morris, *John*, p. 705.

[16] Dick Staub, *Too Christian Too Pagan*, p. 113.

[17] Elisabeth Elliot, *A Path Through Suffering*, p. 89.

[18] F.W.H. Meyers, quoted by Elliot, *A Path Through Suffering*, p.42.

[19] Steve Saint, "Did They Have to Die?" *Christianity Today*, 9/6/96, p.25.

[20] Kent and Barbara Hughes, *Liberating Ministry from the Success Syndrome*, Crossway, 2008, p.144.

[21] Jerry Sitser, *A Grace Disguised: How the Soul Grows through Loss*, Zondervan, expanded edition, 2004, p.42.

CHAPTER TWENTY: HAVE YOU ASKED?

[1] Wiersbe & Perry, *Preaching & Preachers*, pp. 210-211.

[2] Hughes, *Success Syndrome*, p. 73.

[3] The verb is εϱωτησετε. The word was used to describe conversation, and it generally meant to ask a question of someone in a dialogue between two people in close relationship with each other (NIDNTT, 2:856-857). The implication of the word was to seek information.

[4] R. Kent Hughes, *Disciplines of a Godly Man*, Crossway Books, 1991, p. 96.

[5] Wiersbe and Perry, *Preaching & Preachers*, p. 214.

[6] The clause is introduced by "truly, truly" (αμην, αμην) which generally starts a new thought. The verb is αιτησητε which means to ask for or even demand something from someone (BAGD, *Lexicon*, p. 25). Whenever the disciples make requests to God the verb αιτεω is commonly used. Whenever Jesus asks God anything, the verb εϱωταω is used. The verb αιτεω refers to a suppliant making a request of a superior while εϱωταω refers to a person in a relationship of general equality (NIDNTT, 2:857).

[7] Philip Yancey, *Prayer: Does it Make a Difference*, pp. 45-46.

[8] Yancey, *Prayer*, p. 42.

[9] A textual problem occurs with placing the phrase "in My Name" (εν τω ονοματι μου) in the sentence. Does it modify the asking or the giving? Do we ask in Jesus' name or does the Father give in Jesus' name? Some manuscripts place it after the giving so there are those who argue that God's answers to our prayers are in Jesus' name making them more certain (Morris, *John*, p. 708). The stronger manuscript evidence is for the asking to be in Jesus' name. The evidence is more diversified across the geographical spectrum for this reading (Metzger, *Textual Commentary*, p. 248) making it the stronger reading. This reading also fits better in context because the next verse (16:24) clearly associates "in My name" with asking.

[10] Yancey, *Prayer*, p. 137.

[11] John Piper, *Desiring God*, pp. 144-145.

[12] Piper, *Desiring God*, p. 146.

[13] Hughes, *Success Syndrome*, pp. 73-74.

[14] Simon Chan, *Spiritual Theology: A Systematic Study of the Christian Life*, InterVarsity Press, 1998, p. 140 cited by Klaus Issler in *Wasting Time with God*, p. 217.

[15] Hughes, *Success Syndrome*, p. 72.

CHAPTER TWENTY-ONE: TO BE LOVED BY GOD

[1] Vaneetha Rendall, "If I Only Knew Why," *Desiring God Blog*, www.desiringgod.org, December 9, 2015.

[2] Jesus says that He has been speaking in "figurative language" (παϱοιμιαις) and promises to speak later in plain language (παϱϱησια). John uses the word for figurative language (παϱοιμιαις) to mean "dark sayings" where "lofty ideas are concealed" (BAGD, *Lexicon*, p. 629). The word is sometimes synonymous with a proverb or even a parable. The LXX uses παϱοιμια for the title of the Book of Proverbs (Prov. 1:1). It

comes from two words παρα and οιμος meaning "beside the path" to indicate a wise saying alongside a truth (NIDNTT 2:756-757). John, however, uses παροιμια more in the sense of a dark saying or riddle (John 10:6, 16:25,33, Morris, *John*, p.709) in a similar manner to the word "mystery" (μυστηριον) in the other gospel writers. The contrast with speaking plainly (παρρησια) leads to this conclusion since proverbs were normally quite clear in meaning unlike riddles or dark sayings.

3 NIDNTT 2:758.

4 R. Kent Hughes, *James: Faith That Works* in *Preaching the Word*, Crossway Books, 1991, p. 66.

5 Hughes, *James*, p. 107.

6 Carson, *Farewell Discourse*, p. 164.

7 The pronoun "himself" (αυτος) is emphatic both by usage (Moule, *Idiom Book*, p. 121) and in position as the first word of the phrase preceding "for" (γαρ).

8 Hughes, *Success Syndrome*, pp. 74-75.

9 The verb "loves" (φιλει) indicates ongoing affection in the present tense. It is the only place where John uses φιλειν as opposed to αγαπαν in order to communicate God's love for us (Bernard, *John*, 2:520). While an absolute distinction cannot be maintained between these two verbs, it is generally true that φιλειν implies the idea of human affection more than the higher form of willful love (αγαπαν) normally used for God by John.

10 The οτι is causal and introduces two perfect tense verbs indicating two reasons the Father loves us. First, He loves us because *"Me, you, yourselves, have loved."* The "me" (εμε) and the "you" (υμεις) are both emphatic. The perfect tense tells us that the choice to love (πεφιληκατε) was a past event (for the disciples) with ongoing results in present time.

11 Morris, *John*, p.711.

12 Thomas Kelly, *A Testament of Devotion* in *Devotional Classics* edited by Richard Foster and James Bryan Smith *A Renovaré Resource for Spiritual Renewal*, Harper Collins Publishers, 1993, pp. 205-207.

13 E.M. Bounds cited by Hughes, *Disciplines of a Godly Man*, p. 95.

14 "Have believed" (πεπιστευκατε) is another perfect tense indicating a past choice with continuing results in the present. The content of the faith is defined by "that" (οτι) - a content not a causal usage as earlier. the preposition (παρα) means "from the side of" (Robertson, *Grammar*, pp. 579,614).

15 Cited by Hughes in *Success Syndrome*, pp. 163-164.

16 Used by permission. Jacob's surgery was successful. He is doing well and continues to be a delight to all of us.

CHAPTER TWENTY-TWO: BATTERED BUT NOT BROKEN

1 *"An hour is coming* (ερχεται) *even has come* (εληλυθεν),*"* but this hour is not merely any hour (John 16:32). This hour is "the" hour! Jesus prayed, *"Father, the hour has come"* (εληλυθεν) for the glorification of the Son (John 17:1, cf. John 2:4; 7:6).

2 H.B. London, Jr. and Neil B. Wiseman, *Pastors at Risk: Help for Pastors, Hope for the Church*, Victor Books, 1993, p.73.

[3] Henry and Richard Blackaby, *Spiritual Leadership: Moving People on to God's Agenda*, Revised and Expanded, B&H Publishing Group, 2011, p. 334.

[4] The conjunction can be translated simply "that" indicating the content of the hour coming upon them, or it could be translated "when you are scattered" (Dana and Mantey, *Grammar*, pp. 248-249). However, the original and most common use of ἱνα was to introduce a purpose clause. In fact, ἱνα plus a subjunctive verb became "almost the exclusive means of expressing purpose" (A. T. Robertson, Grammar, p. 982). The scattering (σκορπισθητε) and the abandoning (αφητε) are both subjunctive verbs so this is best understood as a purpose behind the coming hour.

[5] J. Oswald Sanders in the foreword to Isobel Kuhn, *Green Leaf in Drought: The Story of the Escape of the Last China Inland Mission Missionaries from Communist China*, OMF International, 2007.

[6] Elliot, *A Path Through Suffering*, p. 74.

[7] Jesus says, *"you have"* (εχετε) pressure in this world. The present tense indicative verb implies an ongoing reality. Jesus says, *"you might have"* (εχητε) peace in Him. The present tense verb is subjunctive in mood which is the mood of probability or possibility.

[8] The "I" (εγω) is not only emphatic but contrastive as well. "I" contrasts strongly with "you" (Robertson, *Grammar*, p. 677).

[9] John 16:33 is the only time John uses the verb νικαω in the Gospel, but he uses it six times in 1 John (cf. 1 John 5:4) and seventeen times in Revelation (Morris, *John*, p. 714, fn 82). Here in John 16:33 the verb is a perfect active indicative form (νενικηκα) indicating that Jesus has already won the victory with ongoing results for us.

[10] Brian Melley and Pauline Arrillaga, "Watch Over Us: Stories of Survival," *The Associated Press* in the *Maine Sunday Telegram*, December 6, 2015, p. A2.

[11] Issler, *Wasting Time with God*, p. 167.

[12] Moulton & Milligan, *Vocabulary*, p.427.

[13] Michael McCabe, "Paraplegic Scales El Capitan," *San Francisco Chronicle*, July 27, 1989.

[14] Jerry Sittser, *A Grace Revealed: How God Redeems the Story of Your Life*, Zondervan, 2012, p. 138.

Made in the USA
Lexington, KY
07 June 2017